Letters from Tel Mond Prison

AN ISRAELI SETTLER DEFENDS HIS ACT OF TERROR

Era Rapaport

Edited and Introduced by WILLIAM B. HELMREICH

THE FREE PRESS

New York   London   Toronto   Singapore   Sydney

THE FREE PRESS
A Division of Simon & Schuster Inc.
1230 Avenue of the Americas
New York, NY 10020

Designed by Carla Bolte

Manufactured in the United States of America

10   9   8   7   6   5   4   3   2   1

Library of Congress-in-Publication Data

Rapaport, Era
    Letters from Tel Mond Prison : an Israeli settler defends his act
of terror / Era Rapaport ; edited and introduced by William B. Helmreich.
        p   cm.
    ISBN 0-684-83180-5
    1. Rapaport, Era   2. Terrorists—Israel—Correspondence.
3. Prisoners—Israel—Correspondence.   4. Religious Zionist—Israel—
Correspondence.   5. Terrorism—West Bank—Case studies.
I. Helmreich, William B.   II. Title.
HV6433.I75R36   1996
364.1'31—dc20
    [B]   96-27869
                                                                CIP

Contents

Editor's Foreword

I first met Era Rapaport thirty years ago when we were both students at Yeshiva College. He was a year ahead of me, and I would probably not even have gotten to know him casually were it not for the fact that he was a co-captain of the school chess team, and I was one of its members. It was an excellent team with at least one nationally ranked player. We even played against Bobby Fischer in a simultaneous exhibition (Fischer won).

I did not see Rapaport or speak with him for more than twenty-five years. Upon graduating from college, I entered the Ph.D. program in sociology at Washington University, where I did my doctoral dissertation (later to be a book) on a branch of the Black Panthers, living, working, and traveling with them as a participant-observer. This experience was the beginning of a long-term professional interest in social movements and extremist groups.

I also developed a specialization in Orthodox Jewdaism and wrote two books on that subject as well. In addition, I spent two years doing research and teaching at the Hebrew University in Israel. The settler movement in Judea and Samaria represented a combination of all of the above topics and led to my interest in them and their leaders' motives and activities.

Thus, it was almost fortuitous that I traveled to Israel in January 1992 with my department chairman, Steven Goldberg, who had not been to Israel since his Bar Mitzvah in 1956. Curious about the West Bank, Steve asked me to arrange a tour of the area. I had read in the *New York Times* about Rapaport's terrorist activities and had heard that he often set up trips in the West Bank for visitors from abroad. I phoned him and inquired if he could serve as our guide. Although we hadn't spoken in a quarter of a century, he remembered me and agreed to show us around.

Era picked us up the following day. His car had shatterproof glass to protect it from rocks, and he was armed with an M16 rifle. "We don't take chances here," he told us. We spent the day touring the countryside, learning about the different communities and why, in his view, the land was important to Israel, from both a historical and a security perspective.

To improve my understanding of the issues surrounding the territories, I visited Israel again in January 1996 and spent some time in Samaria, most notably Shilo, where Rapaport was my host. I got to know him and the members of his family quite well. Observing their interaction and traveling through the area with him was extremely helpful in sharpening my focus on a whole host of issues. The letters in section 6 are based on conversations I had with Era Rapaport during that trip.

The letters in this book represent Era Rapaport's views, although I have added some parenthetical explanations of various points. Many of the quotes in these letters are reconstructions of the conversations that occurred as Era Rapaport remembered them, or as recounted to him by others. The introduction to the book is based on my own interpretation and thoughts and in no way reflects Rapaport's thinking. We have come together to do this book, but we each retain our own independence and varying opinions. We do, however, agree on one thing: that a true understanding of the problems and challenges facing the Middle East requires that all points of view be given equal time.

Introduction

How does a nice Jewish boy from East Flatbush, Brooklyn, a gifted social worker, a marcher for civil rights, a loving husband and father, end up blowing off the legs of the PLO mayor of Nablus?

Some three thousand years after Simon and Levi took revenge on that same Biblical city, also known as Shechem, for the rape of their sister, Era Rapaport slipped quietly out of his house on the mountain of Shilo to help plant a bomb under the car of a prominent Arab who had encouraged a reign of terror against Jews and had vowed to dance on Jewish graves.

What makes a man leave a wife and three children in the dead of night, knowing that he will have to spend years without them in prison? What drives him to leave his native country and to raise his children in a dangerous and harsh environment?

Era Rapaport's book, *Letters from Tel Mond Prison*, many written over a two-year period while he was incarcerated, offers some interesting answers. You may not agree with the author, but it's a captivating story you won't hear from anyone else. A remarkable document, it consists primarily of letters that he wrote to friends, family, and those who criticized him for what he had done. The letters provide a fascinating portrait from the inside of how a seemingly normal individual evolves into a person willing to maim others in the name of his ideals.

Of equal importance, the book provides a clear and well-reasoned analysis as to why thousands of Jews have decided to risk their lives and settle in what is known as the West Bank, or Judea and Samaria. This is augmented by several letters written recently that reveal his thoughts about the contemporary Israeli scene.

Era Rapaport was raised as an Orthodox Jew in Brooklyn, New York. His father was a religious teacher and his mother a homemaker. The family environment was warm and nurturing and deeply committed to Israel and the Jewish faith. Rapaport's father had been born and raised in Jerusalem, and he imbued Era with his devotion to that city and to Israel. His grandfather, Baruch Rapaport, also a native Jerusalemite, was a Talmudic scholar who spent his life giving classes to adults and running a grocery store. Very charitable, he and his wife suffered starvation because they shared what little they had with the poor. And like his grandson, Baruch Rapaport sent letters to rabbis urging them to move to Israel.

In 1966, after graduating from Yeshiva College, Rapaport went to Israel to study in a yeshiva (advanced school), intending to leave after a year. While there, he came under the influence of Rabbi Tzvi Yehuda Kook, a revered figure among many Zionists. The Six Day War broke out while Era was in Israel, and he spent it working as a medic in war-torn Jerusalem. It was to have a profound impact on his life.

In the span of two decades, from Era's first visit to Israel to his imprisonment, Israel's borders expanded. The divided capital of Jerusalem was reunited, with the Jewish and Arab sectors both coming under Israeli rule. It was a tumultuous period in the Middle East as wars were fought and thousands of lives lost.

Returning to New York in 1967, Rapaport completed his studies for a master's degree in social work and returned to Israel four years later, this time for good. His goal was to use his education to help underprivileged Israeli children. Along the way, he married an Israeli woman from a pioneer Zionist family, and together they decided to move to the West Bank. Their home was a windowless trailer on a deserted windy hill. Their goal was to establish the first permanent Jewish settlement in Samaria after an absence of nearly two thousand years.

Today Era Rapaport is a leader in a movement with tens of thousands of devotees. It is a movement whose adherents regard the Old Testament as their constitution, who literally walk in the footsteps of the Biblical patriarchs, and who live the life of the ancient Jewish zealots. It is as if the land itself elicits this spirit in its residents.

While living there, Rapaport became an internationally known activist and a leader in the Underground (also known as the Machteret). He was part of a larger, loosely connected group whose planned actions included using car bombs to maim Arab West Bank mayors, killing Arabs as they rode in buses, and destroying El Aksa Mosque in Jerusalem, Islam's third holiest shrine. Rapaport's involvement was limited to the mayors.

Eventually he and the others were caught. As with the more recent arrests of Yigal Amir and the others accused in the murder of Prime Minister Yitzhak Rabin, the country was shocked when it learned the identities of those involved—twenty-seven people in all, including war heroes, teachers, graduate students, scholars, and respected builders of pioneer towns. Like Amir, they cited the Bible and the opinions of contemporary rabbis to justify their actions.

Rapaport was accused of planting the bomb that crippled Nablus mayor Bassam Shaka for life. He confessed and went to jail for his crimes. One of his justifications was the Biblical command: "If someone comes to kill you, rise up and kill him first."

As the *New York Times* speculated in the week following Rabin's murder in 1995, today's Jewish underground in Israel appears to have "almost uncanny parallels with the earlier Jewish underground . . . that set off car bombs . . . partly in hopes of provoking a war so cataclysmic that it would hasten the arrival of the Messiah." While such apocalyptic visions are not shared with equal fervor by all those involved in the movement, actions of this sort are rooted in the same general ideology, but they can be tempered by personal values. For this reason Yigal Amir's act would have been unthinkable to Era Rapaport.

Rapaport's violent actions seemed radically inconsistent with his general lifestyle. He is a family man who loves his wife and children and whose greatest joy seems to be spending time with them. Deeply religious, he prays in synagogue three times a day—morning, afternoon, and evening—and works hard in his job as mayor of Shilo, a town that now has over a thousand residents. Unlike the notorious Rabbi Meir Kahane, he is not a rabble-rousing politician but a social worker who continues to harbor a dream of building a center for poor Israeli children.

Terrorism can assume many guises. In this case Rapaport spent many years thinking about the appropriate response to provocation. His decision to plant that bomb was neither hasty nor unconsidered. Other men of violence frequently lack the ability or motivation, or both, to evaluate their deeds fully, articulate their views, and convey the passion that drove them to commit their horrible deeds.

Rapaport is an exception. His book is brutally honest and deeply personal. It is written in an authentic and idiosyncratic style that is alternately emotional and coldly calculating, logical yet irrational, charming yet horrifying. Above all, it is an astonishingly revealing profile of a terrorist and a movement. It would probably never have been written had Rapaport not found himself in prison with time on his hands. As a free man he clearly preferred acting to writing about the things he did.

Rapaport's actions put him in a category sometimes referred to as "convictional criminal." These are persons who commit their acts out of a deep conviction or belief that what they are doing is morally right and in the best interests of their group or nation. And in fact they can point to their otherwise unblemished records as proof of the correctness of their actions. They will readily agree that their act of terrorism is, on the surface, detestable. But they will use that admission to justify what they have done. In other words, what they are saying is: "I know that what I did seems awful, and the fact that a normal person was willing to do it is proof that conditions were so terrible as to make it absolutely necessary to do so."

Although Era Rapaport had great difficulty justifying what he did, he was ultimately able to do just that. What makes his letters so intriguing is that they expose very clearly the process by which he reached his decision to act. He had to balance his fears for the safety of his family and his deeply held religious beliefs, plus his view of history, with his nonviolent nature, his ethical beliefs about the sanctity of human life, and his inherent respect for governmental authority.

This internal battle is one that confronts people who are in the vanguard of other social movements as well. These acts, which because of their violence appear irrational, are often the result of a highly rational and complex process of decision making. The writings of Eldridge Cleaver, George Jackson, Ernesto "Che" Guevara, and Menachem Begin are excellent examples of such struggles.

The driving force behind Rapaport's decision was his religious passion. The fact that he had been brought up in America as a Zionist, that he had studied in a nationalistic Israeli rabbinical seminary, and that he had also, by happenstance, been in Jerusalem during the Six Day War all helped to strengthen his commitment to bring to life the Old Testament that he had studied as a child and in which he continued to absorb himself as an adult. As he sees it, God has chosen this time to allow the children of Israel to return to their ancient home.

Looking out on the land that surrounds Shilo, Rapaport observes, in a matter-of-fact tone, "The mountain belonged to me before, many years ago." His map is literally a Biblical one. Every hill, every field, every village represents to him a place where an event took place, where a prophet prophesied, a priest prayed, an ancestor was buried, and a nation lived. Clearly Palestinians who can point to their families having lived in the cities of Nablus, Hevron, and Bethlehem for generations can find similar justifications for their actions. Yet Rapaport uses historical, archeological, and geopolitical evidence to override their claims.

Rapaport had no trouble justifying his decision to settle in the West Bank. With the other settlers, he worked and fought to establish his home there. He moved at first to a windswept outpost with no electricity, becoming a pioneer, just like his sectarian Zionist predecessors who came to Israel at the turn of the century. He not only gave up a comfortable existence in America to emigrate to Israel, but he spurned the relative comfort of Jerusalem to settle in the West Bank. Rapaport could have been a good Zionist had he stayed in Israel proper and in the holy city of Jerusalem Yet he chose to fulfill what was, in his eyes, the ultimate dream: an opportunity given to his generation by God to resettle the land in the barren hills of the Shomron.

But how could Rapaport rationalize the uncomfortable and hazardous life in a trailer home, to both his family and himself, if he was unwilling and unable to defend himself? The actions of the Israeli army, which initially arrested and evicted the settlers from their makeshift homes, further radicalized Rapaport.

Rapaport was also driven by the long history of violence against Jews. There was the specter of the Holocaust in the immediate past, with its images of Jews unable to fight back, for whatever reasons, which served as a powerful reminder of what happens when Jews cannot protect themselves.

Rapaport's immediate family did not go through the Holocaust. His father and grandparents came from Jerusalem, and his mother was also living in the United States long before World War II. But for Rapaport that was unimportant. His parents could well have been killed if they had lived in Europe during that period. This image was juxtaposed with that of the ancient Maccabees, whom Rapaport cites repeatedly as examples of proud Jews who did fight and who populated the very hills in which he had now settled.

In fact, even while growing up in New York, Rapaport had acted to protect Jewish life and limb by helping to form the first Jewish protection organization in Crown Heights, Brooklyn. Armed with walkie-talkies, he and other Jews patrolled the streets of that neighborhood to prevent Jews from being mugged and otherwise harassed. The Arab enemies, with their vows to "drive the Jews into the sea," were the contemporary enemy.

In the years preceding his attack on the mayor, hundreds of cars had been stoned, orchards had been uprooted, and many individual Jews had been assaulted and, in a number of cases, killed. Students of social movements, like the sociologist Neil Smelser, have often observed that direct, violent action is often sparked by a precipitating event. In its investigation of the urban riots that rocked America in the 1960s, the Kerner Commission found that most mass riots were touched off by a simple precipitating event, such as a shooting or arrest by a police officer in the ghetto.

This was true here too. On May 2, 1980, six Jews returning from prayer services in Hevron were murdered by Arab terrorists. The National Guidance Committee, made up of Arab mayors, was widely believed to have ordered or, at the very least, to have sanctioned the attack. The Israeli government nonetheless regarded them as legitimate representatives of the Arab population in the West Bank and did nothing to punish them. Feeling abandoned and convinced that a failure to respond forcefully would lead to the deaths of more Jews, Rapaport and his friends decided that the time had come to act. They did so one month later, on June 2d, when they planted the bombs in the various mayors' automobiles.

Because Rapaport sees himself in the continuum of Jewish history, he feels responsible not only for the present but for the future as well. He worries that he will be held responsible by God for not having done enough and for not having learned from history how to respond to the challenges of today. This combining of past, present, and future was best expressed when he stated, one month after a number of major Arab towns reverted back to Arab control, "Before and during the Holocaust, no one said, 'Run,' except the Zionists," says Rapaport. "Yet in retrospect, it was so obvious. Fifty years from now people will ask: 'Why didn't we see it coming?' " It is not surprising that he perceives an urgent need to act when he feels threatened.

The combustible mix of protest, religion, and nationalistic ideology that fueled the settler movement helped make it possible for Era Rapaport to move from legal to illegal activity. But what differentiates Rapaport and others like him from the rest of society is his literalist view of religion and history, one that has difficulty divorcing thought from action where deeply held values are concerned. For Rapaport, ideology is too serious a matter to be treated abstractly. Ideas must and can be realized only through concrete action. Moreover, people like Rapaport genuinely believe that their own acts can determine the course of history.

This last point is crucial. Though all of them are religiously observant, the settlers are quite different from the Hasidic Jews, or those who live in the world of the Lithuanian-style academies of Jewish learning. These two groups take a more fatalistic approach to political and military events in the Middle East, relying chiefly on prayer and study. By contrast, the settlers believe that the goals of the Jewish people can be achieved only by a partnership in which Jews do their share by settling and defending their land but also depend on God to help them. Thus, the failure of the Jews of Judea and Samaria to hold on to their territories because the nation as a whole does not support them would be acceptable as God's divine will, provided everything humanly possible has been done to prevent that from happening. Naturally, when things go wrong, Rapaport and his co-religionists often find themselves questioning whether they in fact did all they could.

Many of the same factors are at work for Arab terrorists. They have endured almost fifty years as refugees, often living in squalid camps, scorned and hated by Israelis, and often despised by the Arab nations that presumably champion their cause.

These conditions have spawned terrorists who can easily justify their actions, especially when they are influenced by friends and relatives whose experiences parallel their own. In addition, like the Israeli settlers, they have leaders who have asserted that they too are descended from Biblical nations and figures. Their heroes are the ancient Philistines and Canaanites, as well as Ishmael, the son of Abraham, or Ibrahim. Cutting across ethnic and religious boundaries, the root of terrorism is the individual's own worldview, one in which belief is inextricably linked to deed.

To Rapaport, a literal interpretation of the Bible forms the basis for his behavior in every area of his life, as well as his overarching view of the world itself. Therefore, once he concludes that a particular course of action is mandated by the Torah, he feels fully justified in carrying it out, even if it is a terrorist act.

Rapaport differs from other religious fundamentalists in one crucial way, and it is this that makes his story so compelling. Divining the wishes of God as expressed through the Bible is no easy matter, to say the least, and it is in the letters themselves that we see the difficulty Rapaport experiences in determining just what that mandate is. What distinguishes him from so many other fundamentalists is that when confronted with the feeling that he must take direct and violent action, he finds himself wrestling with his conscience.

It is that part of Rapaport committed to respecting other human beings, the very part that made him aspire to be a social worker, that often clashes with the Biblical imperative. We see it as well in the individual conversations he has with his Arab neighbors and in his efforts to teach his children tolerance for the Palestinians while simultaneously viewing them as the enemy. And it is the efforts in which he engages to resolve such conflicts that make for such a compelling portrait.

And what of the larger context? How do we locate what Rapaport did within the historical development of protest in Israeli society? By recognizing that these events and actions are part of a more general pattern of escalating levels of terrorism, one in which each stage legitimizes and makes possible that which follows.

In the first stage there is general opposition to the established order: protests, demonstrations, even sit-ins. This is what happened in the West Bank in the early years.

Stage 2 is characterized by targeted violence. Rapaport and his coconspirators attacked the mayors, and this act was supported by large segments of the Israeli population, especially those living in the territories who saw the mayors as terrorists who used their offices to support bombings and the murder of Israeli civilians.

The third stage is marked by random violence. Subsequent to the attacks on the mayors, several members of the same loosely tied-in West Bank Underground Movement killed several students at random in an Islamic college. They also planned to place bombs under civilian Arab buses. Their objective was to call attention to the situation in general by the very desperation of their actions and to give Palestinians "a taste of their own medicine."

Rapaport, though he knew those who planned these acts, was not part of their plot, and it is doubtful, given the distinction he draws between targeted and random violence, that he would have approved of it. When asked how he would feel if it could be demonstrated that his own deeds might have set the stage for random violence, he replied: "It would have to be proved to me that this was the case, and if it could, it would be a problem for me personally."

The fourth stage of escalating terrorism was the Rabin assassination in which one Jew killed another Jew. It can be hypothesized that each stage of protest makes possible the subsequent one. This inevitable process is motivated not only by the need to find new and dramatic ways of expressing one's position but one that is also conditioned by the response, or lack of responsiveness, on the part of the perceived enemy.

We see here how the players in the drama of terrorism and protest emerge and evolve. And Rapaport's letters provide an invaluable and detailed description of how participants move from thought to speech and, finally, to action. There is something even more significant at work here. These acts represent the extreme manifestation of a more general quest— a yearning of sorts—to find deeper meaning in life.

Although Israelis appear to want normality and peace more than anything else, it is questionable whether they are psychologically ready for a world in which there may be no clearly identified enemies. The Jewish people, who have endured centuries of antisemitism and a Holocaust, may find this to be one of their greatest challenges. In truth, a society whose conception of its enemies had been fundamentally altered, whether by independent forces of history or through negotiation and realpolitik, must also exorcise the demons of fear and insecurity, as well as the habits of stereotyped thinking. The powerful and visceral reactions of the Israelis to terrorist bombings are clear evidence of how close to the surface such apprehensions are.

For Era Rapaport and the settler movement, the meaning of life is clear. They feel they know who their enemies are, but their raison d'être is not shaped by that fact. Rather, it is based on a vision of creating a society resembling that one of the days of old, one grounded in religion, land, and a deeply rooted sense of peoplehood.

For most Israelis, secularized and ambivalent at best about the relevance and even validity of Biblical history, such a vision is unworkable. To be viable, Israeli society must create an alternative worldview that gives positive meaning to the existence of its members, not one that depends on the presence of enemies from the outside. In fact, only an understanding of this process will enable the Israelis to forestall a descent into the violence and chaos of civil war.

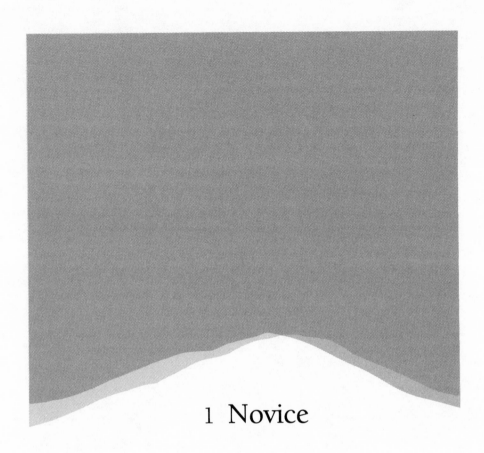

1 Novice

My dear friends, Shalom and Ruth:

We were sitting in the second row of the airplane. After landing in Israel, the aircraft suddenly stopped taxiing on the way to the terminal. The head stewardess addressed one of the other flight personnel. "I don't know why we've been told to stop the plane out here." The other asked, "Why are there so many police cars out on the runway?"

I knew.

My wife, Orit, and I walked down the steps of the plane. Three more steps, two more, one more, and my feet touched the land of my beloved country.

"Shalom, Era," the police officer said. "You are under arrest for your involvement in the 'Underground.' Please follow us."

Quickly, I bent down onto my knees and kissed the Holy Land. I was home. Then I followed the special undercover agents to their car and to Ben Gurion Airport jail.

The moment I had anticipated for over two and a half years had come. I had come home to jail.

It's 11:30 P.M. and I'm lying in my cell bed. Years ago, if you had told me that I would be in an Israeli prison for protecting myself and my family against Arab terrorists, I would have told you that you were crazy.

The flight from New York was okay. Orit and I decided to meet in Europe before my return to Israel. We hadn't seen each other for two months after she returned home with the kids, and I stayed on in New York to be with my sick mother. After six days of being together in Europe, we flew to Israel.

We were whisked off in the police car. I spent ten minutes with Orit and her father, and then the country I love locked me up. The next morning, a judge freed me on bail, after I had confessed in writing to my actions. I was freed for ten days. During that time, the trial was to be held. My father-in-law drove me to my home in Shilo to see my family and my five gifts from G-d, my five kids. Before walking up the steps to my house, I looked out over the valley I love, the valley of Shilo, the first capital of the Jewish people in Israel, where the Tabernacle once rested, where Samuel the prophet learned from Eli, the High Priest.

Shalom and Ruth, as I stood gazing out at the green pasture land and surrounding mountains, an amazing feeling swelled up inside me. My legs started trembling, tears rolled down my face, and in half a minute, the three years of my exile in America, all the anguish and confusion and fear I had lived with were shaken off. I was home. Back where I belonged. I remember the trip we took with the kids, before they went home to Israel, so we could all be together before I went into prison. I remembered the beautiful vistas and mountains we had seen in the Grand Canyon and Yellowstone, Glacier, and Zion National Parks, but for all of their beauty, there was a very big difference. They were somebody else's mountains. Here, in Shilo, the mountains were mine. They belonged to me and my people. Their power rose from the ground up into my feet, up through my body, and all of the bad feelings of being away from Israel, of being a stranger in a strange land, were washed away. A maaseh Hashem, an act of G-d.

I turned and started walking to my house. My little girl, Atarah, was the first one to see me. She ran down the stairs toward me and I ran up to her. And then, finally, she was in my arms; no words, her tears and mine mixed together and watered the holy soil beneath us.

I didn't suffice to hold her when Yitzhak, all two-and-a-half years of him, came running down. More tears. Then David, seven years old, jumped down from the stairs. I put down Atarah and Yitzhak and held David, letting our love and tears flow from one to the other. Then Moriyah, our oldest. I hadn't seen her in over four months. We both held each other and nurtured that ecstatic moment. I had no words and no way to thank G-d. I took a look around at the mountains beyond my house and held on to four of my five wonderful gifts and wondered if there could be any pleasure greater than this.

That evening, all the residents of the village threw a surprise welcome for me. We danced and sang continuously for a full forty-five minutes. It was really a tremendous high to feel so much love and their happiness that I had come back.

The next day I went to my city—Yerushalayim. First, I went to the Mount of Olives, to the gravesites of my family. To my father, may the memory of the righteous be for a blessing. It was an unreal meeting at the grave. I didn't know that I had any tears left, but they came, like water from the snows of the Hermon. Like it is written, "In the merit of the fathers, the children shall return." I thanked God and asked him to keep me strong.

From there, I went to the grave of a true builder of Israel, my uncle, who was three times sentenced to hanging by the British and each time escaped. He had much to do with my being in Israel. Then to the graves of my grandfather and grandmother, and of my great grandfather and great grandmother, buried on the hills where they lived, the holy hills of Jerusalem.

The next day in court I pleaded guilty to charges of grievous bodily harm and membership in a terrorist organization, which really never existed, but the court insisted it had. I was released on bail, and the court case was to continue two days later. The time was filled with phone calls of encouragement from all over. Newspapers interviewed me, and, over and over, I repeated that for a Jew it is better to be in jail in the land of Israel than to be free in America.

And that statement, my friends, is true. I sit in my jail cell, forcibly being kept from my country, my people, and my family. Is it hard on me? Is it hard for a father not to be able to hold his children, to kiss them, to teach them Torah and the traditions which have kept our people together for thousands of years? Is it hard for a husband not to be able to hold his wife? Not to be with her? Is it hard not to be able to take care of your sick mother and to fulfill the great commandment of honoring your father and mother? My wife will give birth in the next two months. For the first time, I shall not be at her side. Is it hard not to be near your wife on the days before birth, to strengthen her and share with her the exquisite moments of God's creation—the birth of a new soul to the world?

For me, my heart and mind are being torn apart. It has been many, many a Shabbat since I have not been able to hold my children, one at a time. To say that I miss this doesn't even begin to come close to describing the pain

15

every Friday night when I am alone, separated from my family by the prison fence.

Our holy land is right outside this prison, but I am not able to walk her, defend her, or build her. Rather, I sit here in prison. Because I did what any normal Jew would do—protect himself and his family and his people against PLO killers.

And yet, my dear friends, I would not exchange your position with mine. It sounds crazy to you? You can't understand? Here, even in prison, I'm with my people, and I go to sleep secure, that here, in Israel, my children will grow up to be strong and proud Jews. Be truthful with yourselves. Think about your kids. What Jewish future do they have in America? What's the chance they'll marry Jews?

Please write to me—through Orit. She'll bring me the letters. Otherwise the prison gets them.

In friendship and love,
Era

January 1987
Tel Mond Prison

My precious children:

What does a father in prison write to his children? Will what I write be understood? And even if it is understood, will it make it easier for you?

Will you forgive me for bringing you back to Israel when we knew it meant that we would be separated? And if I tell you that part of my action against the PLO mayor, Bassam Shaka, was for your sakes, will you understand? Will it make it easier for you to explain to the kids in school why your father is in prison?

The three years we spent in the United States away from our homeland were hard for your Ema [mother] and me, but harder for you. At least your mother and I had the conviction that we were on an important mission— to help other Jews come to Israel. But you were uprooted from the holiness

16

of Eretz Yisrael [Israel], from the beauty of Shilo, from the closeness of our nation. In its place, you found cold, self-centered New York. Instead of being able to come home from school and go outside to play with your friends like in Shilo, you came home to four walls. Visiting friends meant calling and arranging for an appointment. Your school sent us a welcome letter: "We want permission to fingerprint your children." So that in case of kidnapping, God forbid, they could identify your bodies. After that, who dreamt of letting you go outside to play?

And did you understand the reason for our going to America? We told you that we came to further Aliyah [immigration to Israel] and bring more Jews to Israel. Even though it was a hardship for all of us, it was a mitzvah [good deed] to do so, and you were contributing too. I think you understood that we needed more Jews in Israel. We explained that when our homeland was returned to us after two thousand years, the Jews from the West didn't come. And how it was our duty to show them how important it was that they come, how important it was for themselves, and for their children. But still you wanted to go home. The luxuries of America didn't mean anything to you. The bigger car, the color TVs, the amusement parks and endless toys . . . you preferred your own country, Eretz Yisrael.

And my Moriyah, do you remember the first Chanukah in America? When it came time to play with the dreidel, you refused to play with the one we bought in the store, because on it were Hebrew letters which spelled, "A great miracle happened THERE." You couldn't accept the fact that we weren't at home, where the letters on the dreidel spell out that the miracle happened HERE, in Israel. In New York, we lit our menorah by the window. In Shilo, we lit two. One outside the door, because we weren't afraid that someone would come by and smash it or take it, and one we lit at the top of the mountain, together with everyone in the village, overlooking the battlefields and homeland of the Maccabees [Jewish warriors who fought against the Greeks between 200 and 100 B.C.E.], the heroes of the holiday of Chanukah.

Remember, Moriyah, how you fought with us? You wanted to return to Israel, even without us. When our six-month assignment was finished, you wanted fly back. "Abba," [Father] you said. "You taught me that a Jew lives in Israel. What are we doing here?" At seven years old, your logic was sharper than ours.

Because you didn't know English so well, school was difficult in New York. And you had trouble making friends. You came home sad, day after day, not wanting to return. And you didn't want to go to the synagogue there. You said it was too fancy, and that the people didn't pray—they talked.

You couldn't understand why there were such big houses with so few children in them. Birthday parties seemed more extravagant to you than Bar Mitzvahs in Israel. You said the parties had nothing to do with the child. And when your birthday came, you wanted your party in the house and not in some restaurant.

One day, toward the end of May, we told you that we were going on a vacation. When we came back, we'd be going home to Israel. First we went to a friend's house on a lake. Than another friend gave us a car, and we traveled across America, camping out. Wherever we went, I would glance up to the rear-view mirror to see if we were being followed by the police, but your mother and I were careful to keep our worries from you kids. You were all so delicious, we never wanted the trip to end. Then one Shabbat, near Glacier National Park, Ema and I sat you down and told you why we were traveling. You know, we said, that Uncle Yehuda, your Ema's brother, is on trial in Israel, and he's locked up in jail. Yes, you said, we told you plenty of times. Well, we said, do you know why? Yes, you answered. Some very bad Arabs did a lot of bad things and the police didn't stop them, so Uncle Yehuda did. Right, we said, but for that he has to sit in jail. You couldn't understand that and neither could we. And we continued, there are other brave Jews who are also in prison, and others who helped Uncle Yehuda stop the bad Arabs and not all of them are in jail. And then we told you—your Abba is one of them. When we go back to Israel, I will have to go to jail. Because sometimes, I tried to explain, one has to undergo hardships to build Eretz Yisrael [Israel]. Finally the tears came, both yours and ours. Then you, Moriyah, and David complained to us. Why did we have to tell you on Shabbat? Shabbat was supposed to be a day of joy.

Then we asked you the question; would you rather stay in America, and

Abba won't have to go to jail—or would you rather go back to Israel, where Abba will have to go away to jail for many years? All three of you answered, we want to go back to Israel, even if Abba has to go to jail.

Later that night when you were sleeping, Ema and I couldn't find the words to thank God enough for all of you. We were sitting on the porch of the motel room, looking at the stars, holding each other close, asking each other how do you say thank you to God.

To you, my children, being in Israel is natural because that is where you were born. But I had to fight the pull of America, the greatness of America, the opposition of friends, and yes, even my mother, who wanted me to stay. I came alone to Israel, returning to our country, to our land, but I had to make it mine in a way that it is yours by birth. To hear my children tell me that they would rather live in Israel than in America, even though it means that their father will be in jail—I was so proud of you and thankful to God. You, my children, and your desire to go back to Israel were my proof that I had truly made Israel mine.

I love you my children with the love of a father for his children—thank you, God.

Abba

January 1987
Tel Mond Prison

Dear Aaron, Shalom:

I must admit, I was surprised very much, and pleasantly so, to have received a letter from you. It has been years since the day when we first met at the Jewish Theological Seminary library fire. You, the Conservative kid, and I, the Orthodox Jew, working together to save books.

By the way, when and how did you get my address? I have followed your trail through the grapevine. During my recent three-year stint in America, I wanted to contact you.

From some of your writings which I have read, I know we have gone different ways over the last twenty years. You write me, "About five years ago, I read an article on the West Bank by the *New York Times* reporter, David Shipler. You were interviewed. I showed the article to my wife and told her, 'It can't be him, but it is. What happened to him?' " In your letter, you ask the same question. I'll try to answer.

First some basic facts. As you remember, I finished Yeshiva University in '66. I studied in Jerusalem at Mercaz HaRav Yeshiva in '67, returned to New York to get my master's in social work, then went back to Israel and started working with juvenile delinquents. That's when distance and time did its own, and though I thought of you often, no contact.

I married Orit, a Sabra [native-born Israeli], in '74. We have six children now, from ten years to five months. The baby boy, Dvir, was born while I've been in prison.

Yes, I remember our discussions at the library and afterward. We were both greatly concerned about the future of Judaism. This shared concern brought us close. We came from different backgrounds, and we were studying in different schools, whose philosophies were far apart. But we felt a bond.

Looking back, Aaron, we had a lot of ideas and good times together. You were more surprised at my attitudes than I was by yours. Y.U. guys were supposedly close-minded and not worldly. But in your opinion, I was different. I remember you saying, "You mean you also think about girls?"

Interestingly, we agreed on non-Jewish matters and differed on Judaism. We both grew up in mixed neighborhoods. I in East Flatbush, and you in the Bronx on the Grand Concourse. We both had our share of gang fights and were familiar with the slur, "Dirty Jew." You surprised me on that one. You, the peacenik who demonstrated against Vietnam, slugging someone because they called you a dirty Jew.

The old men in my synagogue and in your temple couldn't understand our decision to fight for Black rights. In those days, they were called Negroes, but we called them by the name they preferred—Blacks. As sensitive young men, we couldn't stand that our parents and neighbors called them "shvartzes."

We decided to go down to Washington D.C. together in 1963 for the great March for Freedom. It was on Shabbat, and we startled each other. You didn't believe that I would march on Shabbat. I didn't believe that you would take a hotel room with me on the outskirts of the city and walk with me five miles each way, which you didn't have to because you traveled on Shabbat.

I'm not sure—did you agree with my joining the "Maccabees," the Crown Heights street patrol, or were you against it? As I'm writing, the memories return. We both got beaten up down in Washington Square Park in another protest. You made a point of wearing a yarmulke [skullcap] so people would know you were a Jew. I told you that I didn't accept your reason for wearing it—just to make a statement and not out of religious belief. Anyhow, if you had listened to me, you wouldn't have been beaten up that day.

And do you remember—a couple of months later—you and your date met me on the Staten Island Ferry. It was Saturday night after Shabbat, and I was with some fifty Jewish teenagers, some with kippot [skullcaps] and some without, some girls in jeans and some in skirts. You joined us in singing, "Am Yisrael Chai" [Long Live Israel], to the accompaniment of someone's guitar.

In your letter, you wrote that you were surprised I was arrested for attacking Arabs. You would not have been surprised, you said, to learn that I had been arrested for demonstrating for their rights.

Before I continue, I want to reveal a secret. When the "Jewish Underground" case broke out in Israel, I was in America with my family, counseling Jews who wanted to move to Israel. I remained in the States to be with my mother who was fighting a brain cancer. I also used the time to elicit help for the "boys"—the fathers, and husbands, and teachers, and rabbis, and war heroes and pioneers who had been arrested in Israel. Once, because of your position as a Conservative Rabbi, it was important that you sign a petition to the President of Israel asking for a pardon on their behalf. I hesitated for two days before deciding that I personally wouldn't call you, and so one of my co-workers called, and you know what you said—jail was where they belonged.

You wrote in your letter, "Era, what did Israel do to you? You, the freedom fighter. You who walked arm in arm with thousands of Blacks in D.C. You, one of the best drug-prevention workers I've chanced on. The devoted social worker who could make a desolate human being feel like his life was worth living. Who got beaten up for defending the underprivileged. What happened to you? How could you? Are Arabs not people? What about them? My Judaism teaches, "Love thy neighbor." Is the West Bank more important than that? Who are you to throw those people off their land?"

You've asked me some hard questions, and I'll try to answer them. I won't try to convince you that I'm right.If you can try to understand me, that will be sufficient. But it will have to wait for another night.

From prison in the land of our forefathers.

Era

February 1987
Tel Mond Prison

Dear Aaron,

At the outset, I shall tell you unequivocally—I am proud to be doing my share in the rebuilding of our homeland.

Yes, there are problems. So what? Yes, we make mistakes; who doesn't? We are confronted by difficult and serious problems. Not always do we have the opportunity of being Monday-morning quarterbacks. In football—a mistake and you lose the game. Here, a mistake and you lose a life—lose parts of Eretz Yisrael. Sometimes we are hasty, even brash. We, Aaron, are fighting a war for our life, for your life, and for the Land of Israel, upon which our life as a people and nation depends.

To this very day, we cannot afford to make a mistake. You seem to forget that. In Lebanon, we made a mistake. We listened to the U.S. and didn't destroy the PLO in Beirut. Over 500 of our soldiers paid for that, and we are still paying for it today.

You write me that settling Judea and Samaria, or the West Bank, as you call it, forces people into doing what I did, and will cause apartheid and make Arabs second-class citizens. You say it will force me into physically and violently controlling the area, and chasing the Arabs out, or using them only as laborers.

You have read well what the press is disseminating, but there is a world of difference between the press and the truth. If there is anybody trying to bridge the gap between Arab and Jew it is us—those of us living among the Arabs in Judea and Samaria. What do you expect me to do, Aaron? Put down my gun and let the Arabs slaughter me? Or stay in the States, where you don't have that problem?

I, like you, am the product of a Western civilization. When I first came to YOSH [Judea and Samaria] and became the Mayor of Shilo, I said to myself, now is the opportunity to instill some of my Western values into the area. (As if the Americans have treated their minorities well. Only twenty years ago, you'll remember from our marches, Blacks were in the backs of buses, wouldn't be served in many restaurants, and on and on. But why do I have to go further than ourselves? As a kid of fourteen, I remember in our house the family discussing that Yeshiva University was putting up a medical school, because Jews weren't accepted in other places. And it isn't over today. My mom has an apartment in Cedarhurst. Nearby is Atlantic Beach, where we stayed for some six months. Opposite the house that we rented was a beach club. Atlantic Beach is some 70% Jewish, but the beach club has, to this very day, a no-Jews-allowed policy!)

Shilo is located some 30 miles directly north of Jerusalem. That's pretty close—less than the distance from your Long Island house to New York City. When we arrived in Shilo there were eight other families. The men traveled to Jerusalem to work daily. The only method of communication was an old British telephone line from Ramallah to Singel—the nearby Arab village. From there we connected our telephone via an army telephone line. The line went through another Arab village—Turmos-Aya. It was hung on some trees. This was our only means of speaking to the outer world. There were women pregnant, and if there was a need for a doctor or ambulance, the phone was our only connection. If there was a security problem (and there were), we could notify the authorities only via that phone. So, as you can well understand, that phone had to be in working condition.

Some two weeks after arriving at Shilo (and many times earlier) the telephone line was cut down in Turmos-Aya. That afternoon we repaired it. Within two hours it had been cut down again. In the past, we had complained to the police, but aside from reporting our complaint, nothing was done. In Shilo that evening, at a village meeting, we discussed our possible reactions.

Almost all of those present suggested "illegal" measures—all the legal methods had been of no avail. It was my chance. Here I was—the "Westerner." I would teach them all some democracy. I suggested that we drive over to our Arab neighbors, meet with the mukhtar, the village chief, and solve the problem on a friendly basis.

It was laughed at. "Are you serious?" they asked. "You are trying to introduce Western values into an Oriental/Middle Eastern society. It won't work." But I pressed. In the end I convinced them to allow me to try. It was decided that I and two others would go to Turmos-Aya and speak with the mukhtar the next evening.

The next day, the telephone line was cut down twice. During the day, Shlomo Levyatan had spoken to the mukhtar and arranged the meeting. When we arrived at the house, I was surprised to find some 15 of the village notables present. Aaron, you have heard, I assume, of Arab hospitality. So it was. The table was laden with some of the best fruits that our holy land has to offer. After formalities and introductions, we talked. Our discussion was held in three languages. Shlomo, born in Syria and raised in Beirut, knows Arabic perfectly and translated when necessary. Shevach and I alternated between Hebrew and English and a few of my broken words in Arabic.

I spoke first and told the mukhtar that I requested the meeting for two reasons. One to complain about the cut telephone lines, and second, to discuss mutually important matters.

The mukhtar related to us that some of his villagers complained we had taken away their land to erect and expand Shilo; and that we drove through his village too quickly.

For me, Aaron, the mukhtar presented some very serious moral problems. Before coming to Shilo, Gush Emunim had completed an extensive legal search of the land in our area. For our purpose, the history of the area in the last eighty-five years is sufficient. As you know, at the turn of the century, present day Israel was part of the Turkish Empire. The Turkish registered land claims but much of the land remained unregistered. When the British and Turkish fought, each was interested in Arab and Jewish support. The British promised them both that in return for their help they would receive huge parts of Israel. After the war, even though we had helped the British much more than the Arabs, the British gave the land to Farouk, King of Saudi Arabia. He in turn took out the British maps and gave nice portions of it to his supporters. For some reason, unknown to anyone, the area of Shilo fell between some of these areas and was not divided. Some of the Arabs living in the area, after seeing that no one toiled the land, squatted on it and took it over. However, officially, the land was government owned. In 1948, when Jordan illegally occupied our country, that land became Jordanian Government land. When we returned in 1967, it became Israeli Government land.

For years, some of the Arabs in the area toiled the land and claimed it to be theirs. If I remember correctly, in the States there is a law of squatters' rights. In this part of the world, the law isn't that simple.

When we returned to Shilo there were two options. To settle on the ancient site of Shilo would have meant destroying the remnants of the first capital of Israel. Besides being illegal by law, it would destroy a legacy of our history. (Against the law, the Arabs had been farming on the site and destroying some of its archaeological remains for many years.) Or we could settle the rocky mountains near the site. As I wrote, those mountains were not registered to anyone at all. And, because the land was rocky, it wasn't being used for agriculture at all.

We're talking about a three-acre piece of land which was the home of our first eight trailers. That's an area smaller than your Temple parking lot! And yes, there was some illegal Arab agriculture in the vicinity. And what did we find there? Graves of our grandparents from the period of the Maccabee. The only reason that Yehudah the Maccabee left was because he and his children were murdered and massacred by the Greeks. Since then, save

25

for some grace periods, waves of conquering nations have never allowed us to return. When we finally started blasting the road up the mountainside, I was directing the massive bulldozer. At one point, the bulldozer pushed aside a huge boulder. I quickly signaled the driver to stop. The boulder was protecting an entrance to a cave. As I bent into it, I stopped short and gasped in astonishment and rubbed my eyes to reassure myself that I was seeing correctly. In the cave, hewn in the walls were six smaller caves. I was looking at a Jewish burial cave. Goose pimples covered my body. Do you understand me, Aaron? I, American-born Era Rapaport, was the first Jew to find this cave of our forefathers of over 100 generations ago! We were re-turning to build, to continue the legacy of the first capital of Israel. It's symbolic if you like; just as we were going forward into the future, we had to first touch base with our past. The Ba'al Shem Tov [the founder of ha-sidism] put it this way, "Remembrance is the secret of the redemption."

I came out of the cave and ran to call our rabbi, whose name is Bin-Nun (just like the first leader of the Jews in Biblical Shilo). He was as excited as I was. So was the bulldozer driver. Who wouldn't be? To this very day it is hard for me to grasp the reality of that moment. Our forefathers in Shilo lived and died for practicing the Torah in Israel. The Holy Tabernacle, which held the tablets of the Ten Commandments, was located in Shilo for 369 years. Do I have the right to even consider giving away that which is not mine but my grandparents'? When one of the founding fathers of Is-rael, Isaac Tabenkin, was asked about giving away parts of Eretz Yisrael, he answered, "I have to ask two people: my grandfather who is no longer alive and my grandson who has not yet been born."

Aaron, we have gone different ways, but have you gone so far from your roots that you can consider giving away your history? Which is also your future?

Shlomo responded to the mukhtar's charge of taking Arab land. If any of his villagers have specific complaints and proof of land ownership, we will solve the problem together. Shlomo continued that we were not inter-ested in taking away their land—there was sufficient land for all of us in the area. We came back to live here in peace and together we can success-fully develop the area. The mukhtar and the notables expressed a willingness to work and live together. One of the notables told Shlomo, "We welcome you here. We know that your grandparents many generations ago lived here. We even know that your prophet Eli, the High Priest, lived here. We call the wadi riverbed in the valley wadi Eli."

Over the years, I learned that the Arabs did us a favor. Throughout Israel, they named many of their villages in accordance with the name of the ancient Jewish village that was located on that spot. For example, Beit-El = Bitin; Shilo = Silon; Livonak = Labun; Givon = Gabah. They are well aware of the land's true owners.

This started out to be a two-page letter and is already a Megillah [a long story]. But your questions deserve answers.

After the discussion about the land, we discussed mutual problems; the bad state of the road leading to our villages, difficulties with water and electricity.

At that point, I brought up the cutting down of our telephone line by some of his villagers. The notables listened intently and after a few words between them, the mukhtar said, "That is no problem. Tomorrow, I will speak to the villagers and there will be no more of that. If you have connections in the Military Command, maybe you can influence them to improve and add to the telephone system; the situation is terrible." Shlomo, who worked in the Command, told the mukhtar that he already had turned to them, but they could do nothing for there were not enough lines in the area. After a few more minutes of plain talk, we said goodbye.

As we drove back to Shilo, I turned to Shevach and Shlomo. "See, I was right. A little Western methods. No need for retaliatory measures. After we explained the problem to the mukhtar, he immediately agreed to solve it." Shlomo smiled and said to me in Arabic the equivalent of, "Don't count your chickens before they hatch."

"You see, Orit, a little American culture is so helpful," I told my wife when I arrived home. The next day my resolve was strengthened as the phone worked perfectly. I suggested to Shevach that we drive to the mukhtar to thank him for taking care of the problem. Shlomo was scheduled to return late that evening and so we delayed it for another day.

The next day, the telephone line was cut down three times!! As soon as

Shlomo returned, we drove directly over to the mukhtar. He tried to seem surprised, but it was obvious that he knew what happened. Aaron, although you are the spiritual leader of a large congregation in Long Island, I highly doubt that you have the power or control that a mukhtar of an Arab village has. He knows exactly what is going on and his word is "holy." That's part of the culture.

The mukhtar said that he was surprised and would do his utmost to punish the vandals and stop their actions. "Just two nights ago," I said, "we met and, at least in words, we agreed that we have been destined to live near each other and must accept one another. You promised that you would put an end to the cutting down of the telephone lines. Is this the way that we are to trust in each other?"

On the way back to Shilo, Shlomo enlightened me. "The quicker you learn it, the more you'll understand the Arab culture and the better off you'll be," he said. "Talking, requesting nicely, cajoling for something that is yours is seen as a sign of weakness and fear. If you act, you are respected. If you only talk, you are weak.

"Throughout the Arab world, there is no democracy. The Arab child is born to listen to authority. In a religious Arab family, if a girl has premarital relations, her father or brother will kill her. You wouldn't dream of that in Western culture, but that is the given, the expected, the required by law in Arab culture; if one doesn't act that way, he is wrong. It may seem barbaric to you, but as I said before, it doesn't change the fact.

"Because there is no democracy and because the Arab child is brought up from birth to rule by force, where actions speak louder than words, your method is simply not understood by them. The last two nights of our meetings with them, you have presented yourself as a weak leader. They'll talk to you and do the exact opposite."

I went to my caravan and guard duty that night a lot more uncertain about my Western methods.

After prayers the next morning, we found that our telephone line had been once again cut down. Shevach and I drove to Turmos-Aya to repair the damage. Why burden you and lengthen a lengthy letter—that day the line was cut five times! Late that night, sitting outside our caravan, with the telephone line cut once again, I turned to Shevach. "I drove into Ramallah today and spoke with the military commander and police chief, advising them of the situation and requesting their help." The police chief in Ramallah told me, "If I had a policeman, which I don't, he would be like all of our beat policemen—an Arab. Do you think that an Arab policeman is going to stop some Arab kids from cutting down your telephone line?"

Then I went to the military commander of the area and, to an extent, I was more upset by his words than by the police chief! "I can put an end to the vandalism in your area in just a few hours, but I have orders not to." "What do you mean?" I asked him. "We have women and children out there, pregnant women, with no method of communication, and you're telling me that you have orders from above!?" By a slip of his mouth, he blurted out—"Go speak to Ezer" (Ezer Weizman, then Minister of Defense). Shevach answered, "We've already spoken to Ezer—he's politically against us and therefore he has given orders to the army not to interfere." There was a general consensus in Shilo that if no serious action was taken, soon our neighbors would make things much worse. "How about turning to some cabinet members so they can use their influence?" I suggested. Shevach enumerated some eight ministers who were approached and who understood our predicament but couldn't help. Maxim, originally from Russia, spoke up. "For weeks, time and time again, our telephone lines have been cut down; all the nice words in the world have gotten us nowhere fast. Do you want to wait until there is an emergency and no phone is available? If we don't do something and soon, the Arabs will escalate their 'battle' against us.

"Why do we have to wait until somebody is hurt or killed until we respond?"

Rivka, mother of one and pregnant, spoke next. "Almost all of you leave in the morning and return at night. Often, I am left here in the village alone without even a car in case it's necessary—something has to be done."

Tami, one of the pillars of the community, spoke up. "We have to look at the situation not only from our personal eyes. Why did we come back to Shilo? Why are we living in broken-down caravans? Why do we live half a day and night without electricity? Why are we willing to live without water for close to two to three days a week? Why have the Gurs brought their family to Shilo where their oldest child has absolutely no friends? Even more—Maxim is foregoing saying kaddish [the mourner's prayer] for his father, 'cause we have no minyan [quorum for prayer] here. I can go on and on, but I hope you understand my question and point. We have come here to return to parts of the Land of Israel that have been left unsettled by Jews. We have come here to fulfill the commandment of settling the Land of Israel, to make sure that there isn't an area of our land that's not populated by Jews. That's what the Torah says.

"If I was here for my personal convenience, then I could decide to do something or not. Every time that telephone line is cut down by an emissary of the PLO, it is a blow against the honor of the Land and People of Israel. The PLO is responsible for this provocation. However, every time that I don't react, then I am also responsible for that blow. Does anyone of us have the right to abet this?"

There was silence. While I was still digesting Tami's words, Yosaif, one of the volunteers, spoke up. "With your permission, I'd like to say a few words. I agree with everything Tami has to say . . . but we are part of our State and government. Do we have the right to act by ourselves and, if I understand right, to take the law in our own hands?" Again, there was silence.

Shlomo works in the military command of Judea and Samaria. As part of his work, he meets daily with Arabs of our area. The majority of them, he explains, tell him over and over that they want to live in peace. If we didn't respond to the vandalism we would be strengthening the hands of the PLO. You see, the PLO wields great physical fear over the villagers. The youngsters who cut down the telephone line are paid by the PLO for their actions. When nothing happens to them, it strengthens the PLO. At the same time, it weakens those Arabs who want to live in peace with us. On the other hand, if we do respond and the Arabs of Turmos-Aya realize that for every action of theirs, a response of ours follows, it gives them strength to face up to the PLO.

Aaron, I personally was unsure what to do. While living in Ofra, we had reacted a few times to stone throwing by PLO emissaries. But I had grown up to law and order. I remember "walking the beat" with some of the policemen in the East Flatbush section of Brooklyn where I was born. As a citizen of Israel, could I, we, willingly go against the law of the land? Being unsure, I requested a delay in our decision until the following evening. Those who wanted to react claimed that we had to do so that evening in order to make the villagers of Turmos-Aya realize that we will react swiftly, that we mean business. We took a half-hour break to think. Orit and I walked toward the ancient destroyed city of Shilo. Who knows, I thought, maybe the Prophet Samuel will awaken and give us advice. I felt I was being swayed toward action. Shlomo and Tami's words made much sense. Also, we, the Rapaports, were new to Shilo. The other families had been here some seven months and had suffered through the cutting of the telephone line in the past. They had, indeed, spoken to the government officials over and over, with only negative results. It really wasn't taking the law into our own hands, for there wasn't any law. The PLO did what they wanted to and nobody even attempted to stop them.

We returned to the caravan where the others had gathered and I was promptly asked if I decided. Yes, I responded—we should act, and tonight. I could see shock on some of the faces. My suggestion that the action be left to three of us was accepted and the meeting broke up.

Shevach and I stayed on and discussed what kind of action and who would be involved besides ourselves. Aaron, as a rabbi, you have been in situations where you acted in a manner that you didn't want to—but had to. So, you'll understand when I write you, that I was going to perform an act that evening that I didn't want to—but had to. You do not agree with the action; that I imagine. At least, to the best of your ability, try and put yourself in my place.

We had decided that we were going to cut down the electric line directly opposite the spot that our telephone line had been cut down—so that all would realize the reason for our action.

"If the police come and ask if anybody from Shilo cut down the line, we'll probably have to sit in prison," Shevach warned. "Shevach," I said, "the police don't even know the way here and besides—we are doing the right thing; we have nothing to worry about. But, if they ever do come, I'll be the first to admit to the action."

31

We arrived at the cutting spot with our ladder and cutting tools. Here, Aaron, a little historical background on the electricity situation. The Jordanians "cared" so much about Judea and Samaria that they paved almost no new roads, laid very few sewage pipes and erected no national electric grid. In fact, before we returned, almost none of the Arab villages had either electricity or running water. With Jewish money, generators were installed in almost all the Arab villages and electricity supplied to the homes. The generators were run by the individual Arab villages, who had to pay for their upkeep. Therefore, most villages would shut down the generators at midnight until the morning. Here is an interesting and sad side fact. Almost all the new Jewish villages were supplied generators for electricity. Since we were also required to pay for the upkeep of the generator, we, like our Arab neighbors, shut them down for almost eight to ten hours a day. The difference between them and us? We shut them down during the day, for we had to have it on throughout the night, so that security projectors would work. It's comparative, in a way, to the fact that the Arabs need no guard duty in their villages, while we must have them. Because the Arabs attack us, and they know that we won't attack them.

Getting back. We arrived at the village after the generator had been shut down for the night. Out came the ladder and up it went, but even with my height, there was no way I could reach the lines. Ehud, who had joined for the action, suggested that we delay it for another evening and bring the proper equipment. Shevach suggested that we travel to Ofra and bring pole climbing shoes. "Maybe they're on loan to another village, and besides it will take us at least one hour to do so," I responded. Shevach and I came up with the same idea. "Maxim is a sharpshooter; let's get him and he'll shoot down the electric line." We decided to do it ourselves.

The line was only about eighteen feet in the air, and no one is around to get hurt. After a few minutes of thought, the three of us fired at the electric line and succeeded in cutting it down.

On the way back to Shilo, I turned to Shevach. "Do you think the Arabs will understand and stop?"

I wouldn't have burdened you with the story, Aaron, if not for the results. About a half-hour after the morning prayers, a police car showed up in Shilo. Two detectives from the Ramallah police department were interested to know whether anyone from Shilo shot at the electric line in Turmos-Aya. Amazing. For some six months, we had been complaining about attacks on us by Arabs—financed by the PLO—and not even once did the police come. Yet the same morning, maybe an hour after the Arabs of Turmos-Aya complained, the police showed up!

Shevach and I confessed. But we weren't prepared for the next step. "You are under arrest," they said. I was flabbergasted. For protecting myself? In the police station, after fingerprinting, a statement, and confiscation of our Uzi—we were released. The order to arrest us? From above.

I'm photostating for you a copy of the newspaper article on the court case that we went through—it speaks for itself. The judge himself realized our predicament and therefore gave us a very light sentence. You are right, Aaron; living in the area "forces people into doing what I did." You want me to leave? Just pull out of YOSH and there will be peace? Aaron, from Long Island, it may seem that way, but the Arabs want Jerusalem, too. During our college days, you called me the dreamer and claimed that you were the realist. It seems we have changed positions. You are the dreamer and I the realist!! I write this fact sadly, for it means that I will be at war for many more years and that my children will serve in our army. If my neighbors in Jordan and Syria, etc., wanted peace and not land, we would have smoked the "peace pipe" long ago.

You are right, Aaron, if I pull out of YOSH and the Galilee and Tel Aviv, Beer-Sheva, in short, all of Israel, the Arabs will leave us alone—for that is what they want—Israel Judenrein, free of Jews.

I believe those who tell me that they want to run me into the sea. When the neighboring Arab villagers throw rocks at my car and cut down my telephone line—THEY ARE NOT PLAYING A GAME. They are DEADLY SERIOUS. And, like every healthy normal human being, I must protect myself. In sum, it is not "living in the area" that forces me into a physical and violent reaction. It is LIVING, period.

I have not finished responding to your letter; however, acquaintances of mine are leaving for the States tomorrow. I'll give this letter to Orit, who's visiting today, and I'll continue, please God, to write. I'm glad you have written. Write me about your position. You know, Aaron, we need you here—you, your wife and children and your congregation. And—you all need to be here soon.

Era

March 1987
Tel Mond Prison

Shalom Aaron:

I ended my last letter by suggesting that I would continue to answer your letter. I have received some 70 letters since entering prison and have tried to answer almost all of them. Yours has been, far and away, the longest. Sometimes I hope, through our letters, we can, once again, deepen our relationship and maybe I can help you understand what is happening here in Israel.

I wrote to you that the shooting of the electric power line in Turmos-Aya had a dramatic result. For six months after our action, the telephone lines to Shilo were not cut down—even once. Truthfully, it bothered me that they weren't. For, in this case, Shlomo and the others were right. It showed, exactly as Shlomo had said, that my Western way expressed weakness, not strength. For four months, residents of Shilo had spoken to our neighbors, police, army, Ministers and who not? The sum total—a constant increase of attacks on Shilo. One action—and not even a serious one—by us, and the attacks stopped. No more cutting down telephone lines and no more rocks thrown at us or our cars. For six months—total quiet.

I had the urge to go to the mukhtar and ask him why. I tried convincing Shlomo to go with me, but he laughed. "You still don't understand and are trying to impose Western values on a society that has a different value system." But you know me—stubborn. If Shlomo didn't agree to go, I searched for another way to reach the mukhtar. I drove over to meet and talk with Husni, an Arab I had befriended from a neighboring town. I had been to his house often and had gone to his son's wedding. And he had been our guest in Shilo. I was sure that he would agree to talk with me and the mukhtar.

The gist of my conversation with Husni surprised me. "Husni, I want to speak with you, as they say in Arabic, doogri [straight]." There were two other villagers with him—Ahmad and Ibrahim. Husni asked me if it was okay with me that they could hear the conversation and I agreed. I proceeded to discuss my dilemma with him and ended up requesting him to go with me to the mukhtar.

I could see that Husni was bewildered. "What is your problem? You want to ask the mukhtar why he didn't keep to his side of your deal?" He looked at me like you look at a child.

"I heard about your meeting. What the mukhtar said and what was done by the villagers is normal and your reaction was the right one for you, of course." It was my time to be bewildered. "You're telling me that the mukhtar's promise that there was to be no more telephone cutting was right, and that the villagers' action—cutting down the lines—was right also?

"Husni," I said, "your story reminds me of a Jewish joke. Two people with a disagreement came running to the rabbi. After the first told her side of the story, the rabbi said you're right. In came the second and after hearing her the rabbi said to her, you're right. After the woman left, the rabbi's wife questioned him. How is it possible that both women are right?" "You are also right," responded the rabbi. We all laughed.

Husni said to me. "Let me try and explain. You were born in the U.S. and are used to a democracy. Islam is not a democracy. Nowhere in the entire Arab world is there a democracy. We have had only dictators. Nowhere in the Arab world does an individual choose his way. In all our villages, our parents command their children what they are to do. If a child doesn't listen to his parents, he gets beaten. We teach obedience by the power of the hand, not by the word of the mouth. That is our way. To you it is strange. I know, for my brother and some cousins live in New Hampshire and I visit them."

"But all of what you have said means that the villagers should have listened to the mukhtar," I interrupted. "Generally speaking yes, but you came and spoke pleasantly to the mukhtar. To him, to us, we understand that the situation wasn't too bad. Talking, for you, is the proper way; but when it comes to obedience, that is not our culture. Simply, we come from different backgrounds. The mukhtar knows what the kids are doing. It was done with his permission; so coming after our attacks, to talk and ask us to be nice is seen as a sign of weakness."

"Why are you telling me this?" I asked. "I am learning from you that only by using force will we stop your actions—you mean that talking has no chance?"

"Before actions, sometimes it can be helpful, but afterward, talking is a sign of weakness."

"Then why are you telling me all of this?"

"First, friends of yours in Shilo, who know our culture, will tell you, if they haven't already; and second . . . wait, let me explain differently. I believe that most of us want to live in peace together with you. The PLO wants to take over the entire area, and therefore they pay the youth and their families to cut down the lines and throw rocks at your cars. Only by reacting strongly, as you have done, will you convince the elders, that they have to stop the PLO and not accept pay. We are afraid of the PLO and if you force us to reject them, we will do so. If we don't throw them out, there will be constantly escalating tension between you and I.

"Therefore, it is better for us, and for you, if you act. Talking is not effective. Now do you understand?"

Ibrahim spoke up. He seemed to be around twenty-five to twenty-seven years old. "Truthfully, I want us to run our own lives. I don't want Arafat, Hussein, or Begin to run me. But since you people, you religious Jews, are here and since you've built those villages and houses, I know that you will stay here. I can continue to fight you, and that will bring more and more problems and more injured and dead people. I want to stay here and am willing to live in peace, but the PLO doesn't allow it. The best you could do would be to get rid of the PLO."

"Tell me, doogri," I said. "On a day-to-day basis, does my living here interfere with you? Does my government hurt you?" Ibrahim thought for a moment. "On a day-to-day basis? We go our own way and do what we have to do. In our own villages, there really is no bother. But when we have to travel to the city, then there are the roadblocks; it is the feeling that another people control you. When there is an explosion and you're in the area, you worry you'll be arrested. You don't feel that this is your land."

"Ibrahim," I asked him, "how was it when King Hussein was around?"

"I'm embarrassed to tell you—you Jews have been much better rulers. Do you see these?" He pulled up his pants trouser and pointed to some deep scars on his legs. "They wanted information they thought I had and so they cut up my feet. If you ever spoke back to one of their soldiers, you would be immediately beaten up, taken away—sometimes to return, sometimes not. In many cases, they wouldn't allow anyone from our villages to work outside of the village. There were many executions by their soldiers. They raped many of our girls." I stopped him. "Ibrahim, I noticed that you say 'they,' about King Hussein and his soldiers. Why? Aren't they your people?" "No," Ibrahim said. "They are not one of us. Hussein doesn't even belong in Jordan and the way that they treat us—I told you just a little. But because it was bad with Hussein, that doesn't mean that I enjoy the situation today. As I said, you are better rulers—but you are rulers. You try and travel to Ramallah; if there is a roadblock we must all get out to have our identity cards checked. Then all our packages are opened. Sometimes we are frisked. At the same time, we see your cars passing us by and not needing to stop at the roadblock. Whenever there is a bombing, your soldiers come searching in our villages. It's a feeling of being a second-class citizen!"

"Ibrahim," I said, "I don't like those actions of ours. There have been times when I have been the soldier at the roadblock. Do you think I enjoy it? Do you think I enjoyed cutting down your electric line? But look at my side. You turn off your lights at night and go to sleep soundly. I, on the other hand, put on huge searchlights and stay up on guard duty. Yes, the roadblocks are degrading, but if we were more strict at them, then your neighbor here in your village wouldn't have succeeded in planting the bomb in Jerusalem that exploded and killed thirteen of my people. You are bothered by inconveniences—serious ones, but we are not out to kill you. I, on the other hand, am fighting a battle for my very survival. You're right; it would be preferable for you to rule yourself. But I can't give away this part of my country, for patriotic reasons you may not understand and for security reasons. The PLO and their backers would use this area to attack the rest of Israel. If you received an order to do so, wouldn't you? You would attack us as you have done so many times in the past. If you want a place to rule, it has to be in Jordan with Hussein."

There was silence as we all contemplated our discussion. I looked at my watch. "Like usual, Husni, I say to my wife that I'm going for a half an hour and I've been here close to two. I came so that you would go with me to the mukhtar and I understand a little bit why you won't. Inshallah [please God] we'll find the way to get along with each other peacefully." "Inshallah," they both responded and I drove back to Shilo.

What can I tell you, Aaron? In your letter you make me feel like an aggressor, maybe even one who enjoys this situation. You are so far from understanding the difficulties and intricacies of life here. Have you ever been to the West Bank? No. It's so typical of the "liberal" attitude. Why are you liberal to everybody but us? You can understand everybody, except of course—us. Why are you not willing to understand that YOSH is part of the State of Israel and that the tens of thousands of Jews who live here feel that this is our home? Why can't you understand that we have a need for safe borders, that to the victor belong the spoils also refers to Jews. The Arabs have constantly attacked us and, with God's help, we have defended each time. The land that we freed from their illegal occupation is ours! Both times the Arabs vowed to drive us into the sea. In both situations the West Bank was in their hands. Now they claim that there is no peace because of our being in YOSH, and you swallow their lie. Over and over they claim that YOSH is just a first step in the dismantling of the Jewish State. Why do you not believe them?

I'm sorry about the harsh tone, but your *j'accuse* to me calls for direct answers. You write of the terrible conditions that we "occupiers" are inflicting on the "poor" Arabs living under our control. Aaron, I'll start with the words of the saintly Rabbi Abraham Isaac Kook [religious Zionist leader, founder of the yeshiva attended by Rapaport and widely regarded as a spiritual leader of the settler movement] of blessed memory. "The people of Israel are returning to Israel not as refugees, but as a lion returning to its den." I am not an occupier. Travel the length and breadth of YOSH. You can't travel more than 3 miles in any direction without literally stepping on or falling over remains of our living here for the last 4,000 years. Judea and Samaria is a walking history tour of Judaism throughout all the generations.

I'll return to your letter and your accusation about the terrible conditions that we are inflicting on the Arabs. You have, of course, read of these conditions in the American press and in the leftist Israeli press. I live here and can give you a "slightly" different picture of the situation. A good number of the 650,000 Arabs living in YOSH are not exactly pro the State of Israel. However, they are not at all interested in living under the control of Hussein or the PLO. A good percentage of them are afraid of any Arab rule over them. If that surprises you, it is because of their being "spoiled" by Israeli rule. There is no Arab country in the world whose citizens have so much freedom as do the Arabs of YOSH. My Arab neighbors know it. As my former car mechanic (we no longer have a car) from Shechem [Nablus] told me, "I would like to rule ourselves, but I'm afraid. We destroy and kill ourselves all over. You are better for us than we are for ourselves." Look at the situation in the Arab states in our area. Lebanon—a total shambles; Syria just last year massacred some 20,000 of their own citizens; Jordan is a total dictatorship and in "Black September" of 1970 killed 100,000 Arabs. Iran and Iraq—over 1,000,000 killed in the war. Egypt—police crackdowns all the time, no democracy, no real personal freedom, one of the worst economic situations of all. Libya—a great place to visit! Do I have to go on?

In the entire Arab world, there is one place that the Arab is really safe— in Israel. The majority of Arabs living in YOSH want to live peacefully. Among them, however, are PLO terrorists. They, in fact, do more harm to the Arabs in YOSH than to us. They threaten Arabs who try to live peacefully with us. They support families whose children attack us. They pay and supply their local representatives with armaments. They do their utmost to overthrow our country and stir up the general Arab populace against us.

Yes, there are roadblocks which stop Arab cars and check to see if armaments are being transported. Not pleasant? That's an understatement. I'm saying that as one who has manned those roadblocks. Sometimes I've even had to check the cars of Arabs who I know from my neighboring Arab villages. There were even three times that I drove, as a hitchhiker, to Jerusalem with my Arab neighbors and was stopped for inspection. Yes,

Aaron, it hurts, very much, to check them. Not to do so would mean to allow explosives into our main cities. Is that better?

I have been involved in home arrests during my army stint. If out of fifteen who are arrested, two or three are released because our security forces informed us incorrectly, does that mean that we have to stop that method of preventing terrorism? If your child was killed by a terrorist whose attack could have been prevented by an earlier arrest, would you then feel better about these home arrests? Maybe not, but you'd understand its necessity.

Stopping of riots by force: Would it be better to allow these PLO-led activities to continue? I know that it's hard for you, up there in Long Island, to understand. But remember the Weathermen—the New York City police and the FBI didn't use rubber bullets or fire in the air first.

Collective punishment—the closing of an entire block of stores near an area where we are attacked. Or a curfew on some town. Once again, your Western culture will make it difficult for you to understand our situation. In 99% of the attacks upon us, the attacker(s) must have the help of those in the immediate surrounding area, either to perform the attack or to escape. Closing off the area allows us to hasten in finding the attackers. Blowing up houses. Didn't the U.S. blow up an entire block in Philadelphia to punish Black activists? Yes, there is loss of life during our preventive and responsive actions. Because we are fighting a war. And in war, people get killed. What about the Arab children who have been shot? What are we to do? They send them out in front of their fighters like shields. What kind of civilized people use children this way?

I want to give you one more example where collective punishment works, while warnings, etc., are worthless. Some one and a half years after we arrived at Shilo, cars from Shilo were once again stoned, day after day, by residents of the neighboring Arab village of Singel. Once again, we spoke to the mukhtar and to the school headmaster (the kids generally stoned the cars during recess). It was like giving aspirin to a dead person. One day, after four cars were stoned (and as usual, the police and other authorities did nothing) and the attacks escalated, it was decided in Shilo that action was necessary.

That evening in Singel, two buses and four private cars were burnt, and the windows of some five private homes were smashed. Not at all proper! You're right! But the result? Total quiet for a year. The roads were safe once again.

You wrote that you are very much upset that the YOSH Arabs have no voting rights. This will surprise you—it bothers me more than you! I'll surprise you even further. I am against them voting! Let me explain. The Arabs in YOSH are not citizens of Israel. Therefore, they do not vote. (Almost no Arab country allows voting at all and I don't hear you yelling about that.) Can any healthy country allow proposed citizens the right of voting, if those proposed citizens are actively involved in the overthrow of the country they are going vote in?

"I pledge allegiance to the flag of the U.S. of A." Almost every citizen of the US knows and respects that pledge and if I'm correct, it is a requirement of every new immigrant-citizen to recite it. Can I require my Arab neighbor to recite the Israeli National Anthem? "As long as my heart beats, I dream of being a free people in our country, in the Land of Zion and Jerusalem." Would your congregation allow a sizable number of new members to join, and act publicly to break up the congregation and its existing membership? And that situation, even if it were to occur, would still be way out of comparison with ours. For the leaders of the PLO are out to destroy us.

I know what you're thinking, Aaron. "No voting rights! That can't be. Your living in YOSH means taking away the rights of other people. Therefore leave, would be your retort to me. But before you continue, let me finish. I would suggest the following. Let my Arab neighbors living in YOSH vote in the "Jordanian elections." Oh! There are no elections there. You're right.

When we came back to YOSH, there was not one Arab university. Today, there are six. The unreal thing about it: the lecturers, teachers, and professors at these universities are almost all members of the PLO! And the Ministry of the State of Israel paid for the founding and pays for the upkeep of these places of "learning." Once I posed as a writer for an American college paper and visited Bir Zeit "University." It reminded me of army courses on preparation for war.

By their own admission, there is more freedom of the press for the PLO in Jerusalem than any other place in the world! Don't ask me why. We Jews have always been crazy. Do you know that Hussein kept the local populace within their villages and did not allow them to venture out? Only with special passes could one leave. Under our "occupation," there are no such limitations. Some 80% of the Arab villages in YOSH had no electricity, running water, sanitation, paved roads, or medical clinics during Hussein's time. Today, during our terrible "occupation," almost all have the above facilities. Paid for with taxes from Israeli citizens!!!

I'll let you in on a secret. The Arabs in YOSH have the lowest death rate in the world!! Check the UNRWA [United Nations Relief Works Agency] records. See how many refugees have died. The more who live, the more money they receive; therefore they almost never report deaths. By the way, they need UN money like Israel needs more sand and rocks. The Arabs in YOSH have one of the highest standards of living of any Middle East country.

I would agree, Aaron, that the present situation in YOSH is not the optimum—far from it. I would not want to be in my Arab neighbor's place living in Turmos-Aya. For that matter, I would obviously not want to be in any Arab's place living in any Arab State. I and my Arab neighbors are not for the situation continuing as it is presently. However, I cannot accept your complaints without the circumstances being taken into account.

Well, believe it or not, Reb Aaron, I'm going to sign off. It's now "your turn" after my lengthy scroll. Write soon—even if you are busy.

With blessings,
Era

April 1987
Tel Mond Prison

Dear Moriyah, David, Atarah, Yitzhak, Tsofiyah, and Dvir, my baby boy who came into this world while his father was sitting in prison, may God be with you all:

Some thirteen years ago, I was visiting a social worker supervisor of mine in Jerusalem. During the conversation, he told me that he spends fifteen minutes a day with each of his children. Each child knows that he has time with him to do whatever is possible. I looked at him with a question. Only fifteen minutes? He smiled and said to me, "When you are married with children, we'll see how you do."

That statement of his took me back to my childhood. I have a memory of my Abba playing with me. It was in the schoolyard opposite the apartment we lived in. Abba was teaching me how to play soccer. I was about eight years old. That's all I remember. I don't remember Abba talking very much with me. Abba was a teacher. He left early in the morning and came home late. Then he went to his desk and prepared the schoolwork for the next day. He also worked late at night at extra jobs to afford sending us to Yeshiva. As a child, he didn't have many years with his parents. They both died when he was about thirteen. Abba just didn't have the time to spend with us. Yet, he taught me so much.

I promised myself that when I had children, I would tell them about my Abba and about myself. I told myself that I would spend more time with you—maybe more for my needs than yours. I love you all so much and need to be with you. Every moment I spend with you is a world for me. Every smile, every laugh, every tear, every anger, every question you ask, every step we take together—everything. I love it.

I admit that I haven't been so successful in keeping my promises. Sitting here in my prison cell and being so physically far from you gives me the opportunity to reflect and realize that I haven't spent the time I need with you—the time which you deserve. Not that I don't want to! You know that I'm crazy about you. But the first twelve years with your mother have been spent helping to build Israel. By spending time building our beloved country, I have deprived you, rather us, of much precious time together.

But that also makes you part of the mitzvah of building Israel. Yes, I could close us up in our home and spend the time together. We would all love it. But that would be selfish—totally so. The State of Israel is only thirty-nine years old—there is too much to be done for us to worry only about ourselves. God didn't give us the great privilege of returning to Israel only to enjoy it for ourselves. We are building and preparing the land for all of our millions of brothers and sisters who will follow us in the near future.

Yes; you can say, let them come and do it; let someone else do all the hard work. But that is not your family's way, and I hope I can teach you not to make it your way, or the way of your children.

Your family, on my father's side, were all builders of Israel. My father's Abba taught Torah in the neighborhood of Beit Yisrael, in Jerusalem, and there is a street in his name. The holiest place in the world, Yerushalayim, and you have a street there in your great-grandfather's name! When I think about that I shiver with pride and fear. Pride that he was my father's father. Fear, because he gave his life so that we can live here. Can we continue his way? Can we also be builders of Israel?

Do you know that we have had many offers to sell the house that my father was born in? But it is ours; it is our roots, and it will be yours for you to guard for your great-grandchildren, please God.

Your grandfather's sister would get up every day at 4:30 in the morning to prepare food for the poor people of Jerusalem who didn't have any. In the dark of the morning, she would bring it to their doors, so they wouldn't know where it came from, so that they wouldn't feel embarrassed or feel the need to pay it back.

I promised you that I would tell you about myself—so that you will know. From behind my jail bars, I will write to you. When you will be older, it will be yours to read. To read and to continue, God willing, your people's way.

When did my love affair with Israel begin? I say love affair because that's what it feels like. Like the love for your wife or your children. For our land is like a person, with a soul. This is what makes it holy. No other land is like this. That is why, when you are away from Israel, you feel sad, like being away from your wife or your kids—you miss the land in your heart.

Where did I get this feeling? From whom? My earliest recollection? My grandmother, on my Ema's side. Sarah was her name. Atarah Sarah, you are named after her. My grandmother gave me a Jewish National Fund charity box and stood me on a corner in East Flatbush in Brooklyn. I would say to every passerby, "Please help the JNF." Days, nights, weeks and years I did that. Did I dream then that one day I would live in the Jewish National Land? I am not sure. My mother would spend plenty of time helping the Hadassah organization. She collected clothes and money for them. The closets and other rooms of the house were always filled with clothes and other things for the bazaars. As a child, I used to go to the bazaars to help.

My Abba, maybe you remember him, Moriyah. Even though he lived most of his life in America, he was Israeli. More than that; he was a Yerushalmi—Jerusalemite. Much of my love for Israel came from Abba, though I can't say exactly how. For we never talked a lot about Israel, at least as far as I can remember. It was a natural process. Just from looking at Abba, you knew that Israel was our home. Abba always spoke to us in Hebrew.

As I am writing, I remember, even vividly, how my Abba would celebrate our Independence Day in the synagogue in Brooklyn. Abba would lead the prayers and he sang them in the melody of a holiday service and people came from all over to hear and celebrate with Abba.

You see, Abba didn't have to talk with us. In many ways, his actions taught us. Abba was so gentle to people. He loved and respected them. Just walking with Abba from the synagogue, you learned from him how to act with people.

I knew that Abba was from Israel, and I knew that I had family there. But for reasons that I'll never know, Abba didn't tell me a lot about Eretz Yisrael. Yet, whenever I heard the Hatikva [national anthem], I stood, mostly with pride, sometimes with tears and I would say to myself that someday I will be in Israel.

Then, as a teenager, came the marches for Soviet Jewry. I participated in every one of them. At every one, we would sing the Hatikva, and once again I promised myself that I would live in Israel—even though I had little idea what Israel was.

The decision to come to Israel was finalized one winter night while sitting in the dormitory lounge of Yeshiva University around January 1966. I and about twenty classmates were watching a film about the boat *Exodus*. Someday you will see the film. It describes what happened to our brothers and sisters in Germany and Europe, and what happened to a boat full of Jews who escaped from the Nazis to come to Eretz Yisrael. The boat was discovered by the British, who forced the boat to stop because they didn't want Jews to return to Israel. All of the Jews on the boat came up on deck, and as they raised our flag, the Star of David, hundreds of people started singing Hatikva. The film ended there. But your Abba, and a friend of his, Chaim, stayed in the room crying. For about ten minutes we just sat there and cried, and then we both said that we were going to Israel.

We decided to go learn for a year in Yeshivat Mercaz HaRav Kook in Jerusalem. Why that school? Why a yeshiva at all? I'll tell you a secret. For years I had studied in yeshiva. My Abba and Ema worked so hard and deprived themselves of things so we could get a good Jewish education. But I wasn't the greatest of students. So I said to myself that I'm going to Eretz Yisrael to learn really hard for one year. Mercaz HaRav was a yeshiva which didn't force you to learn. It was also a place that helped you to love Eretz Yisrael. And it was in Yerushalayim. Yerushalayim—just the name made me shiver. I had heard it mentioned so many times. My Abba was born there. All of my life I sang, "Next year in Jerusalem." And now was my chance.

Yerushalayim was the city of Kedusha, of holiness. At that time, in Yeshiva University, I didn't know and couldn't understand or feel what that meant. It's an interesting thing—ask any Jew, wherever he or she is, and ask of Jerusalem. Their hearts and minds open up. It's part of the essence of being Jewish, the connection to Jerusalem, like family, only mystical, something which many Jews can't explain, but only feel.

That night, looking at the film *Exodus*, knowing that six million of our people had been killed for being Jewish, for wanting to return to Eretz Yisrael; that night I made them all a promise. Their children would return. I would go back. Anything else would be a mockery of their massacre. As the tears came out of my eyes and heart and down my face, I remember smiling. Smiling and crying at the same moment. I said to my brothers and sisters whom I had never met and would never meet, that I, all twenty-one years of me, I will carry on your past. I will go to where the world does not want us to go. I will go HOME.

It is late at night, and cold, and lonely here in my cell, and I am falling asleep. I know that all six of you, my children, are with me, and therefore, inside, I feel warm. Tomorrow, with God's help, I will continue writing, and through my story to you, we shall be together again.

Love,
Abba

April 1987
Tel Mond Prison

Moriyah, David, Atarah, Yitzhak, Tsofiyah, and Dvir,

I was spending my first Yom Kippur, my first Holy Days, in Jerusalem. It was September 1966. I had arrived at the Mercaz HaRav Yeshiva one and a half months earlier to start my "test" year. The year I had given myself to see if Israel was for me. Rosh Hashanah davening [praying] was an unreal experience. The days before the High Holy Days kept on building toward a pinnacle to this special meeting with God. But, no matter how I tried, I wasn't prepared for the relationship between God and man going on at the yeshiva. During the prayers, my fellow students were pouring out their hearts in tears to God. When the shofar [ram's horn] was blown, my heart stopped. Would God hear? Would we hear?

Then came Yom Kippur, 1966. Jerusalem came to a stop! Nothing was moving. The aura of Holiness—always present in Jerusalem—you felt it in the air. The main bus terminal—opposite the yeshiva—came to a stop; hundreds of buses parked as if standing in prayer. Verses which I had said for years routinely suddenly came alive. I thought of my Abba in the U.S. and me having this amazing privilege of being in Jerusalem on Yom Kippur. Then we reached the last prayer of the day, Neilah, the closing of the judgment. I felt that this was my last opportunity to request that God seal me in the "book of life."

Suddenly the cantor was speeding up the prayers, rushing to get in the last blessing on this, the holiest of days. The last prayer was over, yet I realized it was much too early to blow the shofar, which brings Yom Kippur to a close. Suddenly, a huge circle formed, led by our Rosh Yeshiva [head rabbi], Rav Tzvi Yehuda Kook. Around and around the study hall students danced, singing "Next Year in Jerusalem." I was not dancing. Why? Because I couldn't dance. Why? I really didn't understand, but I'll explain my feelings.

I was sitting on my chair at the back of the synagogue and I was crying. Suddenly I felt a hand on my shoulder. I didn't want to be bothered, so I shrugged off the hand. But, once again, I felt it on my shoulder, gentle and strong at the same time. I looked up over my shoulder and there was Rav Kook, some sixty-five years old. When he saw my eyes, he asked me why I was crying. "Dance," he urged. I told him, "I can't dance, I'm crying, for next year you know you'll be here and so you are singing, 'Next Year in Jerusalem.' I don't know where I'll be. How can I sing?" Rebbe pressed his hand hard on my shoulder and actually lifted me out of my chair and pushed me in front of him in the circle. For the next twenty minutes, we danced and danced. "Don't worry," Rebbe said, "you will live in Israel."

It was becoming dark outside and soon the shofar would be blown. At Mercaz, nobody even thought about the end of the fast and eating. We kept on dancing and dancing. Finally, the hundreds gathered, and yelled out, "Hear O Israel, the Lord our god, the Lord is one." Finally the shofar was blown. For the only time that I could ever remember, I knew that the shofar was being heard by God.

Some seven months later, it was Yom Ha'atzmaut, our Independence Day. Hundreds of people jammed the yeshiva inside and thousands outside. Rav Tzvi Yehuda Kook started talking about Israel. He related a story which, my dear children, I'm telling you. It's part of the key to understanding me and my relationship to Israel. In 1948, seven Arab countries started a war against us in order to kill all the Jews and to make sure that there wouldn't be a State of Israel. God helped us and we were able to stop the Arabs. When the cease-fire was signed, thousands of Jews poured into the streets to celebrate. Rav Kook couldn't dance. He said how could he dance when we had lost so many parts of Israel? Where was the Temple Mount? Where was Hevron? Beit-El? Shilo? Shechem? How could he be happy when so many important parts of Israel were no longer in our hands? Rav Harlap, a very holy man from Jerusalem, visited Rav Kook. He told Rebbe, right now, God gave us this much. We have to be happy with that. The rest will come back to us also—right now, we have to be happy with what we have. Rebbe and the Rav Harlap went outside to join the happy nation.

Then Rebbe told us some amazing words. "You will see, very soon, those places will be back in our hands. Soon God will send us tremendous miracles." No one knew what Rebbe was talking about. But just a few weeks later, we all saw. Three weeks later, Nasser, the President of Egypt, closed the Straits of Tiran and started threatening war in order to chase us out of Israel and drive us into the sea. He was joined by Syria, Jordan, and another three Arab countries. They all started preparing for war.

We had no choice. We asked other countries of the world to convince the Arabs not to fight against us. Nobody succeeded. So we had to prepare for war. Your father and two friends of his had not been in the army, but we wanted to fight. So we went to the army office and asked to be drafted, but they didn't agree. We heard that the Shaarei Tzedek Hospital in Jerusalem, needed volunteers to help prepare the hospital for war. Rebbe had told all the students in the yeshiva who were part of the army to report immediately to their units and the other students to help in other ways.

We reported to the hospital and started filling sandbags to place around the windows and parts of the roof. We worked day and night, but who even thought about that? At least we were doing something. While in Yeshiva University, I promised myself that I would never allow a Jew to be killed without fighting back. Now, at least we could fight back.

Other American students in Israel received letters and telegrams and even phone calls from their parents telling them to come back to the U.S. I sent a letter to my Abba and Ema, and they kept it so that I still have it to this very day. "Please don't ask me to return to the U.S. I don't want to transcend the commandment of Honor Thy Father and Mother, but understand that I can't leave now and that I will stay in Israel. Therefore, please don't request me to come, for I won't be able to fulfill your request. God gave me a chance that millions of Jews throughout the generations have always prayed for—the opportunity to fight for the Land of Israel." My father and mother didn't request of me to return to the States.

A few mornings later, the sirens started wailing. We ran from the yeshiva to the hospital and took our positions. The Arabs, once again, were trying to march us into the sea. Soon after the war started, wounded soldiers began to arrive by ambulances.

Some of the soldiers were already dead. Others needed immediate help. When they were able to, they told us of how they were wounded. I will tell you of their episodes, but, right now, it is very late and I am tired. I love you so much and want to be right next to you, in order to kiss you and tuck you in. It'll be another one and a half years before I'll be home—we both have to be strong. Don't forget to say the prayer before going to sleep and to thank God for everything.

Love,
Abba

It's now Sunday afternoon and tomorrow is your visit. As usual, I'm excited about seeing you. Once Friday arrives, the time begins to fly, for we have Shabbat, Sunday, and then you here. But, before the visit starts, it's over, and then I have a long, long week to wait until your next visit.

There are many reasons that I'm writing these letters to you. One of them is for you to understand why I was willing to sit in prison, away from you for years because I attacked Bassam Shaka. Maybe, with all these letters and after you're older, you'll understand a little more.

I have thought, not once, not twice, but many times, about what will be when you grow older. I dream that there will be no more war. Which father doesn't dream that? And in the same breath, I say to myself and to you, especially to you, David, for you are the oldest of our boys, if there will be an army and, God forbid, a war, then go, go my dear sons—go and be like the soldiers whose actions I'm writing you about. Go and be a soldier in our army. Go be the best soldier that you can be. And if you have to fight for the People, Land, and Torah of Israel, then know that Ema and I will be with you every moment in battle. Fight like a proud Jew, like a lion returning to its den, protecting its cubs. Fight, not only for yourselves, fight for all the Jews throughout all the generations who couldn't fight and who were slaughtered just for being Jews.

Know that you are fighting a war of existence. Don't be afraid to give up your life fighting. This world is only a bridge to the next world. There is no greater holiness than falling in battle so that your brothers can live.

On the second day of the Six Day War, a soldier was helicoptered in from the southern front. He had been seriously hurt in the fighting and was unconscious. When, finally, two days later, he could speak once again, he told us what had happened. He was the scout of a jeep, leading a convoy of half tracks and other army vehicles, not far from the Egyptian border. They were on a road that had no resemblance to a road. Suddenly, as they were riding, the scout yelled to the driver to swerve off the path. The driver didn't listen, and once again the scout repeated his warning. Then the scout grabbed the wheel, pulled it to the left—off the path—and signaled the rest of the convoy to follow. The driver got angry at him and said, "Why did you force me off the road?" At that the scout looked at the driver and said, "What do you mean? Didn't you see the hand in the sky?" "What hand in the sky?" the driver asked our soldier. "The hand in the sky pointing and warning us to get off the road." The driver then told him, "You're crazy, you must be war crazy." The entire convoy was now some 50 meters to the left of the path. Suddenly an explosion rocked the entire road that they had just left.

I really didn't believe his story. However, after the war, I was telling some of my experiences to my uncle, Mordecai Shimon, and told him this incident. Mordecai Shimon told me a story. "Toward the end of the War of Independence, I was with a group of soldiers on Mt. Zion. We numbered sixteen and had twenty-six bullets. Around us there were thousands of Arabs massed to attack us. We turned to each other, said shalom, loaded the final bullets, and the Arabs charged. Suddenly, they threw up their hands, yelling 'Ibrahim-Ibrahim.' In a panic they turned around and aborted their charge. After the war, some years later, on one of my missions, I was talking with an Arab. In the course of our conversation, it turned out that we were both on Mt. Zion, during that fateful day. I asked him about 'Ibrahim.' He looked at me and asked, What do you mean? Didn't I see the face and hand of Avraham pointing at them (the Arabs) to retreat down the mountain? I hadn't seen any hands or face, but the fact was that the Arabs turned around shouting Abraham's name. Believe your soldier's story."

The next soldier who we brought in the hospital was almost dead. I was holding half of his brain in my hand. He spoke his last words to me. "Don't forget Jerusalem," he said. I was later told by other soldiers who were with him that he had saved the lives of many of them.

The second night of the war in Jerusalem, I was outside the hospital and the sky was lit up with the bombing of Jerusalem by the Jordanians. We prepared the emergency operating room in the basement, for we were fearful that the hospital would be bombed. During a short lull in the fighting, I had a few moments to think. I was scared and didn't know if I would live through the battle. I thought of the battles for Jerusalem during the times of the Temple. And I remembered the words of Rav Kook, just three weeks earlier, that great miracles were going to happen soon. As I was thinking, I passed the room where the dead bodies of our holy soldiers were placed until their burial. I thanked them for giving their lives for me to live. I promised them that their lives were not sacrificed for naught. Jerusalem would be ours and we would keep it forever.

Some of my friends left Israel for the States before the war, for they were afraid. I was also afraid, but does that allow you to run away from your destiny? To be in Jerusalem during a war for our freedom is a real honor. I thought of my Aunt Yehudit and Uncle Mordecai David, in their bomb shelter in the old Jerusalem section of Beit Yisrael, just four short blocks from the Jerusalem border. They were real fighters. As soon as possible, I would visit them.

I reentered the hospital, and soon after, the ambulances started arriving once again. We knew that we were going to battle to free the Old City of Jerusalem and the Temple Mount. The casualties mounted. Some soldiers were brought in who were hurt fighting near Ramallah, north of Jerusalem. One of them told us of the bravery of a fellow soldier. His platoon was charging up the mountain. The Jordanians forced them down, but a few of our soldiers were left on the hillside. The soldier yelled that he was going to bring them down. Under an incredibly heavy barrage of fire, he started up the hill. Somehow the Jordanians missed him, and he reached the first wounded soldier and brought him down. Then, once again, he started up the hill, but this time he was hit by a sharpshooter's fire. He didn't stop. He continued up and brought down another soldier who was hit. Still a

third time he started up, was hit again, yet succeeded in saving another soldier—then he was sent to our hospital.

One hour later, we brought in many other soldiers who were seriously
wounded. But before I tell you what happened, I want you to know that
members of the hospital staff were working almost two full days without
any rest. One time, we brought in four wounded soldiers. Three were ours
and one a Jordanian sharpshooter. While one of the doctors was trying to
save the life of the Jordanian, one of our soldiers gave his soul back to God.
One of the other soldiers present in the room pointed to the Jordanian and
said, "He was the one who killed this soldier." The nurse turned to look at
our soldier who died. Then she started screaming and lunged at the Jordanian soldier. She was stopped by the doctor and fainted. The soldier who
passed away was her brother!! But we saved the Jordanian's life!! Later that
night I said to myself, what a crazy people we are. Saving the lives of those
who are killing us. Is that also part of being a Jew, I asked myself?

I had little time to continue my thinking, for the war was getting more
brutal. The soldiers who were brought to the hospital told us that our
forces were approaching Jerusalem. Suddenly a miracle happened right before my eyes. Together with another soldier, I was wheeling the stretcher of
a wounded soldier from one of the makeshift emergency rooms into another room. Just as we wheeled out the bed, a shell hit the window and
wall of the room. Both of us were thrown back by the explosion, and then
another shell fell into the room itself. Only the shell didn't explode.

Had it exploded, the entire hospital would have gone up, for there were
gas and oxygen tanks in the room!

During the next day, more and more soldiers told us that we were getting closer to Yerushalayim. The air was full of electricity. All the soldiers
that we brought in, each and every one, told us over and over, "Jerusalem,
Jerusalem." Everyone felt seized by great anticipation. We were afraid to
vocalize the thought. We were going to enter and take back Jerusalem! We
were going to reach the Temple Mount! I guess we were too scared, too
shocked to really accept it. There was one soldier, a parachutist, who refused to stay in bed. He had been badly wounded but insisted on returning to the war. He argued with the doctor "For almost two thousand years,

we have been forced out of Yerushalayim. Are you trying to tell me that on the day that we finally free Jerusalem from the Jordanians and all the other foreigners, on that day, I won't be among the fighters? I have to be there." We calmed him down. At least I had thought so. One hour later, I went up to visit him. The bed was empty! Six hours later, I was bringing in a seriously wounded soldier. I looked at his face, all covered with blood. When he saw me, he smiled. You guessed it, my dear children. It was the same soldier. He fought in Yerushalayim!!

Later that day, we wheeled another soldier into the recovery room. He had lost an arm and a leg in the battle. A while later, I passed his room and I heard him screaming. When we entered his room he told us. "I had a dream that I was in a battle for Yerushalayim. I was hit and lost a hand and foot. Suddenly I woke up and saw that it wasn't a dream. Tell them, tell them, that I want to go back to battle and give my other hand and foot for Yerushalayim."

Then we received a message that a synagogue in the area of Machne-Yehuda had been hit by a shell. It was three blocks from the hospital and we ran over to see if we could help. What a miracle. The shell entered one side of the building and exploded by the side of the Aron-Kodesh [Holy Ark] holding the Torahs. But not one Torah scroll was damaged, nor did even one book fall down off the bookcase!

Time passed, and then the radio announced that we had captured Mt. Scopus and were preparing to enter the Old City. The fighting was fierce. The number of wounded soldiers that we were taking care of was going up and up.

I knew that soon, very soon, one of the moments that the nation of Israel had been waiting for for thousands of years was about to happen. I thought of all the Jews back in the States. I felt sorry for them. What they were missing. Then the question that very often fills me—Why me? Why was I privileged to be here? There was almost no time to think; things were happening too quickly. We were rushing toward another step on the road to our redemption. My mind and body were swirling, and the injured soldiers kept on coming.

Then, over the ambulance radio the message came through. "Do you hear, do you hear, I am bringing in injured from the Old City of Jerusalem." My body froze and I couldn't move. We are home! We are home! I kept on saying over and over. Quickly we ran to the emergency and recovery rooms and turned on the radios all over.

Beep, beep, beep, the music was interrupted for a bulletin. "The Central Army Command announces that our soldiers have entered the old city; the TEMPLE MOUNT IS IN OUR HANDS, THE TEMPLE MOUNT IS IN OUR HANDS, I REPEAT, THE TEMPLE MOUNT IS IN OUR HANDS. THE PRAYERS OF TWO THOUSAND YEARS HAVE BEEN ANSWERED, THE TEMPLE MOUNT IS IN OUR HANDS."

And then even the announcer couldn't keep on talking, and he also started crying. Suddenly, in the middle of the pain, in the middle of the treatment, from both floors of the hospital, the Hatikvah was heard. Soldiers who moments before were in agony from pain stood up somehow, for our national anthem. Those who couldn't stand up asked us to hold up their heads. Never before and never since have I sang our Hatikvah the way I sang or cried it then. The feeling of that moment, I will never be able to explain or relate, my dear children. Holding the head of a holy soldier in my hand, I promised myself. Here I will live. I am back home to stay.

Then we were wheeling a dead soldier to the hospital mortuary. A Jew who gave his life for me, for us. How could we be happy when there are those who gave up their lives for us, I asked myself? As I asked, the words of my teacher, Rav Tzvi Yehuda Kook, came back to me. This is another step toward the redemption and we have to be happy.

That Saturday, as was my custom for all the Saturdays that year, I walked to my aunt and uncle's house. I went early, so I could be with my uncle for the morning prayers. His synagogue was on the second floor of a building overlooking what was, just two days earlier, no-man's-land, and Jordanian-occupied East Jerusalem. As always, my uncle stood by the window facing the Old City, facing the Temple Mount. Suddenly, in the midst of the prayers, he stopped and pulled down a curtain covering the window. He pulled it away from the window, turned around, and told the others who were praying, "For nineteen years, I have covered this window so the Jordanian sharpshooters would not be able to shoot us. No longer do we need the curtain. Never again will we need it. Jerusalem is ours forever." Then he said the age-old blessing on extremely special occasions, Shehecheyonu [prayer of thanks]. Can I succeed in relating to you that unreal moment, my children? As I sit here in my jail cell and write you this, I can see my uncle ripping down the curtain, his eyes filled with tears and happiness. Can you understand this, my children? You, who were born into a Jerusalem totally ours? Do you know that before the war of 1967, almost every day there were sharpshooters who fired into our area of Jerusalem? When I'm released from prison, with God's help, we shall go together to Beit Yisrael, and I'll show you the marks of the shells that hit the house, the shells that the Jordanians fired at us for over nineteen years.

There are those who think it's easier to forget about Israel and live in another country. There are those who think it's easier to forget about being Jewish and be something else.

My parents taught us differently. By their actions. My father taught Torah for over sixty years! And my aunts and uncles fought for the Land of Israel for over sixty years. That was their way, and I learned from them. Please God, my dear children, you will continue that path. So David, Yitzhak, and Dvir, if you have to be soldiers, be the best that you can.

Love,
Abba

May 1987
Tel Mond Prison

A letter to my children:

Abba didn't talk with us much about himself or about his feelings. I sensed that he was happy that I was going to study in Israel, but he didn't come out and say so. A few days before my departure, I asked Abba, Can you tell me where your parents are buried? "You can't go there," he said. "They are in Jordanian-occupied Israel on the Mount of Olives, overlooking the Temple Mount." I continued pressuring Abba, and he finally told me, "When you look from the Temple Mount, my parents' graves are on the left side." He couldn't or didn't want to give me more exact directions.

At the airport, I kissed my brothers and mother shalom and then turned to Abba. My last words to him before boarding the plane were, "Please God, I will be able to go to your parents' graves." It was August 1966.

At least a dozen times that year, I photographed, with my telescopic lens, the Mount of Olives. I was trying to imagine where my grandparents' graves were, grandparents whom I never had the privilege to meet. The Mount of Olives, the oldest continuously used Jewish cemetery in the world, with graves three and a half thousand years old, was closed to Jews. Closed by the Jordanians, who refused to allow Jews even to just visit their dead! And my grandparents, great-grandparents, and great-great-grandparents were buried there. As a young man of twenty-one, I couldn't understand how people would be so mean and not allow one to visit a grave.

Through my binoculars and telescopic lens, I spoke to my grandparents. I kept promising them and myself that I would visit their graves. My roots were there. I felt that a part of me was missing, that I had to be attached—reattached—to my ancestors. Between the Mount of Zion, where I stood, and the Mount of Olives, there is a natural valley, where the city of David stood. The Jordanians made it impassable. Jews who snuck into Jordan, who had visited the Mount, told of the wanton destruction of the graveyard. Tombstones were used for roads and latrines. The Jordanians had bulldozed a road through the graveyard destroying remnants (so they thought) of the oldest Jewish graves known. When I get to the Mount, will my graves be intact? The question was not if but when.

The third day of the Six Day War changed it all. From the ambulance radio, I heard the chief rabbi of our army, Rabbi Shlomo Goren, blowing the shofar at the Kotel [Western Wall]. I knew then that I could fulfill the promise to my father. I will be able to visit his parents' graves and say the memorial prayers—if the graves were there.

But because of the fear of land mines, the graveyard was not opened immediately. And I had committed myself to three more years of studying for a social work degree in the States. My meeting with my roots would have to be delayed.

I came back to live in Israel in 1971. Two weeks after arriving, my uncle and aunt came from the States to visit. I took them for a night tour of

Jerusalem, which ended up on the Mount of Olives. They invited me for a drink in the Intercontinental Hotel on the top of the mountain. I refused to join them, for the Jordanians had built the hotel on Jewish graves. I waited outside for them. Now I will go and find my grandparents' graves, I told myself. I remembered my father's words and general directions. It was nighttime and I entered the graveyard not knowing where I was going. Suddenly I felt a pull—something unearthly pulling me. I started walking—being directed by some outer force. Down and around the graves I went, having no idea what was happening. After five minutes, the pull left me. I was standing in front of a grave. The moon was shining brightly. I bent down to see the grave. It read in Hebrew: "Here lies Reb Baruch, son of Mordecai Shimon Rapaport." I was in shock. Slowly, ever so slowly, I lowered my hand to touch the tombstones, to caress it, and then I kneeled and started kissing the stone of my Grandfather. And then the tears came. Here I was, a twenty-six-year-old man, crying like a baby at the grave of a person I never knew—yet felt so close to.

"It is I, Saba [Grandpa], the youngest son of your son, Yitzhak, my father. I have come back to you, I have come back to your city—my city, your country—my country. I have come back to stay, Saba. Saba, do you hear me? I love you." My body was shaking and trembling. "Saba—I have returned, your children have returned. I bring you love from your son—my father. Saba, I promised my father that I will say a prayer for him at your grave." I took out a pocket prayerbook that I carry with me and chanted the age-old prayer for the dead. Chanted it to the melody that my father had taught me and his father had taught him. All this time, my hands were softly touching the gravestone, and as I moved my hands along it, I felt a rough edge and realized the stone was not whole. My grandfather's tombstone was broken in half by the Jordanian vandals. They thought they could erase his past and mine. I looked around for the other part of the stone. I found it meters away. To this day I don't know how I was able to lift up the broken part and carry it to the grave and place the two pieces together.

I had found my grandfather's grave but not my grandmother's. Then I remembered that my father had told me that they weren't buried side by side. "Not too far away, but not exactly near." That will be for another time, I thought. But, suddenly, I felt, once again, that pull and I followed. When it stopped, I looked down, and, yes, I was standing at my grandmother's grave. I prayed at her grave also and then turned to look at the sacred Temple Mount with the Mosque of Omar sitting on it. "Savta [Grandma]," I said. "If we do our job, God will do His and the Temple will be rebuilt. I have returned and I will live here, Savta, and I will come to your grave."

The Intercontinental Hotel was far above me. I made my way back and found my aunt and uncle. "What happened?" they asked. "You look white as a ghost."

That night, late at night, I wrote a long letter to my father, describing what had happened that evening. I asked if he could explain it to me. He never answered my question, only thanked me for visiting his parents' graves.

That evening, I had found my ROOTS. I knew then that Israel was my home. No one will take away the Mount of Olives from me. Not the Jordanians, Egyptians, Syrians, Saudi Arabians; not the Russians, France, or Great Britain. Not the U.S. or the U.N. My past and future are on that mountain.

Those thoughts came back to me twelve years later on a Friday afternoon. I was with your mother at the Hadassah Mount Scopus Hospital. It was nearing Shabbat and Ema was about to give birth. I stood at her side and said prayers as the baby was born, you, Yitzhak. You were born less than a year and a half after my father was fatally run over by a car in Cedarhurst, New York, on a Friday evening as he was returning from the synagogue. My father was buried in the city he was born in—Jerusalem—on the mountain that his parents and grandparents were buried on. That mountain—the Mount of Olives—is adjacent to Mt. Scopus, where his grandson was just born. His grandson to be named Yitzhak Yehuda—his name.

No, my children, you can sometimes take the Jew out of Jerusalem, but you can never take Jerusalem out of the Jew.

"Judah shall sit forever and Jerusalem from generation to generation."

Abba

November 1987
Tel Mond Prison

Dear Suzanne:

Well, here we go again, another letter from the confines of Tel Mond. Your father told you that my finding Orit is a story worth knowing. Why do you want to know? Are you interested in finding someone? Seriously, I agree, our finding each other was, seemingly, a bit unusual. It's all due to Henry Kissinger! And a little help from God!

Meeting Orit was a continuation of my love story with Israel. I was in the army and had a Shabbat off. My apartment was near the house of the then Prime Minister, Golda Meir. It was June or July 1974 and Kissinger was traveling back and forth, seemingly trying to force Israel into giving away parts of the Golan Heights to Syria and Judea-Samaria to Jordan and, of course, Sinai to Egypt.

I had read in the newspapers that there was going to be a demonstration, on Shabbat, protesting the efforts to give away parts of our land. The demonstration was to be held outside the home of the Prime Minister. It was obvious to me that the Land of Israel is ours and that we had no right to give away any part of it. More than the logic was the feeling, the inner feeling that sometimes cannot be explained. It was all the years of studying about the Land of Israel, of learning how central and important our country is to us. It was praying, at least three times a day, "And our eyes shall see You returning to Zion" and "Rebuild Jerusalem, the Holy City, speedily, in our days." It was hearing my father talk about the Land of Israel. It was the years of standing on the streets of East Flatbush, asking all passersby, "Please give to the JNF." It was twenty-one years of praying in the synagogue near our apartment in Brooklyn, in which there were drawings of Jerusalem, the Tomb of Rachel, and other Israel sights.

All those and more drew me that Friday evening to join the protest outside the home of Golda Meir. I could not know, on the way there, that the evening would be my first step toward dramatically changing my life. That happened within one minute of my arrival. The noted writer Moshe Shamir was lecturing on the Land of Israel. Standing next to him, listening intently, was a young lady. I looked at her listening and saw her eyes. At that moment, as if in a flash, I knew that we were going to share our lives together! I kept looking at her throughout the evening and here and there saw her looking at me. I left the demonstration late that evening, without introducing myself or finding out her name.

Three weeks later, I had a one-day vacation from reserve duty. I found out there was to be a demonstration, against withdrawal, opposite the Knesset [Parliament]. I would be there to do the minimum I could to stop my government from a terrible mistake. At the demonstration, there were thousands of participants. Suddenly I saw her once again—from afar, but there was no mistaking her for anyone else. Once again, I saw her looking at me. (If you ask Orit today, she kind of denies that she was looking at me.) Once again, I returned to the army, without knowing her name, but knowing . . .

Two and a half weeks later, I finished the reserves and two days later another demonstration was to be held outside of Yeshivat Mercaz HaRav Kook and of course I attended . . . and of course, among the thousands, she was there. I worked it so that I signed the petition to our government directly after her name. After a little detective work and after two phone calls, we met. What floored me was her suggestion on our second meeting to travel to a rehabilitation hospital, to meet an acquaintance of hers who had been very seriously wounded in the Yom Kippur War. I remember thinking, what a person, what a people we are, here in Israel. The second "date"—we had only met some twenty-six hours earlier—and instead of a movie, concert, or the like, as it would have been in the States, we were going to a hospital. Every moment with Orit strengthened my resolve and belief that the meeting opposite Golda Meir's house was not by chance.

Five days later—five meetings later—five full days together there was a family meeting at her parents' house and I was invited. Well, her parents' house was on a moshav [cooperative settlement] in the Jordan River Valley—the moshav of Mechola. Boom, I was introduced into a family of today's pioneers. Her father had left a job as the general manager of a cotton processing plant to help a youthful village develop an ironworks factory. They moved there to help develop and strengthen the Jordan River

Valley villages so that the area wouldn't be given away to the Jordanians. A lesson in living Zionism. I thought my work with youth preventing delinquency, in the village of Mevasseret Jerusalem, was important. It paled in comparison with the Mintz family's activities. Orit's parents met during the battle for the State of Israel, right before the War of Independence. Avraham Mintz and his wife to be, Yaffa, were sent by the B'nai Akiva [a Zionist organization] to strengthen the defense of Safed, in the nearby village of Biryah. Avraham soon became the security chief there. They spent the War of Independence in the Galilee, protecting our northern borders from Arab armies.

After the War ended, they continued their studies in Jerusalem for two years. Then they were "given" another job, to help build the kibbutz of Ein-Tzurim. And now, in their early forties, they were being called to give of themselves in the Jordan River Valley.

I drove back that evening to Jerusalem, more than enamored of Orit's family. I was beginning to understand what one had to do to help build our country.

The next day was our sixth meeting and once again it was an all-day affair. What we had both known six days earlier was decided that day. However, we waited another five days before telling our parents, so they wouldn't think that it was too soon!

What can I tell you, my niece? The Jewish People cannot thank Henry Kissinger for bringing peace to Israel; however, he will go down in history as having been the matchmaker between your uncle and aunt.

Orit, her family, and peers were all Sabras. To them, sacrificing for the State of Israel was doing "what comes naturally." Looking back at it, that week I joined the club. That week, without even realizing it, I was taking my first steps in being part of the development of Judea and Samaria. The first steps that were to bring me to being the Mayor of Ofra and then of Shilo.

They were also the first steps that were to lead me some five and one-half years later to get out of my bed in the dead of night, drive through the mountains to Shechem, and plant a bomb under the car of the PLO leader and murderer Bassam Shaka.

And the first steps which brought me to the Israeli Court of Peace in Jerusalem. To hear the words, "You are sentenced to thirty months in prison for maiming Bassam Shaka." All thanks to Henry Kissinger.

Study hard and walk our land.

Era

June 1987
Tel Mond Prison

Dear Beth, Shalom:

I can see that Gush Emunim [literally "Bloc of the Faithful"—the name of the Settlement Movement] has become famous. If you're trying to teach the kids in your Jewish Community Center about us, we are really on the map! Yes, I do have the time to write about the beginnings of the Settlement Movement.

On Iyar 25, 5727 [June 6, 1967] some seven Arab countries attacked Israel, intent on driving us into the sea. In one of the most miraculous wars in all of history, the combined Arab States were defeated by Israel in six days. I know this is not new to you. I'm talking about the war, for the information is important to understand the first steps of Gush Emunim. On the third day of the war, Israeli paratroopers freed the Old City of Jerusalem. Among the paratroopers fighting for the Old City were students of Rabbi Kook—Chanan Porat, Yoel Bin-Nun, and others. In charge of one of the groups of soldiers who freed the Kotel was Yoram Zamoosh from Kibbutz Yavneh. He immediately sent an army vehicle to the homes of Rav Kook and Rabbi David HaCohen to bring them to the Kotel.

Rav Yisrael Ariel, one of Rav Kook's close students and a paratrooper, was assigned by his commander to guard over the Mosque of Omar. He has recounted that he waited by the Mosque, thinking mistakenly that the Army was going to bring explosives to blow up the Mosque. The Redemption is coming, he thought. The Redemption is indeed coming, but as the Talmud states, little by little. Rabbi Kook was able to cry and dance at the

Kotel, but the Temple Mount wasn't to really come back to our hands. Even though Judea and Samaria were recaptured, they were not psychologically freed.

People all over the world, including Jews and Arabs, were waiting for us to destroy the Mosque of Omar on top of the Mount. The ancient cities of Jerusalem, Hevron, Shilo, Shechem and Beit-Lechem were finally ours to rebuild. People like myself, who were in Jerusalem those days, were in a dream. We had the feeling that two thousand years of exile were about to come to an end. Years later, Chanan Porat, who became one of the leaders of Gush Emunim, was to recount, "I arrived on the Temple Mount and after the immediate, unbelievable shock, I said to myself, the Messiah is arriving today. Then I noticed two of my fellow soldiers sitting down at the base of the Mosque of Omar, smoking. When I approached, I noticed that they were handing each other pornographic pictures. I said to myself, if, at this moment, this is what they are doing, then it is not yet time for the Messiah."

Chanan was correct. In one of the most tragic mistakes in our history, Moshe Dayan ordered the Israeli flag removed from the Temple Mount. In the future, all of his legendary feats will be dwarfed by the memory that he gave away our holiest site.

Some six and one-half years later, the Settlement Movement was founded. Yet the seeds were planted that day. In the future, some of the leaders of Gush Emunim would be those same paratroopers who fought for Jerusalem—Rabbi Y. Ariel, Y. Bin-Nun, and Chanan Porat. They fought three hard, long days for the second stage (the first stage was the War of Independence) in the freedom of Jerusalem. They would fight twenty more years to see some of the ancient cities rebuilt.

The Redemption, the return of the Jewish people to Israel and the healing light which comes with it, comes in small doses. Our army was able to rout seven Arab armies in six days. Yet we are not able to rid ourselves of our Diaspora mentality, cowering in fear of what the gentile nations might do. Right after the war, senior members of the Labor party expressed willingness to barter pieces of land for "peace"—a philosophy which in the history of mankind has almost never succeeded. Of course, the Arab Nations did not accept our offer. For them, no matter what they may publicly say, nothing less than the destruction of the State of Israel is acceptable.

More important, the Israeli people did not accept the Labor party leader's plan. Almost immediately, attempts were made to resettle the Gush Etzion Block south of Jerusalem, where hundreds of Jews were massacred by the Arabs in 1948. After one and a half years of determined efforts, Kibbutz K'far Etzion was reestablished one week before Rosh Hashanah 5728. The rebuilders were the sons of those murdered after they surrendered to the Arabs in 1948. You want to know what belief they had? Every year from 1948 to 1967, the sons and daughters of those massacred would meet on a mountaintop, southwest of Jerusalem, near Moshav Mevo Betar. There they could see from afar, in territory occupied by Jordan, the single tree which was not destroyed by the Arabs, marking the location of their home. There, they pledged to return to their home in K'far Etzion.

Our government allowed them eventually to return. Sadly, they didn't lead them in returning. Only the determination of the settlers brought results. Among the leaders of K'far Etzion was . . . Chanan Porat, our paratrooper at the Wall, who left the halls of the Yeshivat Mercaz HaRav Kook in Jerusalem to return to K'far Etzion. He had received the blessings and indeed the instructions of Rabbi Kook to leave the yeshiva and return to the Land. With him was Rabbi Moshe Levinger. It took four full months for Israel's own restrictions to be removed and for the gates of Judea to be reopened to us.

That was only the very beginning. Rabbi Levinger stayed in K'far Etzion only a few weeks and then returned to Moshav Nechalim. Along with attorney Elyakim Haetzni and the writer Aaron Amier, they began preparations for the return to Hevron. More than eight months had passed since the Six Day War, and our leaders did not develop any areas of Judea and Samaria. In their words, they were waiting for a telephone call from Hussein . . . so they could give away a "piece" for "peace."

Rabbi Levinger and the others sought the government's blessing to rebuild the Jewish quarter of Hevron. Neither a blessing nor a permit came quickly. Therefore, in March 1968, they visited Hevron in order to purchase some apartments. On one of their trips, they were joined by an elder of Hevron, a Jew who lived there before the 1929 massacre and escaped, Avraham Franko. He showed Rabbi Levinger and the group the ancient Jewish cemetery in the city. Franko pointed to a spot under a patch of cauliflower. "There lies my father," he said. You see, Beth, as in Jerusalem, the Arabs systematically tried to erase all remnants of our connection to Israel, including our dead.

Years later, when we finally settled in a new suburb outside of Hevron— for our government, at the time, didn't allow settlement in Hevron proper—we "battled" our own government over that cemetery! They didn't want us to use the cemetery. I know that it's hard to believe. Anyhow, a new Oleh [immigrant] from Russia, an internationally known physicist, Professor Ben-Zion Talger, was arrested by our government for cleaning out, by hand, that ancient Jewish cemetery. He told the police and soldiers, "If you think your prisons can scare me, then hear me. I have been to the very worst in Russia and I'm alive—nothing you have is even close to what I have gone through." With his hands and shovel and the knowledge that he was right, he "broke" our government—he cleaned out the cemetery. When he died, the Jews of Hevron and Kiryat Arba buried him in the ancient cemetery that he restored!

He was not the first to be buried in the reopened cemetery. That "honor" was reserved for an infant baby—the son of the Nachshon family, Yedidyah. Yedidyah was the first boy to be circumcised in the Cave of our Forefathers since our return to Hevron. One month later, he died. Our government refused to allow his burial in the ancient Jewish cemetery.

When the hour of the funeral arrived, Sarah Nachshon took her infant boy in her hands and began her solemn walk to bury her son in the ancient graveyard. Behind her were all of the residents of Kiryat Arba. The walk—over a mile—was barred in some five places by army blockades. Holding her dead infant son in her hands, Sarah approached the first blockade. The soldiers couldn't stop her. Their rifles dropped down when confronted with this mother and her baby. Silently they moved aside. The action repeated itself at each of the blockades. Soldiers broke down and cried.

When the grave was finally dug and her son buried, Sarah turned and said, "God gave us our son for one reason. He had a job to do in his short life—to open our ancient graveyard. This he has accomplished and God has taken him back. We are very privileged."

I've strayed a bit, and let me continue writing you about the beginnings of Kiryat Arba. When they were not successful in purchasing apartments, the Hevron settlers tried another tactic. They rented an Arab hotel for Passover and moved families in for the festival. Among the approximately sixty "guests" for the first Pesach Seder [meal] in Hevron since the massacre of 1929 were Rabbi and Mrs. Levinger, Yitzhak and Chaya Ganiram, Rav Chaim Drukman, Rav Eliezer Waldman, Benny Katzover, Shlomo Aviner, and Moshe Shamir. It was these people who became household names throughout all of Israel for their part in the rebuilding of Judea and Samaria. So it was, thirty-nine years after the massacre of the Jews of Hevron, their sons and grandsons began returning home.

Although the government didn't sanction the seder in Hevron, various cabinet members supported the action. Yigal Alon visited them on the fourth day of the Pesach holiday, and David Ben-Gurion sent them a letter of blessing.One month after Passover, the families were still in the hotel. On the 17th of Adar, 5730 [1970], the Knesset voted for the establishment of Kiryat Arba, adjacent to Hevron. We were on our way home.

However, the Government of Israel, headed by the Labor party, refused to allow further development of either Judea or Samaria. Our presence was limited to the Etzion Block and Kiryat Arba.

I'm dead tired right now, Beth, so I'll sign off and have this mailed to you. However, I'm not finished answering your question, so I'll write again.

Take care and write.

Era

July 1987
Tel Mond Prison

Dear Beth, Shalom:

Once I started writing about the beginnings of the Settlement Movement, I decided that I would finish. In the past, other people have also asked me, and I would answer, It's a long story. Who has time for long stories? Well, now I have time. Also I think that it's important that the story be told—so I'm writing. I'll continue where I left off.

Some three years later, during the winter of 1973, four leaders of the settlements of Kiryat Arba and Gush Etzion—Menachem Felix, Benny Katzover, Rabbi Levinger, and Chanan Porat—approached the government with proposals for the settlement of the Shomron. They were rejected.

Then the Yom Kippur War broke out, and much of the country was called to extended periods of reserve duty. In the midst of the war, a letter was sent to the Prime Minister, Golda Meir. It was written by Devorah Arziel. "The topic of what we want to talk about is so important, that we can't even write about it. . . . Our husbands are in reserve duty and we want to help our country." Devorah was one of the members of Garin Shechem, a group of people who banded together with the intent to live in the ancient Jewish city where Joseph is buried.

The meeting was arranged. At the meeting, two women from the garin [seed group] suggested that the Government agree, now, to Jewish settlement in Shechem. "It will raise up the spirit of our nation," said the woman. Golda was taken aback and would not agree to the suggestion. The garin now knew that settlement in the area of Shechem would have to be done without government permission.

The NRP (National Religious party) had for years been led by the "Old Guard," who saw no room for new blood. They were partners in the coalition government but refused to pressure for settlement in Judea and Samaria. Younger members of the NRP banded together to form the "Land of Israel" bloc within the party. They hoped to influence the elders to take a more active position on behalf of the settlement of all the land of Israel. On the 15th of Shevat 5734 (February 1974), this pressure group met in the village of Alon Shvut, in Judea, at the home of Yoel Bin-Nun. Among those present were Chanan Porat, Yehuda Harel, MKs [members of the Knesset], Yehuda Ben-Meir and Zevulun Hammer and rabbis Drukman, Waldman, and Levinger. Late into the night, those assembled agreed on the formation of a Land-of-Israel bloc within the NRP. The name that they chose, Gush Emunim, means, "Bloc of the Faithful." I can tell you, Beth, that those who had assembled that evening left full of high spirits—they were going to settle Judea and Samaria. It is highly improbable that those present that evening imagined that ten short years later, the map of Israel would be totally changed—that their decision that evening would alter the future of the State of Israel. Within half a year, "Gush Emunim" was a household name in all of Israel and throughout much of the world.

Members of the Garin Elon Moreh continued their plans and pressures for settlement in or near Shechem. A site was finally decided on, gear was purchased (tents, generators, beds, cooking equipment—sounds like camp, doesn't it, Beth?), and the garin was ready to go. Meetings were held with Rabbi Tzvi Yehuda Kook, and he gave his blessing to the project. Rabbi Kook tried convincing the Minister of Defense, Shimon Peres, of the value of the settlement, but to no avail.

On the 15th of Sivan 5734, Garin Elon Moreh came to the village of Howarah, some two and a half miles south of Shechem. With the garin was Rabbi Tzvi Yehuda Kook, MKs Ariel Sharon and Geula Cohen, and another eighty to a hundred supporters of the cause. Among them was Yehuda Etzion. I was to meet him in very different circumstances some two months later. I had gone to pick up Orit for our third date, and she introduced me to her brother—Yehuda Etzion. When I asked him what he did for a living, he answered, "I'm helping build Judea and Samaria." He explained to me what was going on and asked if I was interested in helping. I answered yes.

The Garin Elon Moreh did not want a confrontation with the government or army, and therefore informed them of their intentions to settle near Shechem. I'm not sure, Beth, that you can understand the special relationship that citizens of Israel have with our army. Almost all of us are both citizens and soldiers. We didn't want a confrontation . . . fighting against our army is like harming oneself.

The army blocked the major roads leading to the area. However, we had done our homework and took a little-known back road. During the night, members of the garin gathered at the home of Avraham and Yaffa Mintz, parents of Orit and Yehuda Etzion, on Moshav Mechola in the Jordan River

Valley. By the way, none of us knew then that six short months later they were to become my parents-in-law!

At daybreak, the settlers started on their way. Two Arabs friendly to the Mintz's rented us their trucks and drove us loaded with settlement gear to the site. To those that are unfamiliar with the Arab-Jewish relationship in Judea and Samaria and whose knowledge comes from the press, this would seem strange, very strange indeed. Behind the Arab trucks were ten cars with members of the garin. Others came from different back roads and some, via the main roads. The main caravan arrived at the settlement site and within a very short time had erected over fifteen tents. The Israeli flag was raised. Mordecai Lapid, a new citizen from Russia, helped erect the fence around the area. Rabbi Kook himself, who had arrived earlier, planted a tree and recited the blessing, "Blessed are Thou, Lord our God, King of the Universe, who has given us life and kept us and brought us to this time." Euphoria was in the air.

It was short-lived. Within a few hours, the army had arrived. When their demands to leave were not met . . . the soldiers, among them border patrol police, began to forcibly remove the settlers. They were dragged, pushed, and pulled into buses to be taken from the area. My brother-in-law to be, Yehuda Etzion, held onto the rocks while five soldiers pulled him. Suddenly they stopped. Above them loomed Israel's famed war hero, Arik Sharon. One of the soldiers let go of Yehuda and with tears in his eyes turned to Arik and said, "Arik, when you gave me the order to cross the Suez Canal in the Yom Kippur War, I did so under a hail of bullets and didn't ask questions. Now I have received an order. Do I fulfill it or not?" Sharon answered him immediately: "This kind of order you don't fulfill. It is an immoral order!"

One by one, the settlers were loaded on the bus, until there was only one person left—Rav Kook. The soldiers didn't dare to touch him. When they urged him to leave, he opened his long black coat and told them, "If you want, kill me . . . you cannot force me to leave." At dusk, after everyone had gone, Rav Kook entered Arik Sharon's car and left.

The memories of that day are etched in the minds of all those who were present. Traumatic memories of Jewish soldiers sent out by the Jewish State to remove Jewish citizens from our own land. The Jewish people came back to the Land of Zion. How can it be that its government would prevent Jews from living in the Land of their forefathers? The center of Judaism was always located in Judea and Samaria. The settlers that day had returned to the outskirts of Shechem. And it was at Shechem that Abraham was promised Israel, as is related in the Bible, Genesis 12:6. This Biblical record is our eternal deed. Every child in Israel is taught the Bible. To you, Beth, Shechem, Shilo, Beit Lechem, Hevron—these are Biblical places that you have read and learned about. To us, these are places "down the road" from our own house.

We left that evening with traumatic memories, but also with a determination and a knowledge. The determination to continue until we would succeed in settling the Land and the knowledge that we would succeed in doing so.

Garin Elon Moreh attempted six more times to settle in the area of Shechem, and each time they failed. At times, there were serious confrontations with our soldiers. In the spring of 1975, we attempted to settle at Sebastia (Shomron), one of the ancient capitals of northern Israel. At Sebastia, there is an old train station that was in use during the British occupation of Israel. This time, we barricaded ourselves on the roof of the train station. When our soldiers did not succeed in reaching the roof via ladders, they attempted to pull down the roof from beneath us. What did we do? With the possibility of serious bodily damage to all of us, including the soldiers, we allowed ourselves to be removed from the roof.

Just two weeks later, we returned to the train station and were once again removed. We had received strict orders from Rabbi Kook that no one was to lift a hand against our soldiers. We were to passively resist attempts to evict us. Why resist at all? Because a Jew is not allowed to abandon any part of the Land of Israel.

Gush Emunim called the People of Israel to a "March to our Home," scheduled for Chanukah 5736 [1975]. Chanukah was a symbolic time for attempting once again to settle our country. Most Jews the world over associate Chanukah with the victory of the Jews over the Greeks. What is not very well known is that the Maccabees had to convince Jews to battle

71

against the Greeks. In fact, there was a kind of "mini-war" between Jew and Jew. For there were many Jews who wanted to act and live as the Greeks. They took on the Greek ways and culture and weren't interested in the "Jewish Revival." In the village of Modi'in, the birthplace of the Maccabees (approximately half an hour from my home), Mattityahu, the High Priest, had to slay a Jew who went to the Greek altar. It was a small minority of Jews who rebelled against the Greeks and freed Israel from its intruders. Just as the Maccabees in their time kindled the lights of return to our roots, we were hoping to rekindle those lights in our time.

Gush Emunim called Israelis to join together at the railroad station near the ancient capital to urge our government to resettle Judea and Samaria. I remember the weeks before the march. Some fifteen of us split up into different groups of three. By car and foot, we traversed the land, searching and finding back roads and paths leading to the train station. Some of the paths were used by our forefathers over one hundred generations ago when settling the Land. We all had the feeling that we were walking for all the generations of Jews that were unable to walk in Israel. It was a feeling of walking history, of touching our roots, of following the steps of our grandparents. No, we didn't feel that we were walking against our government. Maybe it's hard for you to understand, but we are the people and the government is for the people, not the other way around. We were helping our government do the right thing.

My car rode over donkey paths where no one believed a small car could go. Twice the car sank into the mud. Only with the help of tractors belonging to the Arabs of a nearby village we were able to get going again.

The evening before the march it started pouring. We even considered delaying the rally. The rain continued throughout the day. Would people come? If so, how many? That morning, I drove with Orit to one of the back hills to direct walkers. Suddenly I saw our nation coming. By the tens, hundreds, thousands and more. As Orit and I were standing and directing people to the train station, I suddenly looked at my wife and she at me. Our tears of joy mixed with the rain—who knows, maybe those were tears of joy from heaven. "Orit," I said, "we are a Holy People and with God's help, today, we shall succeed." And I hugged her as marchers passed by with flags waving in the wind.

Over the walkie-talkie, I heard the first report from the train station. Thousands upon thousands had arrived and more were on their way. Over one thousand of our people were marching in the blinding rain from K'far Saba to the train station—some eighteen miles away. They were led by the poetess Naomi Shemer, who some nine years earlier had composed the song "Jerusalem of Gold."

Hours later, totally drenched, we arrived at the train station. Moments after, a helicopter brought the Minister of Defense, Shimon Peres, to the site. He demanded we leave. Rabbi Levinger yelled out to all of us that could hear, "We must tear." (Beth, he was referring to the tearing of a shirt as a sign of mourning. You know, of course, that one tears his shirt on the death of a parent, wife, husband, child, brother or sister. You probably don't know that one tears his shirt on seeing a city in Israel in its destruction.)

Peres and the leaders of Gush Emunim were anxious to avoid violence. An old-new proposal was put forth. Some thirty members of Garin Elon Moreh would be allowed to remain in a nearby army camp—Kadum. They would stay there until the government readdressed their requests in reference to settling in Judea and Samaria. Peres returned with the proposal to his office, and the leaders of the settlement drive continued their discussion at the railway station.

After a few hours, the garin decided to accept the proposal. Among the decision makers, Chanan Porat, Benny Katzover, Rabbi Levinger, Menachem Felix, and my father-in-law, Avraham Mintz. Now we awaited our government's response. The tension rose, and the rain continued to pour down. Groups of soldiers and settlers were seen discussing the possibilities. Hot coffee and cookies were passed around from the settlers' "kitchen"—to soldier and settler alike. Everyone prayed for a decision of nonconfrontation. Still more marchers arrived, and as the time passed, the tension rose higher.

Suddenly the megaphone announced, "The cabinet has agreed to the proposal. Thirty members of Garin Elon Moreh will move to Kadum this evening." For a split second there was numbness in the air, and then the multitudes danced. Swirling around in the circle, I thought to myself, How many people are present even once in their lifetime at a historic moment which changes the lives of his people? All around me, thousands were dancing, many crying. We joined hands with soldiers in song and dance. As I danced round and round looking at our mountains, which had been devoid of a national presence since the destruction of the Temple almost 1,900 years ago, I closed my eyes and imagined my forefather Abraham. A scant six miles south of this very spot, some 3,700 years ago, he was promised by God that his children would inherit the Land. Are we on the verge of that fulfillment? I wondered.

That night, my brother-in-law helped the garin erect some of the wooden huts that were to be used as temporary living quarters, and three families moved in. Orit helped the families get settled.

Later I learned that at the Cabinet meeting which agreed to the proposal, it was the Prime Minister himself, Yitzhak Rabin, who urged his ministers to agree. Beth, listen to his logic: "The constant evacuations give them strength. Let us allow them to enter Kadum and within three weeks they'll fold and go home." Like Herzl and other leaders of the early Zionistic movement who suggested Uganda as the Jewish homeland. Their proposal was legally accepted, but in my opinion it failed. Like them, Rabin and Peres failed to realize that the Land of Israel is not just another piece of land. Rather, it is our heart and an inseparable part of our soul.

The weekly visit is tomorrow, and I've got to start preparing food[*] for my wife and kids. That's one privilege that the prison authorities allow us to have, and all of us look forward to it. I think that I look forward to it so much, for, in a small way, I feel once again like a father.

Take care of yourself, and come over here soon. Beat the Messiah Rush.

Era

---

[*] Editor's note: The jailers admired the members of the underground for what he had done and therefore allowed Rapaport and his co-conspirators the privilege of cooking.

2 Pioneer

August 1975
Ofra

Dear Brothers,

These last two weeks, I've had some very interesting experiences. It's been some five months since we've been in Ofra and we've had some, but not much, contact with our Arab neighbors. Some two blocks down the road there is a lone house owned by an Arab. By the entrance gate, painted on the wall, is the following "KEEP OUT USA CITIZEN PROPERTY." In talks that I had with him, it turns out he was born here, has lived much of his life in the U.S. (mainly New Hampshire), is a citizen of the U.S., and generally spends the summers here. Why the sign? Over the years, before the Six Day War, he had been warned by the Jordanians that the Israelis pillage, plunder, rape. When we started advancing during the war, he painted the sign hoping that it would keep us out of his house! When he told me he's from New Hampshire, I started talking with him about the States, for as you remember, I very much enjoyed hiking those mountains. Suddenly Shukri (his Arabic name) says to me, "You know, we don't want you here. This is our country and you don't have any right taking it away; someday soon we'll throw you out." I was surprised at his frankness. I said to myself, this could be an interesting discussion. Two Americans—one, myself, born in America, one, he, Israeli born. But since he had been living most of his life in the States, could we understand each other, or even better could we see "eye to eye?"

"Shukri," I said, "why do you think this is your country, and why do you want to throw me out? What have I done to you? It's funny that you say it's your country. You don't really live here; it's your summer home!"

"You see that town—Silwad—that's where my grandfather was born and my father, he still lives there in the house I was born in. We have been here for so many years; almost all the people in Silwad have been here for generations. How can you even ask me the question, Why do I think it's mine? Are there any Jewish villages in the area? Suddenly, you start a war against us, and now you want to throw us out also. In what you call Ofra, you have taken away land from us. This is our homeland, and therefore it is ours."

"Shukri, you have been in the States for many years. From you I didn't expect the same garbage that's used here in the Middle East. We start a war? We want to throw you out? Take away land from you? About the only thing that is true of what you said is the fact that your father and grandfather were born in Silwad. You know that the war (the Six Day War) was forced upon us by your Arab States. Come on, how many times did we turn to your King Hussein and request him to stay out of the war?

"We want to throw you out? The sign you painted, did you need it? Did any of our soldiers even come into your house? And Ofra? We took your land? Ofra was an unfinished Jordanian Army base. If anybody took your land, they did! But what am I talking about? This entire part of the country including what you call Jordan was given to us by the British as part of our homeland. Why? Don't you really know? It's comfortable for you to ignore the past. All of this land was always Jewish. If anybody threw somebody out, it's you who threw us out after the Romans, Greeks, and Crusaders had done so. If you want to talk about generations being here, then don't begin history when it's comfortable for you.

"You people believe in the Bible, and you know who came first! Ofra— we called it that because Tiabeh down the road was the original Jewish Ofra! Jewish graves from the Maccabean period have been found in Silwad, half a block from your parents' house! It's interesting, you were born here and yet live in the States, except for the summer. I was born in the States and have come here. Your leaving speaks for itself."

Shukri thought for a moment and then said, "What are you talking about leaving and living in the States? There are millions of Jews in the States, so what is your point? And anyhow, the major factor is, we Arabs are not interested in sharing the land or being ruled by you."

You see my brothers—you American Jews get me in trouble even here!

I asked Shukri, "Why don't you want me to be here? Isn't there, in your opinion, as an American, the possibility of different people living together? The Jews living near you in New Hampshire don't bother you, or do they? And I'm sure you don't bother them. So why not here? If you don't try to undermine our government or our people, there's no reason we can't get along."

78

We continued talking for a few more moments, and then I left after inviting him to visit us in Ofra.

Write soon,
Era

November 1975
Ofra

Dear Moshe,

I'm sorry I left you hanging, but that's the way it is these days. There's much to do and little free time to write. We had made the decision about the work camp, yet we really had no idea what was to be. It was possible the work camp idea would be successful and we would establish a temporary base. It was much more plausible that the government would not fall for the "ruse" and would throw us right out. On a personal level, if that happened, what would we do? I would have no job—the same with Orit. On a national level, if we failed, we might have to wait years to return in great numbers to YOSH.

Orit and I felt great responsibilities. Close to 2,000 years of desolation and emptiness and exile. We were to be among the first to return after all those years. I felt the eyes of millions of Jews over countless generations looking at us, urging us on and waiting with hope. And, of course, that endless question that really has no answer—why us?

Days and weeks went by; the work on the mountain continued. As previously described, it was very hard work. We had no experience in the field, did not have the proper equipment to do the job, and, above all, we were very few. I really should not be using the word "we" for the majority of the work was done by Yehuda. I participated here and there.

As time went by and no government authority knew or intervened on the mountain, Garin Shilo/Ofra began to meet frequently to plan its next steps. I write Garin Shilo/Ofra, for in fact Ofra was a second choice. The garin originally wanted to go to Shilo (for Shilo was Israel's first capital), but all our attempts were foiled by the government. When we realized that there would be continued difficulties with Shilo, we agreed "temporarily" to become Garin Orfa, to settle in Ofra until we could settle Shilo. We were sure that we could settle in Shilo and that it was only a matter of time. There were even a number of the Shilo group who refused to consider any other "replacement." They were willing and wanted to help out but, for them, there was no substitution for Shilo.

At the meeting of the garin, various plans of action were discussed. Finally, Yehuda presented the plan that the secretariat of the garin had decided on. For over five months a small group of workers had traveled daily from Jerusalem to Ba'al Chatzor and back.* We decided that on the afternoon of the 9th of Iyyar 5735 (April 20, 1975) instead of returning to Jerusalem we would put up a "work camp" in an abandoned, unfinished, former Jordanian Army base. (The Jordanians had begun to build the base some seven months before the Six Day War and never finished it.) Instead of the daily four or five fence builders, that day some fifteen male members of the garin would join us. Some other members of the garin were to bring a small generator, portable bathrooms, beds, cooking utensils, and food directly to the camp. No women were to be present, for it was to be a work camp. We knew there would be an outcry from those against the resettlement of YOSH. It was our opinion that the best chance of success would be if everything was kept quiet and if we could successfully explain to the government that our intentions were to put up only a work camp. We would especially have to convince the Minister directly in charge—Minister of Defense Shimon Peres—not to have the army remove us. To help us toward that end, we pulled what turned out to be one of the best moves till then and maybe even since: Chanan Porat scheduled a meeting to begin at exactly the time we were to begin moving into the unfinished army base, with . . . Shimon Peres.

As the day came closer we became more anxious. We had to succeed. Failure could mean an indefinite delay in the resettlement of YOSH. I admit that the overall feeling of ours was that we were to succeed. A "feeling in

---

* Editor's note. The army hired people to help build a base. Rapaport's group was hired to build a fence around the perimeter.

the air," if you like. A feeling of fact, of a people that has been exiled for some 2,000 years. A people which suffered through and triumphed through the worst of what mankind could offer. In 1948, just three years after Hitler and his Nazis wiped out 6,000,000 of us and almost no country in the world was willing to accept us, out of those ashes and the ashes of almost 2,000 years of exile; when the words of the infamous "historian" Arnold Toynbee—"Jews are fossils"—seemed to be fulfilled. Out of all that, one of the greatest miracles of all of modern times occurred—the establishment of the State of Israel. To us, the resettlement of YOSH was a continuation of that step of redemption.

Standing there on that mountain called Ba'al Chatzor, where some 3,700 years earlier my grandfather Abraham was promised this land to his children forever, you have to believe.

It's not a feeling of cocksureness. The Jew, maybe especially the Diaspora Jew, is steeled and prepared for failure. On the other hand, we cannot see returning to Israel as simply another episode. I've told you on your visits here that only here in Israel can one understand the rabbinical statement, "The air of Israel makes one wiser." Only here can one understand the dynamic processes at work between land and people in the reestablishment of Israel. Can you, sitting there in your nice house on the outskirts of Washington, D.C., feel that special relationship?

To me/us, being here in Israel makes you believe. Being involved in the process of rebuilding helps you feel, helps you to grasp the ungraspable, touch the untouchable, see the unseeable.

Remember, Moshe, I wrote you in another letter that in my discussions with Yehuda about the "work camp" I laughed at his proposal. I was sure that it would never succeed. Yet, as I was working on the fence, an optimism slowly began to creep in. The more I was involved, the more the optimism grew. Once again, a combination of time and the strength that being on your own land gives you.

It's a process of understanding that your actions are not just your actions. We are acting in the name of and for an entire people. You can compare it to the cantor and his congregation. In Hebrew the cantor is called shaliach tzibbur, or messenger of the public. On Rosh Hashanah and Yom

Kippur, as during the rest of the year, I have had the honor and difficulty of being a shaliach tzibbur. On these holy days, there is a prayer said by the shaliach tzibbur alone, before the awesome prayers of the day. In that prayer, the shaliach tzibbur tells God, "I come to pray before you as a messenger of your people." Whenever I say these words, a shiver runs through my body. A shiver of fear and awe and yet of strength. For it is not I alone who is approaching God. Together, we approach God and ask Him to answer our prayers. The same feelings went through me those days on the mountain. Those same feelings have followed me so many times in my actions since then. The feeling, Moshe, that I am a shaliach tzibbur, for the Jews of all generations, for those who couldn't come, and for all those, you and your children, who will come in the future.

As the day approached, the more our optimism grew and the more our anxiety increased. Were we perched on the edge of an action that would be recorded in the history of our people; that we had a hand in resettling the first village in the Shomron, or . . . God forbid—would we fail?

The day before our "Aliyah," as we called it [Aliyah, from the Hebrew *oleh*, to go up], members of the garin met together to discuss last particulars. We had decided on a quiet attempt, and therefore we requested all of those involved to remember not to "spread the word." I remember late at night, looking out from our Mevasseret Yerushalayim home at the lights of our city—Yerushalayim—and asking myself, "Will I be back here tomorrow night, or would I be in our 'work camp'?"

As we sat outside, Orit insisted that she be with us that first afternoon and night. "I have as much right as you to be involved," she said. "But you know, Orit, we made a decision—no women. It's a 'work camp' only. Your presence there can risk everything," I responded. "At a work camp there has to be food, so I'm going to be the chef," she said. We had been married only a few months, but I had gotten to know Orit a bit by then. When she was determined—she was determined.

Early in the morning of the 9th of Iyar, I quickly kissed Orit, still sleeping, loaded our Peugeot with equipment, and off I went to Jerusalem to meet some more fence builders on our way to the mountain. I was to meet Orit in the afternoon and bring her to our "work camp."

In actuality, we had already given a name to our work camp. You may have guessed it, Moshe, a Biblical name. The mountain that we were working on was in an area which the great Prophet/fighter Joshua had conquered, located in the land belonging to the Biblical Tribe of Benjamin. We were working adjacent to the village of Ofra, as related in the Book of Joshua. From our previous trips in the area, we, with the help of archaeologists, had identified the Biblical Ofra as the nearby Arab village of Tiabeh. It was only natural that in our attempt to rebuild our ancestral homeland, our village would be called Ofra.

We were fifteen on the mountain that day, and although we did work, our eyes and thoughts were turned toward the abandoned army base, which we could easily see from the mountain. My thoughts kept returning to the Biblical story of Abraham and Lot and their parting. Abraham ascended the very same mountain we were on. "And God said, Abraham, look up and see from where you are. Look North, South, East, and West. For all the Land that you see I will give it to you, to your children, for all eternity."

I took you to the mountain. We were able to see the Hermon snow-capped some 150 miles north of us. You, Moshe, reacted just as I have. The views are simply awesome. Yet it is not only the exquisite views that overwhelm me, but the special relationship that I as a Jew have with the land.

The scheduled hour was fast approaching. Chanan Porat would be entering his scheduled meeting with the Defense Minister, Shimon Peres, in approximately a half-hour. It was time to move. Now the anxiety gave way to the excitement of the mitzvah that we were about to do. The jeep seemed to sense that something unusual was happening. For she also did something unusual—she started immediately! We attached the air drills and generators to the back, threw in our equipment, and drove down to our "work camp."

At the entrance to the camp we met up with another five cars and two vans. Quickly, we drove up to one of the unfinished buildings and began to unload our equipment. The folding cots and closets were put into one room. Kitchen equipment in another. In a third—a portable ark to hold our Torah and siddurim [prayer books]. We were some thirty "workers," and we set up camp quickly. As soon as we finished one of those present called out "Mincha." We rushed into our makeshift synagogue and we prayed the afternoon prayers. Prayers of thanks, happiness, and trepidation. As I was walking out of the synagogue I glanced into the "kitchen" and saw a familiar face—Orit. I was supposed to pick her up later on, but she had hitchhiked in with some of the men and was already at work preparing supper for the crew.

My happiness quickly changed, for as I was talking to Orit, two army cars and four jeeps pulled up. This, to an extent, was the moment. We knew the Military Commander of Ramallah and walked over to his jeep. To his question, "What's going on here?" Yehuda Etzion responded, "I told you a while ago that we work on the mountain putting up the fence for the army. It's very difficult for us to travel every day back and forth to Jerusalem, so we've put up a small work camp here." After some fifteen minutes of trying to gently persuade him to allow us to remain, he turned to us and said, "Either you leave of your own volition, or I'll have to forcibly remove you."

Yehuda then pulled the card we hoped would be our ace. "No, we're serious. We have permission to stay here from on high. You know that. Let's make a deal. You check with your superiors as far as the Minister of Defense. If the answer is that we have to leave—we shall do so, quietly."

Nobody was interested in a showdown, and the Commander agreed to Yehuda's proposal.

At the same time that we were talking, Chanan Porat was beginning a meeting with Shimon Peres—the Minister of Defense. At that same moment, the Minister received a phone call asking if he gave permission for a "work camp" near the army base being built. Just as Peres was preparing to give a negative answer, Chanan asked him to withhold his answer until the end of their meeting, to which Mr. Peres agreed.

Chanan continued, "Whether or not you agree with our point of view, there is no denying the real awakening of the spirit of the people of Israel that has come as a result of our repeated attempts to settle in the Shomron. You have to give some positive response to this reawakening. If not, a violent confrontation will come sooner or later. Permission to establish a work camp in Ofra can help calm down the situation. All in all, we are talking about people who are working in the army base during the day and are sleeping at night in the area."

Peres asked, "How can I know that the permission will not be interpreted and used by you, with great fanfare, as a victory over the government?" Porat answered, "I give you my word that we will keep this as quiet as possible." Shimon Peres thought for a few moments. Chanan sat quietly waiting. And in Ofra we were continuing to set up our "work camp."

Finally, Shimon Peres, the Minister of Defense of the State of Israel, picked up his phone, asked for the Military Commander of Ramallah, and uttered four Hebrew words which will go down in history: "Lo l'hafriah, lo l'azor," "Do not interfere, do not help." Four words which were the opening we were waiting for. Four words which meant that the first Jewish village in the Shomron in two thousand years was to be established.

Fifteen minutes after receiving the message from the Minister, the Military Commander of Ramallah arrived and informed us, "You're right; we are not to help you or remove you." We stood there—some of us in shock. As soon as he left, the dancing and singing broke out. "Am Yisrael Chai," "The People of Israel Live"; "V'Shavu Banim L'Gvulam," "The Children of Israel Return to Their Borders." As we danced round and round and laughed, we kept asking ourselves, "How did Chanan do it?" Out came our flag; two of us tied it to a pole and raised the pole on top of a building. Then from all of us, the resounding words of our National Anthem, Hatikvah—"L'hiyot Am Chofsheey B'artzeinu," "To Be a Free People in Our Land."

Era

January 1976
Ofra

Dear Brothers,

Today has been another very long one and I'm falling off my feet, but I haven't written you in a while and I've had some very interesting experiences.

85

This week, I got a taste of East New York/Brownsville. (Of course, I'm exaggerating.) Remember what happened to us in the last few years before we moved from the city? We used to travel through East New York and be afraid to stop at traffic lights, 'cause you risked the possibility of being "approached," your window smashed and the demand for money. After a while, we'd travel through the area with a monkey wrench on the front seat. At a red light we would brandish the monkey wrench to scare off robbers and assailants. Even before that, during the beginning of the change in the area, we joined the Chashmonaeem [self-defense group] which was formed in Crown Heights. We patrolled the area at night to try to catch intruders. To me, however, the "taste" of that period was one Friday night on the way back from Rishon Letzion.

I was walking with Sy Hoffman and you, Yosef, with Baruch. We went, as usual, through the schoolyard of P.S. 252. Sy and I went toward one exit and Baruch and you toward another. Suddenly a group of Puerto Ricans surrounded you both and started calling you dirty Jew, Jew bastard, and more. Well, my brother, you the Y.U. [Yeshiva University] wrestler would not stand to be called those names no matter what the odds against you.

You told them to shut up, and then you were grabbed from behind by some four guys and punched in the face and stomach. Baruch, when he saw you hit, yelled out, "Hey!" and slammed one of them in the nose. Sy and I arrived, and Sy, who knew judo, started flipping some of them left and right. Then there was a lull in the fighting. Baruch yelled, "Let's get out of here," and we started running. But your skullcap had fallen off and you bent down to pick it up. At that moment a couple of "them" jumped you again and then some more came from outside and this time with car antennas. Baruch grabbed a garbage can cover, yelled to one of them with an antenna, and when he looked at him, he slammed him in the face with the cover. You grabbed a cover and started doing the same, and it had a very good effect. They started falling down and even though they were some twenty in number and we were four, we got the upper hand. Then we heard the police sirens and both (they and us) scattered.

We were bleeding and our suits were ripped, so we went over to Aunt Ann's house to tidy ourselves up a bit. When we finally came home Abba and Ema were very worried 'cause they had heard from neighbors that we were in a fight. Abba got upset and told us that we don't have to be champions and we shouldn't get involved in something like that. Let them call us names—we don't have to answer them.

The next morning one of the important members of the synagogue told me, "This is not our country, and we can't do what we want." Those words of caution were repeated to us time and time again by so many different people. My response (inwardly) was that someday I was going to be in a place where all of this wouldn't happen.

So, I'm in my country, and guess what?

Last week on Monday, we were driving through Ramallah (a large modern city populated by Arabs, located three miles south of Ofra) and suddenly some teenagers ran out from a side street and threw rocks at our van. By the time we pulled over, they had disappeared. We continued on to the local police station and military command to report what had happened. They both told us that they would check out the area. That evening I told those residents who had cars to be careful.

The next day, Tuesday, I was driving back from Jerusalem and I was passing the Kalendia "refugee camp" and, boom, a rock goes flying through the front window and, by a miracle, it first hit the front seat and then my leg. I don't know how I succeeded, but I held onto the steering wheel, hit a divider in the road, bounced back to the right shoulder, and then I succeeded in bringing the van to a stop. I was too shaken to do anything. After a few minutes, I drove over to the military command. The assistant in command came down, saw my car, and gave an order to one of his patrols to check out the area where I had been stoned. I then drove to the local police.

You guessed it, my brothers, the situation began to remind me of the "good old times" in East New York, when we kept the pipe wrench on the front seat. With a major difference, I was fighting a battle on my battleground and when you're fighting on your own battleground, you react with a different determination. In the States, I was the "dirty Jew" or "Jew boy," and there was no changing that. I was a stranger and even though I wouldn't stand for being called a dirty Jew, it was a half-battle for me. Even if I succeeded in beating up my attackers I felt that this (the States) wasn't my place. So I fended off another Jew hater—so what? It was important, I agree, but I knew that it was temporary. I couldn't wear the yarmulke freely anyplace. We were always running in the States from one place to another. Remember the discussions we had at home? "Don't you worry; 'they' won't pass the railroad tracks." For some ten years, East Flatbush became more and more Orthodox Jewish. Suddenly, much quicker than it developed, it disappeared. How many years did the beautiful new synagogue of B'nai Israel last? Soon they were offering it for sale! The writing was on the wall. Remember, when Baruch was trying to get accepted to medical schools? It was known that only a few took Jews.

East Flatbush, Brownsville is a good example. Brownsville was the center for Judaism. So many synagogues; every block had one. That's where our Ema grew up. Bubbie told us so many times about the great cantors who davened in those shuls—the "Jerusalem of New York." Millions upon millions of dollars were spent by Jews throughout the generations building the community. Before our grandparents had the opportunity of enjoying the area, "they" started moving in and we were running.

That's why we joined the Chashmonaeem gang. I guess we were tired of being the "weak Jew," the "cheek-turning Jew." I was afraid, but I had two brothers who would fight and protect me. How I looked up to the two of you.

We became the activists to stay in the neighborhood and not run away. However, we didn't succeed. East Flatbush began to empty of Jews. In the end, the shul that our family had built became a church. Funny, they kept Bubbie's name on the iron gates at the entrance. Abba and Ema held out to the very end. Even after Abba was attacked, he didn't leave. Jumped in broad daylight. When "they" left him, he was bleeding, had ripped clothes, and yet no one came to his help.

We left the area—ran away again, as most Jews do. I who promised myself that I and my children would not go through the same situation again. The only place that could be true was Israel.

So here I am, brothers, at home, doing what? Being stoned by Arabs who want to throw me out! The story repeats itself over and over again. Yet there is an immense difference. It can't be compared to Brownsville, East

Flatbush, or any other place Jews have ever lived. In the galut [exile], we were fighting for a place to be a refugee looking for a temporary roof. We Jews always knew that the Diaspora was temporary. That's one of the reasons that we moved so readily. At a temporary residence you don't fight so quickly, you move on—run.

But here, my brothers, it's a totally different ball game. From your home, one doesn't run away. For a Jew in our generation, you don't run, for there is no place to run to. We've learned that lesson. From here, I don't run. Here we are home, our own police and army, and they can handle such situations. You know they are with you. So if rocks are thrown on me, my response has to be, This is my home—I'm not running any place.

I don't enjoy fighting. I never have. But if I have to, then at least here there's a "future" to my fighting. It's not here today, gone tomorrow. So you see, brothers, maybe I never told you, but you've had a good influence on me!

Love to everyone,
Era

March 1980
Shilo

Dear Joseph,

You asked, and so I'll tell you the story of how the present-day Shilo is located where it is. It is an embarrassing story and shows, in my opinion, how we are ready to injure ourselves to be overly fair to others.

The first few portable buildings were placed on the foothills of "Shiloan Mountain," some 200 feet from the ancient archeological site of Shilo. The Minister of Defense, Mr. Ezer Weizman, was adamantly against the erection of Shilo. I think he was "forced" into agreeing to the "temporary" location of our village. However, when it came to a permanent spot, he would not agree to the logical place—adjacent to ancient Shilo where there was plenty of Government land available, large enough for a nice-size Israeli village. He objected strenuously to the erection of the first buildings of Shilo and promised that only over his dead body would Shilo be built here. Therefore, an assistant in the Justice Department was sent to Shilo to check out the possibilities of where the village could be built.

Even though what I'm telling you is true, and I was there to see it, I'll "understand" if you don't believe me. We drove in one jeep and two four-wheel-drive cars to the base of a mountain some four miles from Shilo. From the maps we had, the area seemed to be empty and easy enough to build on. We ascended the mountain by foot, and on arriving, my heart sank. A beautiful mountaintop, flat, no agriculture on it—basically barren. I was waiting for the official to approve, but she said, "No good—this mountain is unsuitable." I couldn't believe what I had heard. "There are five trees on this mountaintop," she explained. "That's a sign that some-one has used this mountain and it has to be Arabs, so you can't use it." On the one hand, I was happy, for if we didn't find any suitable mountain in the area, Shilo would have to be built adjacent to its Biblical site. On the other hand, can you understand the degradation involved? Five trees which were planted, in all probability by the wind, prevented us from building on this mountain. It was empty—no houses, no roads, nothing near the area. I said to Shevach Stern, who was with me, "Are the People of Israel returning proudly to Our Land?"

We descended to our cars and traveled two miles to another mountain. Once again we ascended by foot. At the top, my heart sank once again. It was empty of everything except rocks. "Think," I said to Shevach. "Think of something so that this mountain will be disqualified also." I turned to the official and told her nonchalantly, "This is a very small mountain and there are no roads in the area; let's look elsewhere." She responded, "Bull-dozers solve the road problem, and there is enough room for seventy-five houses." "Seventy-five houses? Shilo is going to be a major center for sur-rounding villages. We need room for 1,000 houses," I responded. "That's not my decision; I'll report to my office that this mountain is suitable for a small village." It really was a beautiful mountain top and it wasn't too far from Shilo. I turned and said to Shevach, "We'll call this Mavoh Shilo or Eli. The name Shilo can only be for the village to be erected adjacent to Bib-lical Shilo." We continued walking around the mountaintop, dreaming up reasons to forestall a government decision. As we were walking, I noticed that the official bent down repeatedly and picked up dirt. She and her assistant talked for a minute and then she casually said: "We'll have to find another place; this is not suitable either." Shevach and I looked at each other in disbelief, not understanding why. The official continued: "Do you see these?" pointing to some balls of dirt in her hand. "These are balls of sheep dung, and the only people who raise sheep in the area are Arabs; therefore they came here with their sheep to graze, and you can't use their land!!!" I broke out laughing, for I was sure that she was joshing. But she was serious.

Dried sheep dung! Thirty years after the establishment of the State of Israel, dried sheep dung was found on an obscure mountaintop, and therefore Jews can't settle there! Unbelievable! I said to myself, paraphrasing a Marlboro cigarette advertisement: You take the Jews out of galus [exile], but you can't take the galus out of the Jews.

God has all kinds of messengers, brothers. This time the sheep were. Even sheep have a part in the mitzvah of building Eretz Yisrael. Because of them, no other mountaintop was found to be kosher for building the village of Shilo. Thus the new Shilo was rebuilt at the site of its original home.

The trip taught me valuable information. If sheep dung was to decide to whom the land belongs, we could use that to our benefit. For the next year, we persuaded the Jewish Agency of the importance of raising sheep—both for the land and as an industry. We succeeded, and two hundred head were purchased. Approximately half a year after our sheep arrived, the same official arrived once again to decide on an area for expanding the village. She was to ascertain if the moutain top near the ancient Shilo was "kosher" for our expansion. On top of the mountain there were no trees—in short, totally barren. Yes, brother, you guessed it, once again she found sheep dung. "One moment, one moment—the balls of dung are Jewish sheep dung," I said. This time the official laughed, and yet I insisted, "Seriously, they are Jewish sheep dung: take a look down toward the bottom of the mountain at that herd of sheep. Who is the shepherd? Use these binoculars." The official looked and was bewildered. We proceeded to tell her about our sheep. The rest is history; my house, among another fifty-five, is on that mountaintop today.

Contrary to what you may believe, it is because of our sensitivity to individual Arabs who live and work the land that I am involved with the Land Redemption Fund. A fund which was founded to buy land from the Arabs. As our forefather Avraham did when he bought the burial field in Hevron, we pay top-notch money. If there were five hundred members of your congregation who wanted to own land in Israel and would be ready to plunk down $3,000 for a quarter-acre of rocky but Holy soil—no problem. The Arabs in YOSH are willing to sell. Is that surprising to you? It is to a lot of American Jews. If you were to live here, you would not be surprised. Eventually, after getting to know the culture, you would then begin to understand their reasons for selling.

My "understanding" was helped immensely by conversations that I had with Husni. He had land some two miles from my house. I had met him one day while driving Shilo's tractor through the valley. His tractor had broken down, and I pulled over to see if I could help. After I towed him home, I was invited for a cold drink. We both visited each other quite a bit from then on. He came to the circumcision of our son, David, and we were present at his brother's wedding held in their village. They even arranged for us to eat kosher food.

We got to talking about his agriculture work. He said that he is one of the few young men (age thirty-five) who still engages in agriculture. When I asked him why, he responded, "For a variety of reasons. Financially there is much better income in industries in other countries; a large number of them don't see their future here."

Joseph, you remember the camping trip we took to the White Mountains? On top of Mount Washington, I told you that one of my dreams is a farm to work. I still have that dream, and here was an opportunity, I thought to myself. Casually I asked Husni, "Is anybody maybe interested in selling his land?" "Of course," he answered. Yet I have not yet succeeded in purchasing land in the valley. Mostly because of the price. The farmers want astronomical prices for it, but they are willing and sometimes even eager to sell.

"You are from America. Why are you here?" Husni asked me. It was, as we say in Hebrew, a moment of truth. I said, "There are many reasons, and I'm not sure that you'll understand them, but I'll try and explain. For all my life until I came to Israel, I prayed every day, three times a day, to God, that He returns us to Israel. My father was born in Jerusalem; so was his mother, so was her father. This is the country that God promised us. This is the only place in the world where a Jew can live like a Jew. Even the valley you plow on, what do you call it? 'Valley of the Girls,' because of a holiday that was held here by Jews three thousand years ago. The terraces that you plant your vegetables and fruit trees on, who built them? The Jews. In other words—I've come home." There was quiet on the porch and then Husni spoke in what, to me, to this very day, was one of the most truthful and sensitive statements that could be said: "I know what you feel. We Arabs, especially farmers, have sensitivity toward the land and like you, we pray. I pray to Mecca and I understand your praying toward Jerusalem."

We looked at each other thoughtfully. After a few moments, I asked, "So why, Husni, are the youngsters choosing to leave?" "There are a couple of reasons, but will you understand them? Doogri, as we say, would you want to live under the control of others and want for the goodness and kindness of others? Don't you want to control yourself? You know, Era, I've never been my own master. We have always been under the control of somebody. First the Turks, then the British, then the Jordanians, and now you. I envy you; at least you can feel what it is to be your own ruler. Don't be hurt by what I'm saying, but it's true. Until you and your friends, how are you called, Gush something? I thought there was a chance that we could be our own rulers here. I now know differently. If you are willing to battle your own government and live in the trailers—you will not leave here. I'll ask you, as we say, doogri, straight, don't you want to throw us out of here?" His question was one that I had been asking myself over and over. Influencing my thoughts were my Western background and my experiences in Ofra and with Gush Emunim. It seemed as if my silence bothered him. "Your not answering is your answer," Husni said. "No, I'm organizing my thoughts," I responded. "Husni," I said, "we have gotten to know each other a bit, and as you have spoken straight, so shall I. You are an Arab Muslim—a religious one. And as you once told me, to you it is natural to live among your own people. Your children study your religion in your neighboring village; you pray together and celebrate your holidays together. The same with me; in short, I want to be among people who share my ideals, thoughts, and plans for the future. On an individual level and on a national level, for close to two thousand years my people have lived as strangers in strange countries. We have always had to turn to foreigners to be good to us. We were thrown out of God knows how many countries—just for the "sin" of being Jewish. We were persecuted, massacred, expelled, and ghettoized all over the world. And in the countries that we were allowed to live in, even there in many cases we were limited severely to what professions we could practice. This is my opportunity to return home and to no longer be a stranger. If I live in Shilo down the road and you live here, that to me is acceptable—under certain conditions."

"What do you mean, under certain conditions? Who are you to make conditions? I have been here with my family, as I told you, for over one hundred years, and you are in Shilo only one year." Husni spoke quickly and angrily, and I knew he was talking from his heart. At that moment, Aziz, a neighbor of his who was sitting with us, spoke up. "That's exactly what Husni said, you'll make conditions and then throw us out."

"Husni," I said. "There are some twenty Arab States in the Middle East. You practice the same religion and customs as they and could easily fit into any one of those places. You have not been expelled from countless countries in the world. In short, you have a place to go, where you and your leaders are the boss. I have none. I didn't come here to uproot you or throw you out. In the last one hundred years that your family has lived here and throughout history, there has never been an Arab country here. You lived as foreigners. I have not said that I will throw you out. I won't do to others what was done to us throughout the generations."

Aziz spoke again and asked, "So what do you mean by 'conditions'?"

I said, "This part of Israel is part of our State and, please God, all the Laws of our State will apply here. Practice your way of life within your village as you like. But if you try to hurt us, injure us, or overthrow our State, that we can't accept. If this was a Muslim State, you wouldn't allow anybody to try and overthrow you. The same with us."

Weeks later in another conversation, I told Husni and Aziz that, in the long run, it may be best for the future of our peoples that we go our own way. That they join an Arab country where they are the rulers. Whoever said that there are simple solutions in life?

Era

January 1980
Shilo

Dear Phil and Sheila,

You must have broken your own world record for responding to letters—only two months approximately and already I received a letter from you. It was really good hearing from you. I needed your ideas quite a bit. A lot has occurred since I wrote to you, and hopefully I'll get to what's going on in this letter. First, however, I want to try and respond to one of your major questions. I've written a bunch of letters, and whenever somebody writes back to me that's the question they ask most often. It's kind of difficult for Americans to understand how we can build a settlement without government permission. Basically, what you are trying to understand is the whole debate here over Judea and Samaria. Is it part of Israel or not?

In actuality, the debate here is not just over land. That would be difficult enough. The debate is even more entrenched than the land itself. It's a national identity crisis.

About a year after we arrived in Shilo, Shalom Achshav [Peace Now] erected a big dove's nest at Shilo. They advertised in the newspapers that "the settlers of Gush Emunim have put up a village of hate and we are erecting a monument of love and peace." They really think that they, and only they, have a monopoly on peace. Only they want peace and we want war. They know it isn't so. We both want peace. The difference is that we see peace through the Torah, and that, simply spoken, doesn't interest them. We see ourselves as you do, the nation of Israel, following the unique ways of all our generations and returning to Eretz Yisrael. To Shalom Achshav, we are just another people, like any other people, and Israel is our land. The difference is blatant in many ways. Walk down Dizengoff Street in Tel Aviv and see store after store with American names

—American Ice Cream, New York; New York Manhattan Restaurant; New York Jeans; Israel-USA and more. You've got to look hard to find something in Hebrew. In the Shomron, everything is history—everything Jewish. It's a clash of values. I take Moriyah down to the ancient Shilo and show her where [the Biblical figures] Yehoshua and Shmuel lived. In Tel Aviv they go to restaurants featuring Egyptian belly dancers.

To most of Shalom Achshav, the Bible is a story/history book and no more. It's all in the past. To us the Torah is past, present, and future. In one of my recent reserve stints, one of my commanders, Aryeh, and I had a long discussion. Aryeh is a teacher in a government school, married, thirty-five years old with two children. "Era," he said, "you are an intelligent person, born in the U.S., master's degree. You explain to me why it is so important to you to have the West Bank. There are 800,000 Arabs there. Who needs them and the problems they bring us? Right, the land has historical value, but that's all. It's nice to visit, but why jeopardize lives for this land? What is so intrinsically important to you?"

Well, like a good Jew, I answered Aryeh with a question. "Let me ask you, Aryeh, why are you living at all in Israel? Beside the fact that you were born and raised here, fought in the army, why stay here? You're surrounded by Arabs who want to kill you. You serve some forty-five to fifty days a year in reserve duty. It's hard to make a living. Why is it so important to you to stay here?" Aryeh thought for a few moments: "I was born here. Isn't that a sufficient reason for living here? You, Era, weren't born here. You came on aliyah, so you need some good reasons to justify your coming here. Therefore, the religious medium is comfortable to you. I don't need any outside help; I'm Israeli, just as you were an American. When you lived in America, did you need a reason for being there? Your being born there and your culture was sufficient. The same with me."

"I hear what you're saying. The U.S. is a good example but in a different way. Numbers-wise, the U.S. has been one of the largest immigrant countries, meaning that millions of people all over the world chose to emigrate from their birthplace, uproot themselves and come to the U.S. To them, the simple fact that they were born in a country was not sufficient reason to stay there. They were looking for greener pastures. In many instances they left countries that were a lot easier to live in than Israel. You asked me before why I jeopardize my life to live here. Aryeh, I'll ask you the same. Why are you jeopardizing your life to live here? Just because you were born here? So what? Tomorrow morning, war can break out and like so many of us you can be killed. You can just as easily go to the States and melt into the great melting pot. Your children won't even feel or remember that they were Israeli."

"Okay," Aryeh said, "you've taken a good tactic; the best defense is a good offense, and you've presented me with some good questions, but you still haven't answered my question. By living here in the West Bank you are jeopardizing not only your life, but you are forcing many others, like myself, to be in the same situation. I'm sure that if we gave back the West Bank, we could find some kind of peace with our Arab neighbors. You're preventing that and causing more of us to be killed."

I admit I get upset when accused by others that my living in YOSH causes more deaths. "Aryeh," I said, "that's rhetoric for your Peace Now flyers. A stronger case can be made for my side—that keeping our land means fewer deaths. One thing we can both agree to: if we leave the area totally—either march ourselves into the Mediterranean Sea or fly to other countries—there will be peace between us and our Arab neighbors. I'm sorry, Aryeh, I'm not a masochist. I also can't believe that an area 125 miles long by 40 miles wide [YOSH] is the reason that we have no peace with the Arabs! Even when they controlled the West Bank, they attacked us again and again."

What's interesting is that all of this is going on as I'm driving our patrol jeep and he was directing me where to go. Aryeh may have very little connection to Judaism, or should I say religious observance, yet he is standing on guard by the borders of our country. Is that not more observant Judaism than what the most fervent observant Jew can do in the U.S.? Doesn't Judaism teach us that the mitzvoth [good deeds] one practices outside of Israel are just to remember how to do them in Israel! And isn't it written in the Gemorah [Talmud], "God said, I prefer a small group (of Jews) living in Israel than a large Sanhedrin [Parliament] in the Diaspora." In a way I can't question his Judaism. He is here in Israel guarding over our country.

We turned off the main road to drive through Gufna, today a Christian

Arab village. "Aryeh," I said, "let me ask you—the village we just entered, what was here some two thousand years ago?" "I know," he responded, "The Maccabees lived here, but that's the past and I'm not going to endanger myself because of what was." I interrupted him. "Who did the Maccabees battle, and for what did they battle?" "They fought the Greeks to be able to live as Jews in Israel. Fine. That's history. Today we have a State, and the only reason for battling is to defend."

"Wait a second, Aryeh. Yes, the Maccabees fought the Greeks, but before that they had to fight the Jews themselves. The great Maccabees were basically fighting to prevent Jews from becoming Hellenistic. They noticed that the Jews were getting further and further away from Judaism and striving to become a nation like the other nations. Gufna was the center of their rebellion for two major reasons. One—militarily we are very high up, and throughout history, whoever controlled the mountain range of Judea and Samaria controlled Israel. The second is for its historical religious reasons. This countryside was, from the beginning of Judaism, the centrality of our people. The Maccabees understood that to beat the Greeks, we would have to stand united as one people. The unification could be achieved only via adherence to the Torah and Am Yisrael [the Jews] being in control of their own land.

"Aryeh, it's not as you say, that I want the land for expansionist reasons, but simply put, it is intrinsically part of us. This may sound strange to you, but how would you feel without your wife? Would you feel a total person, or empty?" "Of course I would feel like an empty person; Vered and I get along very well."

"Any happily married person would feel cut in half if suddenly separated from his wife; it's natural. In the words of the Torah, 'Therefore shall man leave his father and mother and cling to his wife and they shall be one flesh.' In a good marriage, each partner gives of his or herself and together you reach a greater, inner self-harmony.

"I have another love. In some ways it is comparable to my love for my wife. I have a love for this land. Just as I reach tremendous heights and success with my wife, just as we fulfill and complement each other, just as we feel whole together, just as we require each other to fulfill our potential in life, it's the same for the Jewish people and Eretz Yisrael. These are not just words, Aryeh; they are feelings from way down. Only here can we have a Jewish government, a Jewish army, a Jewish police and courts, and a calendar that revolves around Jewish history and tradition. In America, we're well-behaved guests of the goyim [gentiles]."

"Conversely, Aryeh, just as you could not feel whole without Vered, and I without Orit, I could not feel whole without Shilo, Hevron, Bei-El, and Shechem. I could not reach my potential in life, I could not reach the heights that I want to reach. I would feel like half a person. That is how it would be for me without Israel. And, Aryeh, not just me but millions of Jews all over."

Aryeh fell quiet, and we traveled on for a few minutes. "Aryeh," I said, "you owe me an answer." "To what?" "My question." "What question?" "Why are you here?"

"I've been thinking about that since we've been talking. I don't have the belief you have, and for me it's not a question of idealism. Maybe it's an inner feeling that this is my place, or maybe I feel good among my own. I live here because I feel good here, and that's sufficient. What bothers me is that you make everything into deep religious belief, which creates extremism."

My conversation with Aryeh is a good example of what I was explaining to you in the beginning of my letter. The debate isn't only about the land, but differences of attitudes toward culture. As you could tell from our conversation, the land has no special meaning to Aryeh because our culture and past is not special to him.

To a very big extent, our government is a mirror of the differences between Aryeh and myself. Part of the government sees the nation of Yisrael, of the land Yisrael, and even the Torah of Yisrael as the raison d'être of the State of Yisrael and therefore will do its utmost to further those goals. To them, giving away part of Eretz Yisrael is like giving away one of your reasons for living. One can't do that.

On the other hand, others in the government see Western, secular values as supreme and more important than Jewish cultural and historic values. Therefore, giving away part of Eretz Yisrael to gain some modern values is kosher to them.

When I was living in the States, I used to love to go mountain climbing.

The area I especially liked were the White Mountains in New Hampshire. In 1966–67, I spent a year in Yerushalayim, studying at Yeshivat Mercaz HaRav and during that year I traveled throughout Israel, its length and breadth. When I returned to the States, I went to the White Mountains the first opportunity I had and climbed Mount Washington. As usual, it was just magnificent, breathtaking. Yet something was missing. I didn't have the same feeling as in earlier years. I thought about the mountains in Israel, which "objectively" were not as beautiful. It took me a few minutes before I was able to pinpoint the difference. Mount Washington is beautiful, exquisite, but it's not mine. I have no special relationship with it. The mountain in the Negev, or the Galilee, or anyplace in Israel may not be as beautiful, but it's mine. Therefore, it is special to me.

You know, the Beit Knesset in Shilo faces south toward Jerusalem. I sit in the back, and when I turn around and look out the window I overlook the old city of Shilo. On Friday night, during the tefillah [prayer] of Kabbalat Shabbat [welcoming the Sabbath], there is a point where you turn around to welcome the Shabbat who is coming as a guest. When I turn around and see the old city of Shilo, I also see Shmuel, the Prophet, smiling and saying, "My children have returned." I'm not a mystic, but that's what I feel Friday night after Friday night.

Best blessings,
Era

April 1979
Shilo

Dear Avi,

You were in the newspapers last week—a picture of you on a march for the freedom of Soviet Jewry. As usual, you are still involved in important activities for the freedom of our people. I admit that I'm frustrated by the lack of activity here on behalf of Russian Jewry. When I first arrived here on Aliyah, I was upset at the Jews here for not joining marches, writing letters, and more. Over the few years that I'm here, I've come to the realization

that there isn't much we can do here. It's probably correct that by participating in marches, etc., the word would reach our brothers and sisters in
the USSR that we are doing our utmost and making noise. But in terms of
influencing the leadership of the USSR, it doesn't seem feasible that we in
Israel have any possibility of doing so. If our government had an official relationship with them, maybe we could do something, but that is not the
situation. It could well be that this is one of those cases where we have to
depend on American Jewry. Anyhow, more power to you for being involved.

In one of your earlier letters to me, you asked me about our relationship
with the Arabs. Rather, you wanted to know if we have any daily contact
with them. Is there an opening for some kind of positive, ongoing relationship with them? I don't know if I ever told you about an Israeli, who I
served in the army with, by the name of Yoav. About six months ago, I was
hitchhiking in the Galilee and decided to surprise him with a visit at his
moshav [settlement]. He himself is not Orthodox; neither is the moshav,
and politically he is a middle of the roader.

Yoav's neighbor, Yosef, asked me how I knew Yoav. It turns out that he
was very surprised that Yoav was close to somebody like me. One who
wears a yarmulke and lives in a place like Shilo. Well, we got into a discussion which led him to ask the same question that you did: whether we had
any relationship with our Arab neighbors and whether I felt that there was
a chance for an ongoing relationship.

"We have contact with our Arab neighbors," I answered. "Not a lot, that
is true, but there are reasons for that also. Number one, we are very busy
with building and dealing with the everyday problems. I personally have
very little time for my family because of the tremendous amount of time
that I spend working; therefore if I have any spare time, I spend it with my
family. Maybe there is a much deeper reason. I'm not really interested in
having my kids spend time with Arab kids. Why? I want my kids to be Jewish. Look at the Jews in the Diaspora. The moment they began relationships with non-Jews, the amount of intermarriages went sky high. At the
same time, the level of Judaism plummeted."

"What you are saying, Era, is that to be a Jew or a good Jew, if you like, you must separate yourself in a ghetto. That's ridiculous. I'm not willing to accept that," retorted Josef.

I didn't mean that and said so: "No, you misunderstand me. Youths are very impressionable. If they don't know enough of their own beliefs, they can be easily swayed. When my kids are older and are solid in their beliefs, they'll be in a more proper position to reach out into the wide, wide world.

"Still, we do have contact. It may not be sufficient contact, but it's there. Let me give you some examples. They may surprise you. We don't have a grocery shop in Shilo because there are not enough families to support one. Some of the daily products we bring in from Ofra about twelve miles away. We also buy a good amount of produce from the stores in the Arab villages in Turmos-Aya and especially Singel. While we are there we spend time, sometimes sitting and drinking coffee.

"We have one telephone line into Shilo. It is connected to the Arab village of Singel. The switchboard is in Singel and the operators are Arab. If you were to call our number, you would first reach Singel. He, in turn, would plug you in and ring me. If I'm in Jerusalem and Orit is out, I'll call Singel and ask the switchboard operator to leave a message for Orit or to let others know where I am. He would do so simply because of a good relationship. When I go to Singel, I always stop in to see how the switchboard operators are doing. When one of them was ill for two weeks, we paid a get-well visit.

"I've been at the burials of some of their important people and at the weddings of some others. I've taken the children of Shilo to see how their olive press works, and just as they have helped fix our cars that break down on the road, we do the same for theirs. All of what I've said is in addition to the work relationship that we have—especially in the building trade. So, I'm sorry, Yosef, your claim is not all that valid."

Besides an interesting conversation with him, Avi, he showed me how to milk a cow without getting drenched. What very much interested me was his surprise at Yoav and myself being good acquaintances. It seems to me that among the general populace of Jews in the States, there is more of a nonpressure relationship between Orthodox/Conservative/Reform Jews than there is here in Israel. It probably has a lot to do with the fact that in the States there is a separation of state and religion. Here, many religious decisions passed in the Knesset affect the less observant Jews also. It makes for more pressure.

Love ya my dear friend,
Era

January 1979
Shilo

Dear Avi,

The days and nights go by extremely fast in Shilo. I guess that is natural when you are constantly busy with building a village. Yet I feel a necessity, an inner one, to find some time to write of my feelings and actions these days. Maybe because I feel that there are historic times, the rebuilding of YOSH, and I'd like to remember it, to tell my children in the future. Or maybe it's the way I follow after my father, who used to write his feelings.

Since our shooting down of the electric lines in Turmos-Aya, our area is quiet. I wish that were true of other areas. What's so troublesome is the fact that my government is doing little or nothing to stop the actions.

I know, Avi, it's difficult, as you wrote, to understand why. The government in power comprises some twenty cabinet ministers. Not all of the ministers agree on how the government should act. Consequently, different ministers run their ministries according to their own beliefs and not by a general government policy. It can turn out that one minister will give you a no to your request, yet you can receive a yes by turning to another minister in the same cabinet. Sounds crazy? You are right.

Ofra was a great example. Officially the Labor government was against villages in YOSH. Yet Shimon Peres, Minister of Defense, allowed us to stay. When the Likud [government], under Menachem Begin, took over, it was obvious to us that his government would actively push for the resettlement and development of YOSH. I remember, Avi, the ringing words that Menachem Begin yelled out, with his finger pointing, "There will be many Elon Morehs." Our cheering lasted only for a short time. For some reason, which we can't understand even now, a year and a half later, he appointed Moshe Dayan to his cabinet. For another reason, which we can't understand, Ezer Weizman, whom he appointed as Defense Minister, has become a peace lover. When I say a peace lover, I mean one who is ready to give up pieces of land for a supposed "peace." Ezer has gone even further—I believe he has strengthened the radical Arab councils and has allowed the PLO in YOSH to go wild. You don't believe me, my dear friend? I am more bewildered than you, but these are the facts as I see them.

The great change for the worse in YOSH happened after the Camp David talks and signing. Until then YOSH had been quiet. Our promising to give autonomy to the Arabs living in YOSH drove the Arab leadership to band together to fight against the idea and to try and throw us out. Backers of the PLO, Jordan, communists, and religious Arabs—all suddenly worked together. The leaders of the struggle are a group of Arab mayors, militants and radicals, who established in late 1978 the National Guidance Committee. This committee, actually a PLO body, decided on a new tactic. Not only would they use militant methods but also political ones. They are using our democracy for their needs.

They are dressed neatly in shirt, tie, and suit, great for American press. They hold rallies in the main cities in YOSH and call for the overthrow of our country. Arabs in general are passionate people and can be easily roused to action. The NGC leaders called them to riot, to throw rocks at our cars and to burn tires on the roads.

Ezer Weizman knows all of this, but Ezer is "blind" now. Since Camp David he is like a robot. No matter what circumstances, he wants what he considers peace. He is like a man under the influence of a peace drug. Since the "honor" bestowed upon him at Camp David, he can't come off this high. Even though he knows what the NGC is about, not only doesn't he stop them—he helps them! We don't know how to deal with him.

It's important that you understand who the NGC is, Avi. Some of the main members of the NGC are Ibrahim Duak, an engineer living in Jerusalem and a communist. He has been joined by Karim Chalef of Ramallah, Bassam Shaka of Shechem, Fuad Kuwasma of Hevron, Chilmi Chanon of Tul-Karem, Ibrahim Tawil of Al-Bireh, and Muchmad Milchem of Chalchul. These are top-notch PLO members. For example, in 1974, one of our military judges recommended that Karim Chalef be tried for membership and action in the Chazit for the Liberation of Palestine, but the Labor government shelved his recommendations. Shimon Peres allowed this PLOnik to be appointed mayor of Ramallah two years later.

Bassam Shakal!? The Jordanians sentenced him to jail in 1958 due to political involvement, and he ran away to Syria. When he returned to Israel, he began a consistent campaign of recorded terrorist activities against the Jews.

The NGC is calling for a jihad [holy war] against us. In their first public gathering about five months ago, Karim Chalef yelled out to a mass gathering in Shechem, "It's time to return to the hills of Jerusalem, Yaffa and Haifa!" Ezer kept silent, and the military command could do nothing.

Actually, Avi, Ezer didn't stay silent. He did worse than that. Last winter at a meeting in Ramallah of the military command and Karim Chalef, Ezer blurted out to Karim, "Tell Mr. Arafat that we want peace." Chalef began to realize with whom he was doing business. Then he complained to Ezer about the rough hand that the military authorities were showing him. What did Ezer do? He wrote his private telephone number on a piece of paper and handed it to Karim. "If they give you a problem call me!"

Local military leaders backed off. We, the settlers, were left alone.

Chalef, in an interview to the newspaper *Al Fajar,* stated, "There is only one way open to us, as Gamal Nasser said, 'What has been taken by force will be returned by force.' " He calls for a military uprising, and our government sits by and lets him do what he wants.

The result, Avi? Every day rocks are thrown at our cars, buses, and school buses. Sometimes even Molotov cocktails are thrown. Our hands are tied, and if I sound frustrated and angry, I am. Can you imagine, Avi, the U.S. government or your local police allowing the Weathermen or SLA [Symbionese Liberation Army] to operate without doing anything to stop them?

I've written you this before, Avi. We turn to government leaders, police, army, everyone and we get absolutely no help from them. Yes, some of the local commanders try to help out, but they really can't do much, for the politicians stop them. What do they expect us to do? Sit by and get stoned to death? I wrote you about the telephone lines that were cut down constantly. All the meetings and requests for help didn't do any good. The moment we did something, there was quiet. You expect the government to learn, to change their methods of action, but no way. It's as if they want us to be forced into action.

Boker tov [good morning], Avi. It's been about two weeks since I started writing. In the interim we, meaning some other settlement representatives and myself, met again with Ezer Weizman to discuss the worsening situation. I know by now not to expect much from Ezer, and yet I, or we, keep on hoping. I took along a copy of some of the statements of Karim Chalef. Our Minister of "Defense" didn't seem to care.

On rereading my letter to you, Avi, and on rereading your letter to me, I'm not sure if I'm getting my point across. When I wrote you of my involvement in shooting down the electric line in Turmos-Aya, you wrote that you understand. Truthfully, I feel that it's difficult, if not impossible, for you to understand; part of the reason is simply that you are there, and you are not going through the experiences I'm going through. I know that you trust me and say to yourself that if Era did it, it had to be done. You're right when you write me that in one of your talks to your congregation you told them that Era couldn't harm a fly. Well, maybe you've exaggerated a bit, but I admit that circumstances here have changed me. Or rather have forced me to act in methods I would not have chosen in the past.

But, Avi, if we don't react we shall be forced out of here. Shilo these days is about twelve families strong, living in caravans. We truck in water, use a small generator for electricity part time, no road, no medical facilities, no sewage, etc. The army has put up a barbed wire fence around the houses for protection. The problem is, I'm not sure whether it is protection for or against me. Supposedly, it is to keep out PLO terrorists. Sometimes we have the feeling that it's to keep us from settling more government-owned land. As you remember, I wrote you that Ezer Weizman was so mad that the government allowed us to come and remain here that rumor has it he has given strict instructions to the military that we can't do anything outside of the few acres that have been allotted.

Last night, a couple of us were sitting outside one of the caravans, talking about the situation, when suddenly we heard an explosion near the barbed wire fence. Immediately, we made all of the women and kids lie flat on the floor, wherever they were. There were six men armed with Uzis, M16s, or pistols. We spread out—three of us to check out the area near the explosion and three to protect the women and children.

I won't lie, Avi, I was scared. I imagine that if I had gone through full military service, these situations would be more usual to me. But here I am, a social worker from East Flatbush, who knows very little about PLO ambushes. I know what you are thinking—that you met me in army fatigues. That's true . . . but . . . I came to Israel an "old man" of twenty-six! The army "drafted" me at the ripe old age of twenty-nine, and I was given only very basic training and then sent off to be a communications expert. So, thank God, I've had no battle experience.

I crawled my way around the rocks and thorns of Shilo toward the explosion area. If you think too much in these situations, it's not good—I mean thinking about what the consequences could be. Orit and our two babies were back there in the caravan. Had the bomb been placed closer, God forbid, it could have been the end of them and the others. You also think, right now, as I'm crawling toward the PLO, I could be shot down.

The thorns bit into my feet and ripped my hands. Chaim led and we covered for him. Then Shevach leap-frogged forward and then I. Finally, the rocks of Shilo came to good use. Hiding behind them made you feel quite safe. As I crawled and rolled over from side to side, Tel Shilo was in back of me and on one of my rolls I caught a glimpse of that ancient mountain. Suddenly the past mixed with the present. The Maccabees fought here two thousand years ago. It was our turn today. We were getting closer to the explosion site, advancing cautiously.

As we closed in on the spot, I fired off a round to ascertain that nobody was in the vicinity. It was, by now, some fifteen minutes since the explosion, and we had no idea whether the attackers were still around. After some more shots, we felt that they had fled. We stood up and found the remnants of the explosion. Once again, we spread out quickly, jumped the barbed wire "security" fence, and continued searching. After another ten minutes of searching, we returned, carefully, to check with the three guarding the women and children.

One of the women blurted out, "Well, this is what the government wants. Now, maybe, we shall get some protection." While we were talking, four army vehicles showed up, including the military commander of the area and two trackers. One hour later they reported to us that they found footsteps of two terrorists who had come from the road some three kilometers away. Their footsteps led to a car, and that was all they could do. The demolitions expert told us how fortunate we were. The explosive had gone off, but the launcher didn't work. The damage was done near the fence. Had the launcher worked, it could have detonated right among the buildings.

There were those of us who wanted to drive right down to Ezer Weizman's house in Caesarea and those who wanted to wake up Menachem Begin. Rocks are bad enough and can kill, but to have a missile planted at your doorstep!? If Menachem Begin wants to give in to Mr. Peanuts [Jimmy Carter] that's his problem, if he were speaking for himself. But Mr. Begin was elected on a platform of settling all of Eretz Yisrael. To put us in danger and to be afraid to act against terrorists because of what Jimmy Carter says? That's something that we can't accept.

After the army commander and his staff left, we continued to discuss our reaction. Suddenly I throw out the idea that the proper reaction would be one of building. "What do you mean?" I was asked. "What are the PLO interested in doing? Throwing us out, chasing us out." By cutting down the telephone line, by throwing rocks at our cars, even when there are women and children inside, and now by exploding a mine near us, they are trying to scare us and make us move. This time, the proper response to their actions and their motives may be to show them that their actions don't scare us. Even more so, that any action of theirs will be met with our action—to build.

"What you're saying is interesting and I like the idea," responded Chaim's wife, Rivka. "However, we don't have the money to build, and even if we did, the government is not allowing us to do anything, so what can we do?"

Tonight, I said, a few of us will roll the fence twenty meters farther away from our houses. This way, we can include more government land in the village. And the PLO will learn that every time they do something, we'll respond by expanding. It's the proper Zionist response. We are showing the PLO that building life is our response to their activities of death.

The idea was accepted by all of us. About one hour later, six of us were pulling up fence stakes and carefully rolling the fence out from the center of the village. The anger and frustration in us changed to a feeling of satisfaction. Satisfaction in building Israel. On the other hand, I turned to Shevach and Chaim and told them what a bushah, shame, if this is the way we have to build Aretz—under the cover of darkness. I don't know if you understand, Avi. On one hand it was a great feeling that this is the answer to all those who would see us destroyed. Yet my government should be doing it, and in strength. I didn't come to Aretz to build settlements under the cover of night. Last night was one of those struggles of mixed emotions. One of many.

I doubt if they'll find the terrorists soon. The Shin Bet [General Security Services] is superb, but this won't be easy. Will we complain to the government? I'm not even sure. There are those of us who feel that there is no reason to complain, for nothing will be done anyhow. We will be given the same runaround as before. Also, there are those of us who feel that our response last night wasn't sufficient and that we have to have some retaliatory action. I'm against it. I have no proof that the terrorists came from the town nearby. I've got to stop writing: they're calling me outside. Some official visitor to our place.

Shalom, Avi, once again. Orit says I should mail the part of the letter that I've written already, 'cause if I wait until I'm finished, you may never get the letter. She, as usual, is probably right, so maybe after I finish today, I'll send it off.

I want to tell you about an interesting meeting I had about two days after the attack on Shilo. I was visiting Singel, one of the Arab villages nearby, buying some vegetables in the store. While shopping, in walks Ahmad, one of the villagers whom I got to know pretty soon after arriving in Shilo, and along with him, three other fellows. While we were both buying vegetables, Ahmad said to me that he heard about the attack on the village, and he wanted to know whether anyone was hurt. I answered, "Inshallah" [something like, Thank God, no].

Suddenly Ahmad says to me, "We expected you to retaliate against us after the attack on you!" I was taken aback. Ahmad said to me, "You look surprised." "I am very surprised by your frankness. I'll be frank too. We both claim this land as ours. I don't think that we will ever agree on whose land it is. Right now we must live together, so why do you insist on trying to throw us out? Why the rocks, burning tires, and now this explosion?"

Ahmad was silent for a few moments. "Era, on a personal level, we get along well. I respect your ideals. That's on a personal level, but on a national level, it's very different. I want to be my own boss. Doesn't everybody want to be? So the more militant among us will do what they can do to get rid of you. Even if we get along on a personal level, the national level will always remain a major problem."

"Do you ever see an end to it?" I asked.

Again, a few moments of silence. "Truthfully, I'm not sure there will be until you Jews leave or unless you live under our control."

"Ahmad," I said, "I appreciate your frankness, but your words make me sad. You are a religious person, as I am. My being here in Israel is comparable to your trip to Mecca—a religious obligation. For me to leave here is to take away some of myself. I won't do that. Second, there is no comparing the way we treat you vis-à-vis the way you have treated us. You know very well that if you don't attack us, plant mines, and the like, you will be left alone. In fact, the freedom you have here is more than the freedom offered any Arab in any Arab state."

"You may be right that we have more 'freedom' here, but we are part of the Arab nation and therefore we should be governed by an Arab state. Also, this land belongs to the Arab nation, and we can't allow anyone else to control it save ourselves. Let me tell you something else. The more militant in the villages and in the West Bank will continue to fight you with force. Now more than before. When you tell us that you're here to stay, we believe you; therefore, we have to fight."

"You are right. I am here to stay. If you fight me, I'll have no choice but to fight back. Somehow I hope that on a personal level we can keep our friendship, for even though we are both extremists on two different ends, we also have much in common. But I'm not sure—if you were one of the leaders or involved in attacking us, I would have no choice."

"I also have no choice—you are one of their leaders," he said.

He's an interesting guy, Avi, and this is not the first time we have discussed such things. I've eaten in his and his father's house a few times.

110

The first time they invited me, I explained to them the laws of kosher food. Since then they offer me a drink and fruits or Israeli kosher cookies! He, of course, has been in our caravan. About a month ago, I was telling him about our plans to start an archaeological expedition in Shilo, and he says to me, "You want to see something?" Without waiting he jumps up, and I follow him into his car. He drives toward the end of his village and pulls over near a house. He knocks on the door, introduces me, and takes me to the backyard. There he shows me an ancient pillar the owner of the house had taken from the area of Shilo. "You see, before you are going to dig, we have done so." I recognized the pillar as belonging to one of the ancient Byzantine buildings that are located on Shilo's grounds. I asked him where it was from. "It's from Silon (the Arab name for Shilo), and it belongs to an old Arab mosque that was there."

"Ahmad," I said, "look carefully at the pillar and now you come with me." In his car we drove to the remnants of the Byzantine building in Shilo, and I showed him three or four more pillars lying on the ground. "Ahmad," I said, "sorry to disappoint you. The pillar is ancient but not Arabic. It's Byzantine." "No, Era, this building was an Arabic mosque, hundreds or maybe a thousand years ago," he maintained.

Well, you see, Avi, I learned a bit about archaeology. First, during my year as director of the "Field School" in Ofra, and a lot more since coming to Shilo, where we live history and archaeology. The Danish dug here in the 1920s, and their report states clearly that the building is Byzantine.

You remember the story of the beginning of Shilo? Menachem Begin had promised that when elected he would put up the village of Shilo, the first capital of Israel, and we must redevelop it. It was also one of his big arguments with Jimmy Carter, who didn't want Shilo being resettled. Mr. Begin told him that there are five Shilos in the U.S. and you, Mr. Carter, wouldn't dream of not allowing a Jew to live in one of them. Even more so in the original Shilo—not to allow a Jew to live there? Well, they came to an agreement that there would be an army base established in Shilo, and then we could live here dressed as soldiers!

Menachem Begin had to look for another "cover." It came in the form of an archaeological expedition in Shilo, led by Dr. Ze'ev Yevin, the assistant director of the Ministry of Education, Department of Archaeology, and one of Israel's foremost archaeologists. It was during these meetings with Dr. Yevin that I began to learn a bit about archaeology, and we found a way to develop the site.

So when I answered Ahmad, I knew something about the subject. "Ahmad," I said, "you have a mosque in your village. Where is the gumcha?" Gumcha is the niche found in every mosque and facing Mecca as our Ark faces Jerusalem. "Where does it face? North, south, east or west?" He thought for a moment, and answered, "South. That is the way to Mecca."

"Right," I answered. "Now tell me where is the gumcha facing in this building?" Ahmad looked and looked and could not find out where it was facing. I waited a few moments, and when he didn't respond, I said, "You can look as long as you want. You won't find one. That is proof positive that this was never a mosque. It is an ancient Byzantine building. I'll tell you more, Ahmad. I have a feeling that the family who took the pillar knew for sure that it wasn't from a mosque. Rather, he thought that it was an ancient building of ours. Like the farming your people do on the Tel although there is a British law, a Jordanian law, an international law, and an Israeli law against it. The reason for your farming? To erase all memory of our past here. While farming, you destroy the terraces that my great-grandfathers of 150 generations ago built here. That's what your neighbor tried to do also, but it won't help, Ahmad. History is history. We have been here for so many thousands of years, and let me tell you. We will continue to be here."

Getting back to the present, Avi, who knows? Maybe my talk with Ahmad will have a small positive effect, and he'll convince some of the militants to stop their attacks.

Now I'm taking Orit's advice. I'm finishing this letter here. Take care, my dear friend. I miss you mucho. Take your congregation, and bring them over here. We need you and you need us. What can I tell you? Living here is a fantastic experience and feeling. Walking the streets of our forefathers and rebuilding them. What an honor has fallen into my hands.

Come on Aliyah soon; beat the Mashiach [Messiah] rush.

Era

February 1979
Shilo

Dear Avi,

Well, it's been some three weeks since I wrote you. With us things are okay. We are having a ball, building and living in Shilo. Like usual and like yourself I'm working crazy hours from 5:30 in the morning until twelve or one every night. At least once a week I have guard duty. On top of that, recently we've been spending once or twice a week "fence rolling," which I wrote about in one of my letters.

But, my friend, I'm in a dilemma. There are voices calling for preventative action against the Arab village that continues to harass and hit us. There have been members of Shilo who have participated in such actions recently. It's the only thing that helps, but it hurts that we have to act this way.

Last week we had another real scare. A number of the kids are bused to Ofra every day for school. We only have a first grade here, and the older kids have to travel. There are two roads to Ofra from Shilo, a shorter and a longer. The shorter winds up one of the most magnificent mountain roads in the country. On one side are high rocks, on the other a deep gorge. A slight mistake and it's all over for you. By the way, the mountain road is directly through Maccabee country. It's exquisite. Please God, when you're here, I'll take you for a ride on it. Often the school bus is driven by Shevach or myself. Last Thursday Shevach drove the nine schoolchildren and was returning home.

I'm in the office and I hear him over the CB/Motorola, "Help, I'm being attacked by a mob of kids." Then there was quiet. After a few moments, I hear once again, "Help, I'm . . ." and then the words were broken by poor transmission. "Shevach," I say into the Motorola, "what is happening. Where are you?" Finally, he answers, "I'm near Mazraat and being stoned." I grabbed my Uzi and yell to the secretary to send help. I would have been a winner in the Indianapolis 500 at the speed I was going. Some of the potholes that I hit were so deep that I don't know how the car remained in one piece.

The turnoff to the back road to Ofra via Mazraat is some seven to eight kilometers (five miles) from Shilo—half the way on a dirt road. I'm not sure how, but I made it in less than four minutes, turned on the Mazraat road, and took off. As I rounded a ninety-degree bend, I saw in front of me two unreal sights. Two hundred feet ahead of me was Shevach's school van stopped one foot from the chasm. Boulders had been rolled from the cliff to prevent him from continuing. Boulders had been rolled down in back of the van, so it couldn't go forward or back. When Shevach got out of the van, they started to stone him.

I slammed on the brakes, jumped out of my car, grabbed the Uzi, and started running toward Shevach. Suddenly I was bombarded by some fifty "schoolchildren" approximately twelve to seventeen, standing on the cliff above me. Shevach was crouching behind the school bus for protection. Behind me was an abyss two hundred feet straight down, and on top of me were rocks. Suddenly I understood that if I didn't do something, I would be dead. I crouched down and yelled with all the force I have in my voice, "Ruch min hon" (get out of here). The response was perfect. I was bombarded again. I yelled out once again, "If you don't stop I'll fire." And as I was yelling, two rocks hit me, and I was knocked over.

As I regained my feet, I heard Shevach yelling, "Shoot! They're going to kill us." Another stone hit me. I pointed the Uzi straight up into the air. "They're kids," I said to myself. I fired a few shots, and the sounds reverberated all over the canyon. Suddenly the rocks stopped coming. I threw Shevach my Uzi, pulled out my pistol, and began climbing the cliff. Three of the teens saw me climbing and threw rocks. Shevach fired into the air and they scattered.

When I reached the top of the cliff, there were about ten teens one hundred feet in front of me. The rest had scattered. They turned around and ran. I ran after them as I holstered my pistol. I knew I couldn't catch them, but I had to give it the old college try. Also, I wanted to get closer so I could identify them if needed.

Shevach and I split up trying to head them off. I got a good look at four of them before they found refuge in the houses of the village.

We returned to our vehicles and surveyed the damage. After pushing the boulders off the road, we radioed Shilo that we were both okay. Then we decided to drive through the village to see if we could identify any of our assailants. Near the local market, I pulled over to talk with some of the notables. First, Avi, I've got to explain what kind of place Mazraat is. Physically, it is a beautiful place, one of the highest villages in the country. The village is separated into two parts—the older and the newer. The older part of the village is built just like the traditional Arab village. The mosque is on the high spot, and all the houses are clustered around it. During the Jordanian occupation, they were not allowed to expand. However, since we have returned, the situation is quite different: the village has rapidly grown, and they have built some beautiful mansions. A certain percentage of the residents live here part time and part time in the States and they are quite well off.

The local marketplace we stopped at is in the older part of the village, which is also closer to the cliff from where we were stoned. We asked the elders if they had seen some schoolchildren running in this direction, and, of course, we received the expected no. I then told them what had happened and strongly advised them that if they wanted quiet in their village, they had better control their kids. If need be, we can respond very strongly. As we continued our drive through the village and as we turned a corner, I saw a teenager run into one of the houses. He was wearing a red sweater and looked to me just like one of the attackers. Before the van even came to a standstill, I was out the door and running after him. I ran into the yard and watched him dart into a door. We knocked, and after a few minutes it was opened by a middle-aged man. The teenager was sitting on the couch.

The father, who obviously knew what had happened, spoke up. "Please don't do anything to him. He's just a child. The others forced him to do it."

"Forced him to do it!" Shevach responded. "He was standing in front of the group and was among the leaders; I'm going to call the police immediately and let them take him to the jail. Era, you stay here. I'll go call the police."

"No, no, wait a moment," said the father. "Not the police. They'll lock him up and beat him up. Maybe I can pay for the damage, and you'll let him go."

Suddenly I had a good idea. "Shu es mak?" I asked, pointing at the teenager. "What is your name?" "Yosaif," he answered. "Yosaif, if you don't want to go to jail, give me the names of ten others who helped you. I won't give the names to the police, but, if in the future anyone from this village attacks another Jewish vehicle all of your names will be given in." The kid thought for a few moments and hesitated. "Look," I said; "just one half an hour ago, I was almost killed by your rocks. I'm not exactly in the mood to play games, and in a few moments even if you give me the names, I'll call the police. Make your decision."

The boy spoke to his father and then said, "I'll give you some names." Shevach asked for a piece of paper, and then Yosaif rattled off some eight names and their fathers' names.

We drove back through the village, toward my car, slowly looking for other kids. The village had suddenly become empty. Upon arriving at my car, we started to clean the boulders and rocks off the rest of the road. I turned to Shevach and said, "They are really in a jihad against us. The information we have from 'our guys' in the military command that the NGC is paying money to attack us is obviously true. Something has to be done to stop Shaka, Chalaf, and the rest. Damn it, what do we do?"

"Talking about what do we do," Shevach interrupted, "what do we do with the list of names, and do we even report this attack?" I didn't know how to answer. We both knew nothing would be done with the names. The kids were too "young." The other problem was that in publicizing the attack, people would be afraid to come and live in the area. Already, the leftist press was using stoning reports as a way of discouraging settlement. And for Israel to hold onto the area, we needed to have Jewish houses and communities fill up the empty hills.

I suggested we give the list to the police and hold onto a copy. And keep the attack to ourselves.

"I've got a feeling, Era, that soon we are going to have to take some action by ourselves," Shevach said. "I don't like the thought of it, but after today . . . what a feeling! I began to understand the meaning of the Biblical command of skilah—stoning. It was unreal, Era.

"Thank God, the school kids weren't with me. Could you imagine if they were? You saw the situation when you arrived. Now you're telling me that we shouldn't do anything? What do you want to do? Wait for somebody to get killed, or even then you wouldn't do anything about it? I don't understand you, Era. We are the leaders of Shilo. Leaders of many thousands of Jews living in the area. A lot of what we do sets the tone. If we don't react to such an action, do you know what's going to be in the area? The PLO will feel braver. They will try even more severe actions than they have till now.

"Plus, Jews in the area will see that we don't react. They'll be afraid to protect themselves or even to travel around. They won't recommend anyone else to come here. By not reacting, Era, we are taking quite a responsibility on our shoulders. We can't just stand by."

What can I tell you, Avi? There was really nothing I could say to Shevach. I basically agreed with everything he said.

I feel a tremendous need to seek out advice. There are many times that I miss you. Sometimes it is an emotional need to share feelings with you. Sometimes, like now, it's a need to share and seek your advice.

When I came to study in Israel right after YU, I didn't know where I was heading. At the end of my year in Mercaz, I had fallen in love with my country and it was obvious to me that I was going to live here. I also realized that just living here wasn't sufficient; I would also have to give to my country. Therefore, I returned to the States to study social work. It was and still is a field needed in Aretz. So when I finally came on Aliyah I started working with youth. I was doing important work and had much gratification. To an extent, I felt that I was "paying my dues," so to speak, to Israel, for giving me so much. Along came Orit and the settlement movement, and I realized that what I was doing wasn't sufficient. That I had to give more to Aretz. So we came to Ofra, then Safed, and now Shilo.

I never would have imagined or believed, when we sat in class together during our YU days, that I would have to force my government's hand into developing YOSH, to stealthily put up villages at night, so we can strengthen my government hand against your American government's misguided pressure. It has taken me time to realize that giving of yourself to one's country is more difficult and involved than you can imagine. On an objective level we have gone through one heck of a time—at least physically so—living under very difficult conditions—you know, you were here. I don't know how many people would willingly give up all the pleasures of home and live out in the sticks with no electricity, sewage, running water, roads, and the rest for the sake of putting up villages in contested land. Well, Avi, that, it seems, is also part of Ahavat [love of] Eretz Yisrael; you feel it more and appreciate it more. Now, I don't know, do we also take the security situation into our hands? Is that "written in the books" also? Or do we "turn our cheeks" and say that the geula—redemption—and the development of the land comes in stages, and right now we have to retreat?" Retreating in this case, Avi, can mean life or death.

I feel that with a few planned actions against centers of disturbances, we can bring quiet and save Jewish lives. Do we have a right to sit back and not do anything?

I could really use you around right now, but the good Lord has put us in two different places, six thousand miles apart. Write me soon, if you can. I'll try to write you soon.

Era

February 1980
Shilo

Reserve Duty Diary

As I sit here by the light of our portable generator, and by the campfire, I'm surprised at myself that I'm writing. For some strange reason I feel the necessity to put my feelings on paper. Maybe in order to express my anger and maybe to solace myself a bit.

Beside the pain of the moment there is the frustration. This is my second week of a three-and-a-half-week army reserve stint in Judea and Samaria.

A yeshiva student named Yehoshua Soloma has just been murdered in Hevron.

I *am* frustrated. For the last few months we have been warning the government officials over and over and over that they have to put an end to the PLO activities in our area. We gave them names of PLO mayors who are involved in terrorist actions, either by enlisting the terrorists or by paying for their actions. I met with the Minister of Police, Dr. Yosef Burg, and the Minister of Defense, Ezer Weizman. Burg was at least apologetic (not that it excuses him), and Ezer was adamant. Burg says there are political pressures from above. Weizman, with his nose and head sticking up in the air, says to us, "You're not going to tell me how to run security and where to put villages. I'm the expert. Nobody told you to go settle where you are, and I'll appoint who I want to be heads of Arab villages." Just two weeks ago we warned him that we had information about an impending attack. He didn't do anything. It is amazing how political office can blind you.

I spoke also to the Minister of Education, Zevulun Hammer, and he told me, "There are political pressures from the U.S. and we can't do anything about it. They don't want us to put our foot down in the area. When you went to live there, you knew there were risks involved." When he told me that, I responded, "Zevulun, risks we agree to, but you have to do your job also because lives are involved."

This has been my most difficult time at a roadblock. I've been at a few in the past. It is not a pleasant experience, stopping cars, almost all of them Arabs, and checking the contents. Yet this time I want to catch Yehoshua's murderers. It's hard for me to be pleasant at the checks. The murder of Yehoshua hurts more than a soldier killed in war. Or maybe it hurts differently. War is war, and we do our utmost to win, and in a war people get killed. In this situation the opposite is true. Our government has done very little to stop them. To an extent it has strengthened and given the terrorists the go-ahead to act. That's what gets me so mad.

I took a break from writing to relieve one of my co-soldiers. Amram feels just like me. Actually, almost all of us feel the same. If our government would throw out about thirty of the PLO leaders here, the situation would be totally different. Eli said that if the government doesn't do something to stop the PLO from attacking us, we'll have to do something ourselves, and we all agreed to to it. Now that I'm by myself and thinking for a few moments, it seems absurd that we would even bring up such a possibility. Anyhow, it's more of a reaction of anger than anything else.

The thought keeps on repeating itself—it could have been me, just as it was Yehoshua, and it could be my wife or kids. I just heard on the radio our Minister of "Defense" talking about the situation. He says we can't lose control of ourselves because of what happened, and the only way to peace is by having the PLO mayors and the NGC continue in their jobs, and he will not give into the settlers' pressure! How many times do we have to be knifed and shot at until he and others will realize that what the PLO wants is to march us into the sea? As I look out at the stars over our Holy City of Hevron right now, I'm reminded of the massacre of 1929.

Well, I took another break and it's now daybreak. The curfew will continue today, in the hope that maybe, somehow, we can find his murderers. And if we do? At the very worst, they'll get a life sentence. They should be executed. But not here. We are too "progressive" a country! One of the Arabs whose car we checked just a while ago, a taxi driver, asked me, "Why do you keep on bothering us with roadblocks? It makes life so difficult for us. Throw out the instigators, and it will be better for all of us." Oh, how I wished I'd had a tape recorder to record his words and send them to our ministers. If they won't listen to us, maybe they'll listen to this Arab taxi driver.

Yehoshua will be buried today or tomorrow. His short life tells our story. . . .

I just came back from a patrol through Hevron and its environs. We were a group of ten. We got into a heated discussion of what has to be done. Everybody was of the opinion that if we are quiet and do not respond to what happened this time, it will continue. The guys are top-notch fellows; one of them, a professor at the university, said that he was very surprised by his own response. I told him that if you don't live here and go through the experience that we are going through, you wouldn't understand what brings us to the anger we're feeling and to the kind of discussions we are having. In a way what's happening is ridiculous. To an extent we are more upset at our government for its inaction. The actions of the terrorists are to be expected, while our government's action is totally the

Era Rapaport (front, left) with his older brothers and parents.

Era Rapaport and his brother in Prospect Park, Brooklyn.

Era and Orit Rapaport at their wedding.

Era and Orit Rapaport honeymooning at Niagara Falls.

Orit Rapaport holding daughter Moriyah as their trailer home is lowered into place in Shilo.

Era Rapaport's parents and uncle near the Cave of Kings in Jerusalem.

Era and Orit Rapaport with son Yisrael near ancient spring of Shilo. An Arab woman appears in the background on a donkey.

Yetta Rapaport (Era's mother) planting a tree near Shilo Forests.

On left, ancient remains of building at the entrance to the old city of Shilo. On right, trailers in fourth year of the new town of Shilo.

Broken gravestones on the Mount of Olives.

From left to right: David, Orit, Yitzhak, Atarah, and Moriyah Rapaport during a camping trip across the United States.

Moriyah, Atarah, and David Rapaport at miniature golf course near Newburgh, New York.

Era Rapaport with his brother-in-law Yehuda Etzion inside Tel Mond prison cell.

ehuda Etzion in prison courtyard with banner:
*or the sake of Zion I will not be silent
nd for the sake of Jerusalem I will not be
    quiet
ntil its righteousness goes forth like
    splendor*

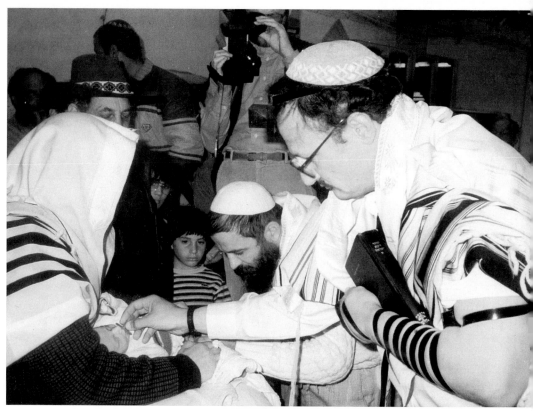

Era Rapaport on leave from Tel Mond Prison, accompanied by six guards, to attend son Dvir's circumcision..

View of Shilo with the Arab towns of Turmos Aya and Singel in the background. In the center of Shilo is the synagogue, built to resemble the tabernacle built in ancient Shilo.

Era, Orit, and Yisrael Rapaport outside their home in Shilo.

Era Rapaport with an M-16 rifle visiting the graves of his parents in Jerusalem.

Orit Rapaport with her children and an Arab neighbor in front of his home.

From left to right: Tsofiyah, Yitzhak, Atarah, David, and Moriyah Rapaport in front of the ancient valley of Shilo.

Era Rapaport with his daughter Moriyah during her Bat Mitzvah at Tel Shilo.

Bat Mitzvah celebration at Rapaport home.

Above, Era Rapaport with his son David during his Bar Mitzvah, the first Jewish ceremony to be held in Mitzpeh in 3,000 years. *Left,* Era and Yisrael Rapaport watching the Bar Mitzvah festivities.

East Flatbush, Brooklyn, apartment house where Rapaport grew up.

ormerly the First Zionist ynagogue, which Era apaport attended as a boy. ow the Church of God of ast Flatbush.

Star of David and inscription honoring the synagogue's earliest members, including Era Rapaport's grandmother, which are now covered by a sign at the Church of God of East Flatbush.

Era Rapaport with the Lubavitcher Rebbe pointing out the Shilo settlement on a map of Israel.

Above, Orit Rapaport addressing a crowd one year after Rachela Druk was shot by a PLO terrorist, at the site of the murder. *Below,* Era Rapaport dancing at a wedding ceremony with a man who has immigrated to Israel from Peru.

Era Rapaport hosting two Russian emigrants at Purim meal.

Era Rapaport filling the water tank of Shilo's tractor-pulled fire truck.

opposite of what it should be. What is for sure—this is a trying moment for us.

Three hours later. We've made two more patrols into Kiryat Arba. The people there are very tense. It seems there were discussions last night whether to react with force or what. Even some of the rabbis were for reacting with force, because it's obvious the government is doing nothing, and it is not going to. On the other hand, other rabbis say we have to wait and pressure the government. I have mixed feelings. Maybe what happened to Yehoshua will wake up the government to action.

We were told the particulars of Yehoshua Solomon's murder. He was on his way to buy fruits for Tu B'Shvat [Arbor Day] in the Hevron marketplace. Eighteen years old. A new immigrant from Denmark.

It's been three days since the murder, and we are still checking cars and doing patrols. Sometimes, during our patrols, the importance of our mission here comes flying through my mind like the shooting stars in the skies above Hevron. I think of my family without me. I ask myself whether a piece of land is worth my leaving them. A simple flat yes would be lying to myself. I love my family, wife and kids, too much to think that either they or I could be killed for this land. Nachon, yes, I love the land very much, but vis-à-vis my family? So as I drive on my patrol I think a lot. On today's patrol we shared thoughts together. Their thoughts are much like mine. Here we are, ten fathers, forced by our neighboring countries into being soldiers on reserve duty and into jobs which none of us want. Almost all of the group are married with kids. The murder of Yehoshua most assuredly has a negative effect on some of the guys. Maybe some of them will question the worthiness of being here in Hevron.

Sometimes I'd like to consider taking the "easy" way out. Simply leaving. Yet I know that I can't. This country is like quicksand. You put one foot in and you sink—you can't get out, you don't want to get out. This place fills me up. On the patrol I looked up at our sky and heard the words of the Torah: "The eyes of the Lord your God are on it from the beginning of the year till the end of the year."

As I was thinking, David spoke up. David is an interesting fellow. A bit older than me, about thirty-seven years old, born in Haifa. An engineer.

"Era, are we always going to have to fight? I remember when I was a kid, I overheard my parents talking. Their most fervent wish was that when their son got older there would be peace and no need for an army. Here I am having the same wish. When will it end? Can't we be somewhat normal? Be home twelve months a year and not ten and a half, and not have to be on guard duty two hours twice a week?

"Just a few weeks ago, before reserve duty, we took the family and went camping, something which we haven't done in such a long time. What a fabulous time. We rented a tent and just spent the time together enjoying ourselves and our country. What a gorgeous country we have. Now, here I am patrolling against PLO terrorists."

I thought for a few moments and then asked him, "Would you ever consider leaving YOSH or the country for that normalcy you're talking about?" He almost screamed at me, "Are you out of your mind? Don't misunderstand. Just because I'm wishing or complaining, that doesn't mean that I don't want to be here. I love this country and our people. It's an honor, a very special and unique honor, to be here. Are you suggesting that because it's hard I check out on my country? Let me explain you something. . . ." "Wait," I interrupted. "I didn't mean . . ."

"No, you wait. I am an engineer and I have been offered many positions in the U.S. I respond nicely to them that I am not interested at all in anything outside of Israel. Listen, Era, 2,000 years we are in galut; now that we have our own country, are you suggesting that I act as if nothing has changed. How many times have you been to Jerusalem? Don't you feel special when you are there? Doesn't a shiver run through you? Just because we Israelis don't show emotion so quickly, don't think that we aren't feeling or don't have feelings. New immigrants do not have a monopoly on feelings for Israel."

Boy, was I taken aback. I didn't mean to hurt him, but it seems I did. On the other hand, it was one of those few times that I heard Israelis talking about their feelings toward Israel.

Another eight hours went by, and I was on patrol again. A group of some ten college-age Arabs came over to talk to us. During the conversation, one of them said, "You know that your traveling around with armaments as a conquering people doesn't help the situation at all." I think it was Chaim who responded: "What do you expect us to do when you brutally murder one of us? Pick up and leave? No way!"

"I didn't say that, and I'm not suggesting it, but why punish us all?" the Arab said. "Do you think that I will be closer to you or understand you better, or live with you better, when you ride my streets with those army patrol trucks?" "I don't enjoy patrolling any more than you don't like being patrolled," I answered. "You guys generally know who is at fault. Stop them, don't help them, don't let them hide out, and the situation will improve. Your actions are not going to make us leave. This is our home and the only place we have to be." The Arab quickly interceded: "That is the same with me."

Chaim said, "Even if I agree with you, that it is the only place that you have, and I don't agree, then fine, live and let live. As I said, control your terrorists."

"Let us say that I wanted to stop them," the Arab replied. "Do you think I could? If I were to even hint in the smallest way that I was helping you, I would be murdered. It's you that has to be strong and throw them out. See, the majority of us want quiet here. When you are weak, what do you expect their response to be? A couple of years ago you used to throw out anybody who was caught. Down the block from me lived a terrorist who was caught after he planted a mine. His entire family was marched across the border and his house was destroyed. Of course, we hated it, but the elders of the area got together and warned everybody not to be involved in activities against you. The parents were afraid so they made sure the children didn't get involved. If you really want it, put your foot down and throw out their leaders. You'll see the difference immediately."

As we traveled on, I said to Chaim, "Sometimes they seem to be as sick of the situation as we are."

In another two hours, I'll be handing in my army uniform and equipment and returning to be a regular citizen. Actually, I don't know if I can return to be a regular citizen. I have "changed" since Yehoshua's murder and my stint here. I am feeling that if my government doesn't do something to curb the PLO actions, then we'll have to do so ourselves. The feeling scares me—it's probably because of the situation I'm in. I'll think differently when I'm back home.

March 1980
Shilo

Dear Avi,

I have not been fair to you, that I agree. I should have written you one or two days after the attack on Yehoshua Solomon. However, there have been objective and subjective reasons for my not having done so. Objectively, for I have been on reserve duty, and it's not really the best time to write. Subjectively, for I have not been in much of a mood for writing to anybody since the attack. I did, however, write myself a letter—kind of an expression of feelings during my reserve duty. I have debated whether to send you this or not, and I decided yesterday to do so.

The feelings are self-explanatory. In rereading them before sending them off to you, I felt myself going through different stages during the days immediately after Yehoshua's murder. The feelings are mixed: anger and frustration, depression, determination, and acceptance. I didn't hide anything from myself, and so in sending the letter to you, I'm hiding nothing from you.

It's been close to a month since his murder. The army, as to be expected, came down hard for a few days, then relaxed a bit, and since then has been relaxing steadily. I really shouldn't state army, for they do what the politicians tell them to do. Real change is not about to happen. It's hard for me to write that, but I feel it. One would imagine that the government would change directions after such an attack. Nothing. No real change. At the very minimum we expected a crackdown on the major PLO leaders in the area. Maybe throwing out the NGC heads. Such small actions would change the situation in the area quite drastically.

I'll admit, Avi, I am past the feeling of frustration. I'm at the point which says we must do something ourselves. It's as I wrote you—a situation of no choice. I am not going to run away from here, that's a given. Second, I have no intention of being the next sacrificial lamb of the PLO. I have to protect myself. There is serious talk among some of the guys in the area to retaliate. Call it a retaliation or self-defense or a preventative attack.

Do I sound like a different or new Era, Avi? I'm not sure. Maybe to an extent I am. Did you ever imagine yourself being arrested by the New York City Police for demonstrating for the freedom of our brothers and sisters in the Soviet Union? And you stretched it even further than that, chaining yourself to the Soviet consulate! That's not the peace-loving Avi I knew in YU. Obviously, I'm joking, Avi, but you get the idea. Situations change a person or bring out different strengths in him. Sometimes to be a lover of peace you must fight. In your case, the preacher of "love thy neighbor" had to take different steps—you had to demonstrate in the street.

To some extent, on a different level, I am changing also, my dear friend. I'm coming, or maybe I've already come, to the conclusion that our inaction cannot continue if we want to protect ourselves. If my government doesn't do something drastic soon, we shall take some action ourselves. I would really dislike seeing that or being part of it. But maybe it's a necessity and has to be done. "In the place where there are no men, try to be a man," says the proverb. In this case, if nobody is willing to act, then maybe I have to.

Era

May 1979
Shilo

Sisterhood Congregation Beth Shalom, Cedarhurst, New York:
To the members of the Sisterhood, Shalom,

Just yesterday I received a letter from my parents which contained a check for $407.00 as a gift from the sisterhood to the settlement of Shilo. As a friend of mine is leaving for the States tomorrow morning, I decided to immediately write you a thank-you note.

Distances divide and separate—generally. Therefore many of you have contributed to a settlement which you have never seen, and this makes your contribution even more meaningful. As you must know Shilo was the most important city before Jerusalem, in Biblical times. Here rested the Tabernacle for 369 years. Here Joshua separated the Jewish people into the portions of land promised to each tribe. Here, the great Samuel prophesied. Here, Eli the High Priest fell dead upon hearing of the defeat of the Jewish people by the Philistines. One mile from here, Judah the Maccabee defeated the Greeks in his first major battle on his way to reclaiming the Temple in Jerusalem.

Here young, vibrant, and dedicated Jews have begun to reclaim the land that Judah and Joshua reclaimed in their times. Thirteen families who have lived one year and six months under very difficult conditions. Thirteen families who demanded and finally brought their government to officially recognize Shilo as a settlement in Israel. Your contribution strengthens us in many ways. Maybe the most important one is your spiritual help. Your contribution makes you, in our eyes, close to us. It strengthens our feelings that Jews all over the world back our determination to rebuild Shilo, and Judea and Samaria.

Our needs are so great it is difficult for us to decide what to do first. However, our children are most important to us. Therefore, we shall use the donation to purchase playground equipment for them. When we receive the equipment, we shall photograph them and send you a picture.

The children of Shilo, twenty-eight in number, would like to thank you themselves. However, they still do not know how to write, and therefore I am their messenger. I can just tell you that every piece of playground equipment makes our children extremely happy. To us, as parents, that is the most gratifying thing to see.

Your contribution helps tell the world that Shilo is ours—forever. It helps build us into a stronger settlement and I am not exaggerating.

We, the people of Shilo, invite you all to come and visit us on your very next visit to Israel. We also invite you to come and be one of the members of Shilo by living here. That would be your greatest contribution to yourselves and to us and to the people of Israel.

We wish you a very happy Shavuot [holiday]. Once again, in the name of the people and especially the children of Shilo, I thank you deeply and sincerely.

Era Rapaport
Mayor

May 1979
Shilo

Dear Yosef and Baruch,

During the past few weeks, it has become obvious to me that no real steps are being taken by our government against the ever increasing attacks against us in Judea and Shomron. I feel that not only during my trips to Jerusalem when my car is stoned, but I feel it is also from the non-results of meetings with army and government officials, where the name of the game is all talk, no do.

We told the Defense Minister that the roads were becoming dangerous to travel on. Every day there are stonings. Isn't it sufficient that one Jew was murdered? Why do we have to wait for more? If he doesn't do something drastic, the Arabs will escalate their actions.

When we spoke to the army commander of the area and told him of the escalating instances of rock throwing against cars by Arab teenagers, paid by the PLO, he said, "I can't do anything against kids who throw rocks through car windows, for, generally speaking, they can't be brought to court due to their age." I couldn't believe my ears.

One week after talking with the commander another serious instance happened. Ilan Tor, age thirty, was traveling home from Jerusalem to Kiryat Arba when his car was trapped in a demonstration of hundreds of Arabs in the village of Chalchul. He pulled his car over some one hundred feet before the mob. Suddenly he was bombarded by stones from all over. An army command car also in the area was similarly bombarded. Hundreds of stones—large ones—were thrown at the two cars. What did our soldiers do? They were afraid to react because new orders had been handed down by Ezer Weizman. Soldiers who fired were going to be court-martialed, and so they were afraid.

As I think about the instance, just imagining our soldiers being stoned and afraid to react . . . Finally, Ilan saw that there was no choice, and he fired three warning shots into the air. It didn't even faze the PLO students, and they continued to throw and get closer. Tor then started to back up to save his life. The terrorists-students suddenly began to run after him, throwing rocks. With his life in imminent danger and the soldiers not lifting a hand but rather hiding behind the command car, Ilan turned once again and fired just above the heads of the terrorists, who this time slowed down a bit. He then yelled to the soldiers that if they didn't do something, he would, at which point they finally fired warning shots into the air. Their lives and Ilan's had barely been saved.

If I was in Ilan's situation, there is no doubt in my mind that I would have acted as he did. His life was in danger. That evening we requested a meeting, once again, with those in charge of security in the area, and once again we left frustrated. Another Jew had almost been stoned to death, and nothing had been done or would be done. This time as we left the meeting, some of us turned to each other. "What do we do? Ezer doesn't appear ready to act. Neither do the police and the other members of the government who say that their hands are tied."

It's getting to the point where our lives are in danger. Either we leave the area or do something is the feeling.

A few hours after the riot, an Arab girl, who had participated in the riots, was found dead. Ilan Tor was arrested and "treated" by our police to some of the worst treatment they could dish out. He was put into solitary confinement, moved from one jail to another so his family would not know where he was, and for a time he was denied reading material. To top it all off, the prosecution (i.e., the government) charged him with premeditated murder!!! When we heard these charges we were in total shock. After the shock came anger. Ilan was a perfect case of a defensive action. If he had not protected himself, he would have been killed. To charge him with premeditated murder!! The charge sheet stated that he planned to go to Chalchul in order to kill Arabs. Nothing could have been further from the truth, and the government knew it. It was an opportunity for the Ministry of Justice, whose leaders are leftists and fierce anti-YOSH, to try and get back at us and scare us.

The leftist press celebrated, and we boiled over—at both the incident itself and the official reaction. It was, to us, another sign of our being thrown to the dogs. After the Ilan Tor incident, even the more moderate among us became a bit more convinced that we were entering a situation of being on the verge of no choice.

I don't know if I'm getting my thoughts across. You get up in the morning, travel to Jerusalem, and your car gets stoned on the way. By a miracle you don't lose control of your car and "only" need some stitches on your hand. This happens almost every other day. Yet when we complain to our government, the response is, "It's a political situation!" This from the "right-wing" Likud. This, from many of the ministers and MKs who are close to our cause.

Ilan has been sitting in jail several months. His case has stretched on and on, purposely so by the prosecution who would do anything to attack our settling of Judea-Samaria. In their effort to do "justice," they got the court to have Ilan remanded to jail until the end of his trial, for he was a dangerous person!*

Who is the prosecution's star witness? Gubrion Shaavan from Chalchul, a student from the local school and . . . one of those who stoned our soldiers and Ilan! The prosecution gave him judicial protection, and he would not be charged for his part in the demonstration. What chutzpah. The attacker goes free, and the victim sits in jail. One needs superhuman patience these days.

Era

February 1980
Shilo

Dear Brothers, Shalom:

You see, you've got a famous brother. David Shipler writes about me in the *New York Times!* Actually, I've been sent copies of a couple of articles that have been written about the Brooklyn-born-and-bred social worker who leaves it all and goes to Israel, and on top of it, to a disputed area in the "West Bank."

---

* Editor's note: Tor's case was heard by a court of three judges. On Friday, February 1, 1980, the defense finished their arguments. The three judges cleared the accused of any crime. Tor had spent eight months in jail.

Be careful of what you read. Papers are rarely objective regarding what is going on. I don't think that the *Times* has ever been a backer of Israel, and that is an understatement. You would expect differently, with some of the top echelon being Jewish. Then again, to quote the Bible, "Your haters and destroyers will come from within you."

I read an article recently by Shipler in which he describes how badly the Palestinian Arabs are treated here. What's worse, he doesn't try at all to balance the article by reminding his readers that the Palestinians are headed by the PLO and that they are actively engaged in trying to destroy us. In other words, even if we are acting sometimes improperly, there is a background to it.

The *Times* writes that we persecute the Arabs here and steal their land for our villages. I wish you were here yourself, my brothers, to see the land that we are "stealing" from our "poor Arab refugee neighbors"! Just last week I guided a group of American rabbis around the Shomron. Barren mountain after barren mountain, Arab villages few and far apart, and Jewish villages fewer and farther apart. The question that they kept on repeating to me was, "Where is all the land that you have been taking from the Arabs? The *New York Times* reported it." I would laugh and answer, "You mean you still believe the *New York Times*? You won't see 'all' the land, 'cause no land has been taken from Arab villages for Jewish villages. You can see for yourself there is plenty of elbow room out here." I then decided to show them some of the houses of the poor Arab refugees. Baruch and Joseph, you should see some of these poor houses. Right next to us in the village of Turmos-Aya are mansions built by Arabs out of Petra stone—imported marble, most modernly furnished and more. Some the size of hotels.

On the tour there was a rabbi from Los Angeles. His reaction to these houses was that they could be put right into Millionaires' Row in Beverly Hills. During the Jordanian occupation of the area, the Arabs were not allowed to build in this manner. It's the persecuting Jews who have raised their standard of living. I asked Shipler at one of our meetings, "Why is it that suddenly Judea and Samaria are 'occupied by Israel'?" From 1948 to 1967, when the Jordanians occupied YOSH, no one used the term "occupied by Jordan" even though that is exactly what the situation was. I "reminded" him that in 1948, the Jordanians attacked, against UN requests and warnings, and captured YOSH. "Why," I asked Dave Shipler, "didn't the *New York Times* call the Jordanians occupiers? Yet we, who in a defensive war, in protecting ourselves in 1967, freed the area and resettled it—we suddenly became 'occupiers.' In the space of six days YOSH became occupied. Nineteen years of Jordanian occupation was kosher. Our returning to our land was no good. How is all this possible?" I asked. You know what he finally answered? He hemmed and hawed and said, "That's our attitude."

What garbage, my brothers! This is exactly what I told the rabbis on the trip. The rabbis were even more surprised when we traveled through Turmos-Aya to Shilo and I stopped at the local grocery to pick up a prepared order for our home. "But the *Times* reported that you have no relations with the Arab villages." "Those were Jews dressed as Arabs and it was all an act," I said to the rabbis. The *New York Times* should change their quote at the top of the front page from "All the news that's fit to print" to "All the news that fits, we print." Anyhow, this wasn't meant to be a tirade against the *New York Times,* just a warning to take whatever they say about YOSH with half a grain of salt. By the way, I once said to Shipler that until I lived in the area I really believed what the *Times* wrote. Now that I've seen how they distort the truth and deceive their readers, not only can I not believe their reports on and about Israel, but the same is true for every other part of the world.

I wrote you, I believe, about the National Guidance Committee. One of their chiefs is Bassam Shaka, a PLO terrorist, who is the Mayor of Shechem. This terrorist has organized and paid for the stoning and firebombing of many of our cars. We have presented Ezer Weizman with proof after proof of his actions, but Ezer has done absolutely nothing. Well, the past few weeks have seen an interesting turn of events. Listen to this. Bassam was summoned to the office of General Dani Mat (in charge of affairs in YOSH). During their discussion, terrorist Shaka said to General Mat that he is for active terrorist acts against Jews, for example, the murderous attack on the Egged bus near the Herzelia Country club in which some thirty-five Jews were viciously killed. "I am convinced that these actions give a chance for results," he said.

Dani Mat needed to respond somehow, However, he was afraid to let

Ezer Weizman know, for he was sure that Ezer would do nothing about it. So Dani Mat let the press know about the meeting and publicized it in the newspapers. Ezer blew his top and screamed at Dani Mat that "you are destroying my policy in the territories." He almost fired him. The press stopped Ezer from doing so.

A couple of days after the incident, the Minister's Committe for Security Matters decided unanimously to evict Shaka from the country. Thank God. However, they afforded him the opportunity of appealing their decision to a special army court. Even Ezer had to vote for the decision. You remember, brothers, that I wrote you how bad Shaka was. This is what our Prime Minister Menachem Begin said: "He initiated use of military methods to exacerbate his political fight. . . . His statements in support of terrorist activities are not by chance; rather they portray his ideas and his support of terrorist activities. . . . The Mayor of Shechem is the major organizer of the underground activities and his part in initiating the activities in Judea and Shomron is great."

Well, you would imagine that he would be evicted—right? Wrong! It was obvious to us that when he would be out of the country our area would calm down dramatically. We were sure, especially after his remarks were made public and after the reactions of Begin and the Minister's Committee, that he would indeed be evicted. I guess we were too naive. "Someone," who later became a member of Weizman's political party, found a way to leave him in Israel. Amazing, they even suggested that he apologize. You guessed it. Of course, he didn't. Our leaders are still very much galus Jews and haven't been able to shake off the attitude that we have to turn the other cheek again and again. I mean, brothers, this is our country. We are not second-class citizens to anyone, and we don't have to be afraid of what the goyim say and yet we act that way—its unreally frustrating.

Shaka, after the Minister's Committee decided on his eviction, was jailed, waiting for his appeal. There never was an appeal. According to reports, there were orders from "high up" for the army prosecutor not to present their file on Shaka to the special committee formed to hear Shaka's appeal. The case was simply dropped—although in my opinion the prosecution had enough evidence not only to evict him but to sentence him for many, many years behind bars.

Not only didn't that happen, but rather, Shaka spent thirty days behind bars, after which the Military Commander, Ben Eliezer, informed him that he was free to leave the prison. They allowed him to return to Shechem as mayor. I was watching his welcoming party, sponsored by the PLO, on TV, when he returned to the city. Thousands carried him on their shoulders, waving PLO flags, calling for the destruction of our State. I couldn't and can't believe my eyes and ears. Are we commiting suicide? And then Bassam started talking, and among his words were, "I'll continue to be a proud Palestinian sticking by the principles of the PLO." I knew, my brothers, that we are in for one hell of a terrorist time.

Excuse my frustration. It's just unbelievable to me that today, in the State of Israel, something like this can happen.

It's been four and a half weeks since I started writing this letter. Since then Bassam and other members of the PLO-NGC have instigated a variety of terrorist activities against us. Burning tires on the main road from Jerusalem to Beit Lechem. An orchard of trees uprooted in Gush Etzion. Just this morning two cars from Shilo were stoned. In one of them, a three-month-old baby was cut from the glass. A miracle he wasn't killed. A couple traveling in Aza were murdered. A hand grenade was thrown at the bus going to Ofra. No, my brothers, it's not the 1948 War of Independence, although it may sound that way. And just last week, an officer of the IDF [Israeli Defense Forces], who was traveling near Beit Lechem, had his car stoned. What did he do? Please don't publicize this—he left his car and ran away! The car was immediately burned. He told his superiors that he "preferred to run away rather than return fire and be court-martialed!!"

The PLO in the area has called for an all-out jihad on us. There is basically no choice any longer. We are going to have to react in self-defense against them. Our very lives are in danger. When I came on Aliyah, brothers, I expected to be drafted into the army here. I never expected or dreamed that I and my neighbors in the Jewish villages here would have to be the Army—Basically, to take the place of our Army, which certain politicians are preventing from acting.

I don't exactly know what will be done and I have to be careful of what I'm writing (which is why this letter will be hand-delivered to you). It's not a game here, like in East Flatbush; it's for keeps. The PLO's out to destroy us. We have no one to talk with. The authorities are not listening. What I can tell you is that I have made a personal decision. If there will be actions taken, I'll be involved. It is a mitzvah. The Torah tells us, "He who comes to kill you, arise to kill him first."

Love you,
Era

Well, here I am again. Each time I say to myself that I can't mail this letter due to some of the statements that I have written, so I keep on waiting to find someone who knows either one of you, so it can be delivered by hand. Since you told me this morning that your neighbor Eli is going to be here this week, I'm preparing a bunch of letters for him. Just to cue you in, we have had to partake in some small defensive actions in the area. The PLO's hired hands were throwing rocks all over the place and firebombs also. Since some of our actions, our immediate area has quieted down somewhat. About the actions, I'll tell you when we see each other, please God.

We have, once again, gained more information that the PLO and NGC are planning a major attack on us. We have passed on the information to Ezer Weizman, other ministers, and the military authorities. However, there is no doubt in our minds that they will do absolutely nothing. If I sound despairing of our government and its authorities, the answer is yes and no. Despairing of our government, not at all. In the specific instance of security in YOSH—yes. Not that they can't do anything about the situation—for sure our government can. Rather, as I wrote you a long time ago—there are those members of the government who don't want to, for their own political outlook; and there are those who are weak and are afraid of what the American government will say.

Because of the information that we have, we are on alert—all over YOSH. Please God, things will be okay.

Era

March 1980
Shilo

Shalom Avi,

There are times when I am really upset at myself for writing you so much about the security situation here. It's just that you are almost the only one in the States save for my brothers that I can be totally honest with. I know you understand the situation and can give some good advice. Well, I'd like to write you that things have gotten better security-wise, but that is not so. Things are continuing to worsen, and far graver is my government's lack of action. I've written you all about this, and I won't repeat it.

Avi, this has to be secret. Therefore, be careful with whom you share it. We have received information from some people close to the security forces that the PLO, through the NGC, is planning a major attack in the Hevron area. What is amazing about the information is that it has been passed on to the proper people in charge of security, and nothing has been done about it. That is frightening. We have considered publicizing the information, but there are problems doing so. One, it could very well compromise the identity of the people who gave us the information. More important than that, those in charge would deny everything and do nothing.

Through our own channels, we have checked the information, and it seems to be 100%. I hope and pray it's not true. We shall be on super-alert during the coming days.

How is your Beit Knesset [synagogue] progressing? You know that I have mixed feelings about your work. On one hand it is a big mitzvah. You are among the very few who can reach the far-out Jews of America, especially the youth. I know how hard you're working and what kind of job you are doing.

On the other hand, Avi, I also know what kind of work you could do here. The chances of reaching the faraway Jews are much greater here, for you don't have to deal with the intermarriage problem. There is so little of it here. I've always had mixed feelings. I know the move would be very hard for you, leaving the position you have and the success you've had. More so, starting all over again here would be difficult. Yet, Avi, that has been our way through history—moving from one place to another, starting

135

and restarting. Now that we finally have the opportunity to come home, the majority of us are not doing so.

Yes, to start again would not be easy for you. However, once you got over the first hurdles, what an important job you could do here. Well, enough of my Zionism right now.

Please keep the first part of this letter between us.

Best Blessings,
Era

April 1980
Shilo

Dear Brother,

In your letter, you asked why our government doesn't act to stop the terrorism directed against us in Judea and Shomron. Right you are that in America or Russia, or any other self-respecting place, if a minority rose up against the citizens of the state, the violence would be crushed in a day. I remember what they did to the Black Panthers in America. We should learn from the Arabs themselves. God knows how many hundreds of thousands Syria has killed of its own people, and Jordan, the "champion" of Palestinian rights, murdered ninety thousand Palestinians during the infamous Black September.

But Israel is different. More moral. The old double standard. We bend over backwards to be fair to our killers. I'll try to explain why.

First, there is great pressure from America. They know we are very capable of destroying the Arabs, and they are afraid that we will. At the Suez Canal, and in '67, and again in Beirut, they forced us to stop. And the reason is simple: American interest. Primarily oil. America is our friend, yes, but what would happen if an oil stoppage shut down winter boilers in New York? How long would their love for us last before the Christians came after the Jews? The rednecks down South are waiting for the chance. And the liberal intellectuals wouldn't be far behind. Plus, America has vast financial, economic, and military ties to the Arabs. So, always, when we start hitting back at the Arabs, the pressure from Washington starts.

And, realistically, we have to listen. It is true we benefit greatly from American aid. Also psychologically, it is nice to think you have a friend. Israel, let's face it, is all alone in the world. God will stand by us for sure, but not everyone has that kind of faith. So when Washington barks, our leaders fall down.

Second, and deeper than this external pressure from abroad, is an inner malaise. The Jews gave justice and humanitarianism to the world. Before Sinai and Torah, the planet was a jungle of despots who worshipped rivers and stones and made gods of themselves. Our people still have that great humanism today and want to be fair to the Arabs. But they have separated this humanism from deeper Jewish sources, Divine sources, which point to a different way. Abraham was all kindness; but he was incomplete until Yitzhak and Yaacov added the traits of valor and truth. Those kind to the cruel will end being cruel to the kind. We bend over to be super-fair to the Arabs, and they respond by killing.

Our leaders want to be just like the goyim. They want to be better than the goyim. It stems from a noble dream, but the destiny of our nation demands something else. Our strength and uniqueness will truly come when we are most truly ourselves.

Judea and Samaria is the perfect example. There are Jews who say we should give it up. To them it's just a piece of land like any other. But deeper than that, it's Jewish land, the heartland of the Bible, our connection to Torah and God. Very few religious Jews would think of giving it away. It's forbidden by Torah law. Just as the body can't survive without a heart, the Jewish nation can't survive without Jerusalem, Shechem, and Hevron. But those of us who want to be like the gentiles, without our unique Jewish character, fail to feel or understand the value to us of the land—the heart from which we draw all of our spiritual identity as a nation with a land and destiny of our own.

We who are living in Judea and Shomron are not simply squatting on land; we are pointing the way for our people, back to our roots, back to our true Jewish selves, and this battle, this educational battle for the souls and integrity of our people and land, is what we are fighting for, and what our government fails to defend.

Best to the family.

Era

April 29, 1981
Yamit

Dear Mother,

It has been at least two and a half or three weeks since I wrote you a letter. During that time Orit, I, and the kids moved down to Yamit in order to help stop the withdrawal from this area of Sinai. Only God knows if we shall succeed. We hope at least to keep this area and maybe force a stopping of the withdrawal from the rest of Sinai.

When I say we "moved" I mean we just threw bedding, clothing, dishes, etc., into the car and drove down. During Pesach we moved to Talmei-Yosef which is a moshav being dismantled. By moving here we stopped the wreckers from wrecking, and twenty buildings have been saved in which twenty families, like ourselves, have moved into. It is now one day after Pesach (your last day of Pesach) and although according to Camp David we should have not been here by now—we still are. We are hoping that God will hear our cries and allow us to stay.

David passed his third birthday last week, and I am thirty-seven today. We made him a birthday party in Yamit. All of these would be happy days except that I cannot really be happy. I think so much about Abba, and whenever I think about him I become despondent. To me the entire situation is still entirely unbelievable. Yesterday I said Yizkor [the Memorial Prayer] for him for the first time. This whole situation is hard on me—so much more on you. There are no words of solace. I believe that God knows what He is doing and will return Abba to us soon.

It indeed has been a very terrible year. Not only did God take away Abba, he also took away Rabbi Tzvi Yehuda Kook. God is gathering great people around him in heaven.

The invitation for the summer obviously includes Baruch also and/or Yosaif and Surri. We have room, that's no problem.

How has your health been, Mother? As you said, you can't afford to get ill. Orit and I worry about you a lot so please take care of yourself.

With blessings from a son to his mother,
with all my love,
Era, Orit, Moriyah, David, and Atarah

138

July 1, 1982
Shilo

Dear Mother, Baruch, Joe and Surri,

Yes, my dear mother, you had to go through another very difficult day. If God had willed it, it would have been your anniversary together. But we don't know God's ways, we just know that they are correct. God wanted Abba with Him and so he took Him. For us it is a void that will not and cannot be filled. The branches of our tree have lost the main stem. For you, Mother, every step and every day are filled with the void—filled with the loss. Abba would not have wanted you or us to mourn him—for life must go on. Trying to fulfill his wish is not easy. Abba had the "opportunities" to mourn so many, and yet he covered his mourning and forced himself and us to go on—to build up from the shattered. That is one of the uncountable things that our father and teacher and your husband taught us and that we shall try to follow.

With you every moment in our hearts,

Era

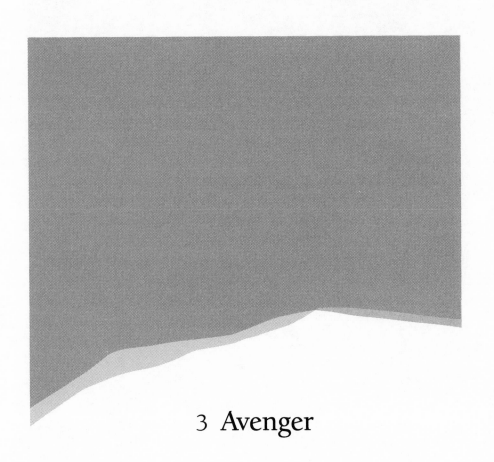

3 Avenger

"Ma'arat Hamachpelah," "The Cave of the Patriarchs"—just the mention of the name brings shivers to Jews the world over. It is one of Judaism's most revered places. The Talmud says that there are three places in Israel which the nations of the world can never lay claim to. They are Jerusalem, bought by King David, Joseph's grave in Shechem, bought by our forefather Yaacov, and Ma'arat Hamachpelah, purchased by Abraham. Genesis relates a fascinating discussion between Abraham and Efron, the cave's owner. Our Matriarch, Sarah, had just passed away and Abraham was looking to bury her. He could have taken one of the many caves in the countryside. But Abraham wanted to purchase his burial place so that in the future the nations of the world could not take it away from his great grandchildren. Efron said no; we are friends—take the cave and bury your dead. Abraham responded, No, please let me purchase the burial spot from you. When Efron realized that Abraham was insistent, he asked for four hundred gold shekels. Without debate, Abraham immediately counted out the money, a veritable fortune, and gave it to Efron.

From the moment in ancient history, till this very day, the Cave has become the most noted cave in world history. The fathers and mothers of Judaism are buried there: Abraham and Sarah, Yitzhak and Rivkah, Yaacov and Leah—the forefathers of the Jewish people. The great King David ruled in Hevron before going to Yerushalayim, and from then on Jews lived there throughout the generations.

In 1929, hundreds of Jews were massacred by Arabs living in Hevron. The British, who ruled the area during that period, did nothing to prevent the massacre. The few Jews who were not killed reached Jerusalem. From then on, until the Six Day War, Jews were not allowed to live in Hevron.

It was only natural, therefore, that Hevron was a focal point for the Jew-

---

Editor's note: On May 2, 1980, terrorists attacked and murdered six Jews in Hevron after Shabbat evening prayers. Era wrote an account of the attack and of the settlement of Hevron for a Jewish newspaper in New York. The article was never published.

ish People in the resettling of Israel. Kiryat Arba, overlooking Hevron, was the second village to be reestablished after the 1967 war, yet Ma'arat Hamachpelah remained off-limits.

During the hundreds of generations that the Tomb was not in our control, we were forbidden to enter it to visit or pray at the graves of our forefathers and mothers. At best, we were permitted to pray on the outside of the building, which was built over the graves. And so, immediately after the Six Day War, we rushed to reinstitute prayers in the halls adjoining the graves of our forefathers.

As great as our expectations, so was our disappointment. The Minister of Defense, Moshe Dayan, refused to allow Jewish prayers at the graves. He explained that since the Arabs were praying there, in a mosque they had built on the site, they had preference over us. No amount of gentle persuasion could change his mind. At the outset, he was not even ready to allow us time to pray when the Arabs weren't there.

We applied a tremendous amount of pressure on the government—political, personal, and mass. We called and visited Cabinet ministers and members of the Knesset day and night, urging them to allow Jewish prayers at the Cave. At the same time, groups of men and children would arrive daily at the Cave, and on Shabbat, women also came to pray. It became a game of cat and mouse. We would use various tactics in order to pray, and our soldiers would chase us away.

Finally our pressure bore fruit. An agreement was reached with the military authorities in which we were to be allowed certain hours of prayer. Very limited hours. Nonetheless, it was a victory for us. We continued our pressure, for at least equal rights with the Arabs for use of Ma'arat Hamachpelah.

But the city of Hevron is not only the Cave. Throughout the generations there have been active Jewish communities in this city of our forefathers. It is natural. Which proud U.S. citizen would not demand the right to settle in, for example, Boston, the site of the famous Tea Party, or Valley Forge, or Philadelphia? Those places are the very roots of American history, which is some 210 years old. The same with us. Except that Hevron is a bit older, a holy city for Jews for over four thousand years. Throughout the generations, Jews yearned to live here and paid dearly for doing so. At the end of the nineteenth century and the beginning of the twentieth, one of the important buildings in Hevron was Beit Hadassah. It served as a hospital for the residents, Jewish and Arab, of Hevron. The massacre of 1929 didn't spare Beit Hadassah. The Jews there were also murdered. Since then the building has remained empty, waiting for us to return.

If, after the Six Day War, certain sectors of the government were against our prayers in the Cave, they were tenfold more against our returning to resettle the old city. The reasons varied. "Now is not the proper time." "It is too sensitive a situation." "You'll be a security problem." "There is no real need, now, to force ourselves into heavily populated Arab areas." "We have no budget for rebuilding houses right now." "The United States government won't allow us to do so." Even the children of the builders of Beit Hadassah were not allowed to return to their parents' home.

As with the Cave, this too was a totally unacceptable situation. Once again we tried peaceful methods of convincing our government to permit us to resettle. We requested entrance to Beit Hadassah, a building for which we have the kushan [deed]. Weeks, months of negotiations proved fruitless, and it seemed that we were at a dead end. It was, as in other instances, the women who brought down the gates.

When our Minister of Defense cancelled a cabinet decision to enlarge the boundaries of Kiryat Arba, Miriam Levinger, wife of the Gush Emunim leader, Rabbi Moshe Levinger, felt that something had to be done to show that we could not accept such a non-Zionist decision. That very night, she, her friends, and their children found a way into Beit Hadassah. The entrance to the building was guarded by soldiers to prevent Jews from entering. The women entered by a ladder perched on the back of a truck that pulled up at the back of the building. The women and children entered through a window, and only later that night did the soldiers find them.

It's been over a year since then, and what total devotion the women, men, and children of Beit Hadassah have had. The situation is comparable to what has been written about Jericho during Joshua's siege. "Ein Nichnas V'Ein Yotzei"—"No one came in or left." After a day, the children ran out of milk, and the decision to allow in fresh milk reached all the way to

Begin. The same thing with Pampers. Husbands took advantage of the diaper okay to send food supplies inside the big boxes.

Day after day, night after night, week after week, and month after month, the women and children of Beit Hadassah stayed in confinement. The women had read the situation beautifully. The government would not forcibly remove them and their children. However, neither would they permit them to stay or have their husbands join them. A Jewish government in the State of Israel would not allow seven men to join their families for over a year, just to prevent the resettlement of one building in Hevron, a building that Jews have a deed to!

Finally, one small compromise was reached with the Minister of Defense. Every Friday night, the husbands were allowed to visit their families. It became a weekly event that the majority of those who prayed at the Cave would visit, before going home to their apartments in Kiryat Arba, the women and children of Beit Hadassah. Every Friday night a procession would wind through the streets of Hevron, from the Cave to Beit Hadassah. And when they would reach the corner of the street, they would always break out with a rousing chorus of *"V'Shavu Banim L'Gvulom"*, "The Children Shall Return to Their Borders."

It was different two weeks ago, as the procession danced its way from the Cave to Beit Hadassah. That Friday night, at the exact time that the prayers at the Cave were ending, Yassar Zaveedat, Machmud Abu-Sininah, Adnan Jabar, and Machmud al Shubu were on their way to the roof of the building overlooking Beit Hadassah. Under their coats, they hid the weapons and ammunition for their mission. They had illegally crossed the Jordan River some ten months earlier. Their instructions were wanton murder of Jews. Machmud had previous experience. He murdered an innocent couple on a walking tour in the area of Beit Guvrin.

Some ten minutes after 7:00 P.M. the Friday evening services at Ma'arat Hamachpelah were ending. The song "Adon Olam," "Master of All," sung by millions of Jews all over the world on Friday night, was happily being sung. Fifty of those present began their procession to Beit Hadassah.

Rabbi Levinger was the first to arrive at Beit Hadassah. He had been seen by Machmud, the lookout, but the commander of the group decided to wait until the majority of the walkers arrived. Among them were Aron Piniel and his recent bride, Meerah; two visiting students from B'nei Brak, Dafna and N'Turah; and Tzvi Glatt, a new immigrant.

Early that afternoon, Ze'ev Chaver (Zambish), one of the stalwarts and founders of Kiryat Arba, had met with the military commander of Hevron. "We are worried about the security situation; things are getting worse," he told the commander. "Don't worry," retorted the commander. "We have strengthened the patrols, everything is okay." That Friday night, Zambish went directly home from the Cave. He had promised his wife he would come home for a celebration. His wife had given birth that week to a boy. In the houses of Kiryat Arba, the traditional festive song welcoming the Angel of Shabbat Shalom was being sung at that very moment.

But this Shabbat there was no peace.

Just as the men, women, and children of the procession reached Beit Hadassah, Adnan and Yassar, standing in the darkness of Hevron on the building overlooking Beit Hadassah, threw their hand grenades. Machmud lit the six detonators and then started shooting with his submachine gun directly into the back of the procession.

The first to fall was Eli Hazeev. An American—a good American—he fought in Vietnam and received the Badge of Honor. He had one life and lived it for his country—Israel. He was shot in the back. The PLO terrorists wouldn't face him. He would have taken them down.

The first grenade exploded and Eitan Arbel and Chanon Gruthamer went down. Eitan somehow managed to get up and run into Beit Hadassah. Aron Piniel fell behind some boulders at the entrance to the old hospital, and his bride followed him. She watched his stomach falling out and handed him her sweater to cover the wound.

At Beit Hadassah, one of the yeshiva students found a submachine gun inside the building and started returning fire. His actions saved many lives. The terrorists fled into the dark.

The ambulance sirens in the background could be heard as the women and men inside Beit Hadassah started running to the victims. Tzvi Glatt was pulled in, but he had been murdered. Shmuel Mermelstein was also dead. Yaacov Tzimmerman was dead with a bullet in his brain. Chanon

Gruthamer was unconscious but still alive. He was laid down on the floor in Beit Hadassah. Miriam Levinger, a born American, registered nurse, and mother of ten, worked over his body trying to save him. As she worked she prayed, "Chanan, don't go." Her prayers weren't answered that Friday night. Even the doctors at Hadassah Hospital, the new world-famous hospital in Ein Kerem to which he was flown by helicopter, couldn't save him.

May 1980
Shilo

Dear Avi,

I don't know that I'll ever mail this to you.* It may be too problematic to do so. But more than ever before, I need your advice.

It's Sunday night now, forty-eight hours after the murders in Hevron. Some of the funerals were today. Besides the anger and the public cries for revenge, you could hear the recriminations: "Had we acted before, after the attack on Solomon, this never would have happened. Now we must react, we must prevent another attack."

What can I tell you? Who knows when one is prepared for life-or-death decisions? Never in my days in the States, and never here, would I have imagined myself dealing with the problem before me. This is not a question of what kind of car to buy, or where to purchase a house, or to what school to send the kids. I remember when we hassled with the question of participating in marches for the freedom of Soviet Jewry, rabbis published positive and negative responses to the question. Yes, it was a difficult decision, but it wouldn't necessarily change your life. In this situation, Avi, I don't really have an illusions. My government is not going to act. That is a given fact. Yes, we'll try to persuade them, but we've had the experience in the past. So I know that I have to act.

But, Avi, there are huge ramifications to such a decision, some personal and some national. Truthfully, I am not sure which is more important. This is not pre-1948 when the Underground acted against the British. We are a

---

*Editor's note: The letter was never sent.

sovereign government, and we are a sovereign state. Do I have the right to assume responsibility for what my government is doing? Would an action by myself and others not be a desecration of the honor of Medinat Yisrael (the State of Israel)? I couldn't do that, Avi; I love my country too much to disgrace it publicly. Even when I come to the States to talk about the situation here, I won't talk negatively about Aretz. You know better than I that there is a halachah [law] against speaking lashon harah [evil speech] about our land. If I were to act, I'd be doing more than speaking lashon harah. All my life I've been taught by my Abba and Ema about the special honor that one must have for Medinat Yisrael and its leaders and elders. Could it be that by one act of mine, I'll throw all of that out the window? Is it also possible that my action will be the basis for others to act as well? Who knows where it would end? Everyone has his "red line." My red line is the present situation, and therefore I feel that something has to be done. Someone else's red line can be something else, and then he'll act. It'll be a situation of no law and order. I have grown up to be a law-and-order person. What right do I have to possibly hurt our country on a national level?

Then there is the personal level. I know, Avi, that if I am to act, there is a good chance, almost guaranteed, that I'll be spending time in jail. Possibly even ten years or more. That will, to an extent, destroy our family. Do I have a right to force Orit into being a living widow? That's exactly what it would be. My kids will grow up basically without a father. Don't they have to be asked? You know that's a rhetorical question; they're too young to understand. Who knows how many years this could take from my parents' lives? And myself? You know me, Avi. I love kids so much. Just the thought of being in jail without them makes me despondent. When I'm on reserve duty and away from them for two weeks or a month, I go crazy. I can't even begin to imagine how I'll live without them. Also, I love the outdoors, working, being active, building Eretz Yisrael. All that will stop.

Even more so, should I give away my life just to maim some PLO leaders? Even if I protect Jewish lives by doing so? Early this morning, Avi, before going to the funerals, I took my child David on our baby carrier (the one you put on your shoulders with the baby inside) and took a walk with him to the top of the mountain overlooking Shilo. What a ball of fun, just being alone together. This little kid is so delicious. I'm crazy about him, as

I am about Moriyah. I have taken David up on my backpack in the past just to play around together. This time, however, I was doing it not just to play around with him. As you can probably feel from my tone of writing, I've come very close to deciding that someone must act against the PLO leaders here in order to prevent more Jews from being murdered. If everybody leaves it to someone else, it will never get done. I am aware of the consequences. I'll spend many years behind bars. I had to "speak" with David about it. I had to explain to him that even though I'll be put into prison for many years and that we wouldn't be able to be with each other, I love him. That I would be sitting in prison because I love him. I admit, my friend, tears came to my eyes as I sat there on top of the mountain overlooking "my" green valley. "David," I said, "only God knows how many years I won't be with you, to hold you and play with you once again. Will you ever be able to forgive me for taking myself away from you? I won't be able to play ball with you. I won't be able to ride a bicycle with you or take walks with you, sing with you and spend Shabbat together. With you and Moriyah, your sister." I've never been in such a dilemma throughout my entire life, and I don't wish it on anyone. Here I am thinking to myself, Era, where do you, Brooklyn born and bred, who studied social work because you love working with kids—where do you even come off thinking about attacking PLO mayors and putting yourself in prison? That's for someone else. You're not a macho man; let someone else do that work. There are many Israelis who went through the army and can do the job. You shouldn't be the guy. You sitting in jail—without being able to see the wife and kids? And what about the plans for putting up a home for disadvantaged children? Who will do that? Everybody has to give in the area or field that he is best in. Isn't working with kids and preventing delinquency more important than stopping some PLO mayors?

After a few moments of total silence, even from thoughts, and just holding David close, I said to myself, Great, Era, do things that are good for yourself, but leave the difficult work to someone else. Everybody can use the same logic you are using right now. The logic is right, but the PLO mayors will continue murdering Jews. I remembered the rabbinical statement in the Talmud, "Israel is acquired via tribulations." The commentator,

Rashi, explains tribulations as tribulations of love. Our history is full of trials and tribulations by Jews. Throughout all the generations, Jews were willing to suffer to remain Jewish and keep Israel Jewish. Am I not part of that people?

Maybe I'm wrong, but I had the feeling that David understood the seriousness of the situation. During those moments of "our serious discussion" he calmed down and remained quiet. It's one of those times in life that you want the clock of life to stop and not move on.

Just to sit there with David and not have the clock move. With its moving I would have to make a decision, one that could possibly take me away from my wife and children, and I didn't want to make that decision.

The clock ticked on, and David fell asleep in my arms. As he did I thought of my uncle, Mordecai Shimon, of blessed memory. David Shimon is partly named after him. I think I've told you about him. He was a real hero of Israel. What would he have done in my situation? What I was afraid to do. If we Jews were to worry and take care only of our personal selves, we would have disappeared long ago. It is precisely because many of us are willing and ready for personal sacrifice that we have existed as a people. I am, I "said" to Mordecai Shimon, a link in the chain. Do I have a right to break that chain? How does the saying go? A chain is as strong as it weakest link. To be a Jew is a big responsibility, and one must live up to it. To be a Jew today living in Israel has even greater responsibility. My uncle was a strong link; my grandfather before him continued the link from my great-grandfather. They did so so that we could practice our faith and pass it on. I looked at David and said to him, "David, you will be a link in the chain only if I teach you to be a link. Teaching is not only words. The best teaching is action." What could I say to David if in the future more Jews were killed by the PLO murderers and I did nothing to prevent it? What could I say to David if in the future Jews wouldn't settle in this area 'cause I did nothing to stop the killer? Could I tell him that I warned others to do something?

I closed my eyes and just swayed holding my sleeping boy David in my hands. A decision had been made.

Era

February 1987
Tel Mond Prison

Dear Cousin,

When I told Orit, she was super. She agreed that we had no choice but to act. Her feelings were almost identical to mine. We can't expect others to do it for us and run away from the responsibility ourselves, she said. When I asked how would she manage if I went to prison, she answered that God would help give her strength. What a good woman. I'm so privileged to have her.

Years later when Natan Natanson was arrested, his wife, Tami, was asked if she had agreed to his participation. She answered, "I told him I preferred a live husband behind bars than a dead one in a box."

I called my brother-in-law, Yehuda, after speaking with Orit and told him I wanted to meet him.

I met with Yehuda, and we agreed that something drastic had to be done about the PLO mayors. He wanted time to do some investigating, and we agreed to meet again in two days. He never showed any hesitation at all. In the meantime, I was supposed to approach Natan about his involvement. We discussed the risks, and he had no delusions about not getting caught. He had been considering a reaction for many months too. The murders at Beit Hadassah had finally convinced him.

Yehuda and I met on the top of the mountain in Shilo, in the same place I had spoken with David two days before. We did so to make sure no one could hear our discussion.

I met my friend Noos (Natan Natanson) in Jerusalem. We drove to the Mount of Olives and walked to the grave of my uncle, Mordecai Shimon. He had given his life for the country and had been arrested six times by the British during our struggle for independence. Noos didn't hesitate and asked what action I had in mind. We both agreed not to speak about the subject to anyone, not even our wives. Noos understood the need to attack the PLO mayors, but he wanted to know who else was involved. Besides having served in the tank corps, Noos came out of a yeshiva background and had been taught to judge a case from all sides. Yehuda had agreed to let Noos know that he was involved. "Who else?" Noos asked. I answered that for the moment I couldn't tell him more.

Noos walked back to the car while I said a few prayers at my uncle's grave. Prayers for guidance and strength. "Even though I walk through a valley in the shadow of death, I will fear no evil," King David taught us to say, but to really feel it was no easy thing. In my uncle's generation enemies rose to destroy us, and in my generation, the same. Just as God helped my uncle's generation in their time of need, I prayed for God to help us now.

I met Yehuda again the next night. He had spoken to a few other people. The consensus was to attack the PLO mayors, to injure them in a way that they wouldn't be able to continue their work. To attack all thirteen of the leaders would have involved too many people with too great a risk of leaks and mistakes. Also, we wanted to act on the thirtieth day after the massacre in Hevron, so that there would be an obvious link and warning, and so there wasn't time to plan a full-scale action. Therefore, the five main leaders were chosen: Bassam Shaka of Shechem; Karim Chalef of Ramallah; Ibrahim Tawil of El-Bireh; Dr. Shamzi Natashe from Beit Lechem; and Ibrahim Dakak of Jerusalem. I told Yehuda that I didn't want to know the names of any of the other participants. That way, if I were caught, the Shin Bet couldn't get any information from me. I told him I trusted his decisions in choosing the right people.

Yet in our discussions I got an idea of the type of people involved: an F-16 flight squadron chief; an underwater commando; mayors of two settlements in the north; two demolition experts; a scout in Arik Sharon's commando division that crossed the Suez Canal in our counterattack in '73; the dean of a yeshiva; a respected teacher and scholar. I felt a lot more confident after learning about the type of people who would be helping. Yehuda mentioned that everyone he asked immediately volunteered to take part.

The demolitions people decided that bombs had to be placed under the cars of each of the targets. The explosions had to be simultaneous so that there wouldn't be time for one to alert the others. We didn't even know where the mayors lived or when they drove to work in the morning. Which meant we had extensive research to do. All of which is time-consuming, necessitates special equipment, and leaves one open for detection.

The deeper I became involved, the greater my inner conflict became. Is this what I came to Israel for? To do my government's job and fight the terrorists? It was so frustrating. I was always against even hitting people, and now I was planning to seriously injure. That's some jump.

Every meeting had to be done extremely carefully. If people in Shilo saw me traveling too often or meeting with Yehuda or someone else too often, they could, after the attack, put two and two together. I told my secretary, and anyone else in the village who asked, that we were looking for more land in the area for the development of some new villages. Therefore, I was traveling more. It was decided to attach a small charge to each car of the five PLO leaders. The bomb was easy to attach and strong enough only to injure—not kill. Noos and I would work together, and our job was Bassam Shaka.

When I came home at night, I'd go to the kids' bedroom and spend an extra few minutes there. It was scary. Who knew how many years I'd spend in prison and wouldn't be able to be with them? As they slept, I put my head next to each one of them and kissed them over and over. In a way, I wanted to close my eyes and have the entire problem be a dream.

When I lay down next to Orit, I looked at her for an extra few minutes. For how long would we be separated, I asked myself? Did we get married in order to be separated by a prison wall? Then I held her closely in hopes that the fear would go away.

Noos and I practiced for the first time on a fake bomb, attaching it to the bottom of my car. If a red light went on, we had succeeded. Both of us "succeeded."

We still had a problem—a real one. We didn't know where Bassam lived. The address that he was listed at was not his. The date of action was drawing closer, and we hadn't been successful. We obviously couldn't go riding into Shechem and ask some of the locals where he lived.

Yehuda told me that he ran into a similar problem in Al-Bireh with the PLO mayor Ibrahim Tawil. There they knew where he lived. The problem? They hadn't found his car there any night at all, although they had done a few stakeouts. So one of our guys decided to wait for him outside City Hall—sitting in a car opposite the entrance. When Yehuda told me the story, I really got upset. That's like saying, "Here I am fellows, trying to blow Tawil up. Come and get me"—totally irresponsible. It didn't make me feel better that he was able to follow Tawil to a garage some 250 feet from his home, where he parked his car. I told Yehuda, why not call up the Shin Bet and inform them of our plans!

Finally we found him, and how! Noos and Yehuda were in Shechem staking out the neighborhood we thought Shaka lived in. It wasn't the first time that we had done so. We had already been there five times. We had thought of waiting for him as he left City Hall and then following him, but it was too risky.

After once again failing to see Shaka come to his listed residence, Noos and Yehuda headed back. It was late in the afternoon and Shavuot was just two hours away. As they were driving up the "S" turns of Ma'aleh L'vona they noticed, going the other way, the Opel Rekord, which they recognized as belonging to Bassam Shaka. Sitting behind the wheel was his wife. Could this be the break we'd been waiting for? Yehuda and Noos made a very quick decision. Even though it was very late and nearing the beginning of the Shavuouth holiday, they decided to follow Mrs. Shaka back to Schechem—maybe she would lead them to the residence. Noos, who could probably come in first or second in the Indianapolis 500, turned around and took off after the Opel. As he was telling me this, I said, "Kaddish," over my Peugot, which they were driving. Soon they were tailing her. Suddenly, after they passed the "Valley of Livona," bang, bang, bang, psss . . . a flat tire. They would have embarrassed the tire changers at the 500—two minutes and they were off. But meanwhile Mrs. Shaka had vanished. Flooring the gas pedal and reaching speeds of up to 125 miles per hour didn't help. They reached Shechem but still didn't find the Opel. They drove through the main drag of town, and once again God was with us. Mrs. Shaka had stopped at a local store. Carefully, in order to avoid being detected, they followed her to the house—one which I was to get to know so well. Then they sped back to Shilo, arriving just before the holiday started.

After Shavuot we began to study Bassam's daily routine. We found a spot on the mountain of Eyval from which you can see Bassam's house. Once I spent five hours staking out his home from the mountainside. You ought to have seen how I dressed—Sherlock Holmes hat or sometimes a

New York City cab driver's cap, a good pair of binoculars, my Pentax with its telescopic lens, and a bird-watcher's book! The binocs are also good for nighttime viewing. We tried to "patternize" Bassam Shaka's moves, to ascertain when he left his house in the morning, whether he was the driver all the time, where he went, where he parked his car at night—in short, everything about him so we could plan well and make no mistakes.

Sitting up here on top of Mount Eyval, overlooking the ancient city of Shechem, you cannot help but be overwhelmed by history. I was back at our first stop in Aretz. Right beneath this mountain is where our forefather Abraham made his first stop in Eretz Yisrael. Right here is where God promised the land of Israel to Abraham. Right here Joshua separated my grandparents of some 175 generations ago into two groups—according to the words of Hashem—and we received the blessing and the curse. Interestingly enough, our rabbis state that Shechem is a city of misfortune. Dina was raped there, and her brothers killed all the men of the city in retaliation. Nearby, Joseph was sold into captivity.

To an extent, this place lives up to its name even today. It is a city of problems for us. It has the largest Arab population of any place in YOSH, a very large number of PLO members and sympathizers, a hotbed of their activities, and has one of the most wicked seminaries of anti-Israel studies throughout the Arab world. In 1929, pogroms chased the Jews out of the city.

Several days before the attack, Noos and I drove to Bassam's house in the dead of night. We left Shilo comparatively early, so there would be no unusual questions.

On the way there, close to midnight, we changed into army fatigues. That way, if someone saw us in Shaka's area, we would not necessarily raise any eyebrows. People would assume that the army was guarding his house. I was a bit scared after we parked our car a few blocks from his house and started walking over there. Albeit nothing much could happen to us if we were caught because we weren't doing anything wrong, but the whole plan might have had to be shelved. Bassam's car was inside the gate to the yard of the house. A quick check revealed no lock on the gate. The garage was also empty. A small light was on in one of the upstairs windows, and we kept our eyes in its area to see if someone was looking. We needed no more than five to seven minutes. Then we retraced our steps to the car and returned to Shilo after changing back into our clothes on the way. Noos and I felt satisfied.

Then we blundered. My car was used for reconnaissance of Shaka's residence. On the way out of Shechem one night, the two guys in the car were waved over by a policeman. Since they felt that they didn't have a good enough excuse to be found in Shechem at this late hour of the night, they decided to speed up and zoom by the policeman. They weren't sure whether he managed to mark down the license plate number. But it meant that my car couldn't be used on the night of the attack or anymore in connection with our activities. I had to prepare a good alibi so that if I was questioned during the next few days, I'd be prepared.

Friday night services in the Beit Knesset at Shilo are indeed special. Beside the added joy that is evident in the prayers there is another "sweet" at the end. We sing and dance for about five minutes. To use an understatement, Noos is not a big singer or dancer and generally stands on the side. Yet this night after praying, he was one of the leaders of the singing and dancing and even introduced a new song.

I told Orit that Friday night that the attack was scheduled for the following night. She was startled; she didn't know it was so soon. We spent much time together on Shabbat, the two of us along with the two kids. We walked together to the ancient city of Shilo and talked there. I said to Orit, "On this very spot some 3,500 years ago Hannah came to pray and to ask God to help her conceive. God answered, and Shmuel, the Great Prophet, was born. For over 369 years, our ancestors came here from all over the country to pray." We spent plenty of time on the Tel and I came away strengthened and more prepared for our mitzvah.

The next afternoon, Noos called me to say that he was on the way out of Shilo and that there might be a change in plans. I began wondering and worrying. Did something go wrong? Maybe somebody found something out?

Noos arrived about an hour and a half later. He drove slowly, for he wanted to make sure that he wouldn't receive a speeding ticket or be stopped.

We drove out into the country. Noos told me that as an extra precaution, two of the bombs were tried in the late morning and didn't work. Our expert who devised the bombs instructed us to add another battery. Noos had one with him. Afterward we returned to our office.

A half-hour later we got a phone call. "All the doctors had successfully operated on their babies."

There would be no delay.

Era

March 1987
Tel Mond Prison

Dear Brothers,

The town meetings at Shilo are held once a week, and from the length of our meetings, one would assume that we are the U.S. Congress with so many important matters to handle. There are important things to decide upon, but the length of the meetings doesn't necessarily have to do with that. It's probably more connected to the joke about the lone Jew shipwrecked on a desert island who had built two synagogues. When asked why, he responded, "So if I'm angry at one, I can go to the other." Jews have a passion for differences of opinion.

Noos and I are both on the council. We couldn't afford to have the meeting last too late this night. We had other business. On the other hand, we couldn't seem to be too anxious to finish early. Two other members of the council came to our rescue. They weren't feeling well and requested a short meeting. "Reluctantly," we agreed.

I needed to talk with Orit about the action. From the very beginning I had decided not to speak about the attack in any building or automobile. Oversensitivity? Only time would tell. My field in the army is communications, and I'm aware of what listening devices are available these days. I wanted to be overly sensitive and free rather than less sensitive and behind bars. Orit and I held each other tight, sensing, together, the seriousness of the action that we were going to undertake in just one short hour or so. I looked in her eyes and said to her, "Thank you for all you've given me."

I rechecked my gear to see if everything was in place and then went to the kids' room for two last kisses. Oh, how I love them! I told Orit to get some sleep. Then I slipped out the door.

Noos and I met some fifty yards from the entrance to Shilo. We walked swiftly to a waiting car. With us, in a plastic bag, was a wooden box carrying the bomb. Mekorot Water Company was digging a well along the road on which we were walking. They had a guard positioned there to watch the equipment at night. On our trial runs we found that he generally slept, and the equipment guarded him. We were hoping that would be the situation tonight. It was, and we passed him without any problems.

Seven minutes later, after a sharp bend in the road, we saw a flickering of the parking lights of a car. So far everything was perfect. Without a word we sat in the back seat and our driver headed north to Shechem. Then I noticed who the driver was—Moshe Zar. I hadn't seen him since we worked together in Ofra—I as the mayor and he as an electrical contractor. "I see that we meet only while doing mitzvot," I said.

Quietly, as Moshe drove, I thought to myself, what a person he is. In his middle forties, he was one of the big backers of Gush Emunim. In 1956 he was the first parachutist to be wounded in the Mitlah Pass. It cost him an eye and pain in his head every day. He was hospitalized for months in critical condition. Yet he refused for years to accept money as a war cripple. I felt good knowing that he was our partner.

Down the "S" turns of Ma'aleh L'vona we drove. Here, 2,000 years earlier, the great warrior Yehuda Ha'Maccabi destroyed a vastly superior, well-armed Greek army and paved the way for the sanctification of the Temple. Some three miles farther north, near the Arab village of Yutma, built on the ruins of a Talmudic village of the same name, we asked Moshe to turn onto a side road and turn off his motor and lights.

Quickly Noos and I jumped out and opened our army bags. We had practiced doing this over and over at night in the mountains surrounding Shilo. At any moment a car could pass by; we had to work fast.

Three minutes, and we were on our way, dressed as soldiers in army fatigues, gloves on our hands, and knitted caps ready to be pulled over our faces.

We drove past the army base where I had done my basic training. If the guards were doing their job, a powerful spotlight would soon shine into the side of the car. The spotlight discourages unwelcome visitors. The lights of Shechem could easily be seen now. The city nestled beautifully between two towering mountains, Har Gerizim, the Mountain of the Blessing, on the left, and Har Eyval, the site of the Curse, on the right. It was here that God promised Abraham all of Eretz Yisrael for his children.

We had to be careful in Shechem. We could be pulled over by the police and questioned. It was unlikely, however, for there are very few people and cars out at night in YOSH, and consequently few policemen. Still, just a few weeks ago, my car had been pulled over. Obviously we could not afford any chances tonight. Earlier Noos and I had decided on using back roads through the city to avoid such detection.

We guided Moshe to a side street about three blocks from the Bassam house. He parked between two cars about one-third of the way up the street. This way a passing car couldn't make out the Israeli license plate. We both quickly stepped out of the car. We told Moshe that if we were not back in twelve minutes he should leave, or if he heard shots and we were not back within three minutes, he should also leave. We checked our watches, and then Noos and I were on our way.

As expected, we were greeted by barking dogs from different houses. But since we were walking quickly, they quieted down as soon as we passed the house. Suddenly we were at Bassam's house. Yes, the car was in place. Bassam was home. Noos whispered to me to stand guard in front of the garage wall. Since the car was not in the garage but behind the yard gate, if the bomb went off by mistake, I would be shielded. No reason for both of us to go. "Tell Tami I love her," Noos whispered to me. A noncharacteristic remark for him; so personal.

A small light was on in Shaka's house, but I detected no movement. My M16 was loaded, cocked with the safety off. In all of our stakeouts we never encountered a guard, but we didn't intend to be surprised by one now.

Noos was under Bassam's car. A wrong move, and the bomb would go off with Noos beneath it. Seconds passed slowly. I squelched the need to ask him how things were going. Noos had attached the bomb by magnet to the car and was stretching the trip wire. The slightest mishap, and it was all over. I heard him placing the rock on the wire and slipping out from under the car. He had successfully attached the bomb. Hopefully, no dog or cat would crawl under the car during the night and move the rock or pull the cord. One last check. Everything in place and Noos had rejoined me. I gave him a big, hard squeeze, and we were off. I attached the safety and pulled out the cartridge of my rifle. We reached the car. "Moshe, get us out of here quickly," we said. Within a minute we had left the area and were heading, via side streets, toward south Shechem, on our way back to Shilo. From what we could tell, no one had seen us, and everything went off well. Now we had to wait and see if everything worked as well in the morning.

On the way back to Shilo, four or five cars passed us going in the opposite direction. Once again, out of supersensitivity, we ducked when the car approached us. In addition, Moshe turned on the high beams as the car approached. Once again, Moshe pulled the car over into the side road, and we quickly changed back into civilian clothing. We still had to get into Shilo without being detected. Moshe left us at almost the same spot where he had picked us up. With a big "yasher koach" ["More power to you"], we left him and walked back to Shilo. Once again we found the Mekorot Water Company equipment watching over the guard. Orit was sleeping when I climbed into bed. She awoke and asked me what happened. "Everything went okay. Sleep. We had a good meeting, I'll tell you about it tomorrow." Although Orit was anxious to know particulars, I wouldn't talk in the house.

I was dead tired, but my mind was racing. The main thought and hope was that the explosive would go off. We had done intensive information gathering and knew that Bassam drove the car by himself to his office. The explosive was built to maim only. Would it go off? Would it do the job?

Now, I was a bit scared. The action was over. How long would it take until the police would find me? Yet, I said to myself, you made a decision. But I was floored at my action. Where did I get the nerve to do what I did? I dislike any type of violence. As a social worker, I constantly tried to influence youth to reject violence. Here I was, doing what I've abhorred.

Yet I know, as Ecclesiastes says, "There is a time for everything under the sky . . . a time to throw stones and a time to gather them . . . a time for war and a time for peace . . . a time to kill and a time to heal." We would all prefer to be nonviolent all the time, and that day will come. Sadly, until then, there are times when force must be used.

The last thought I remembered was my wish to make sure the bomb exploded under his feet.

Yours,
Era

April 1987
Tel Mond Prison

Dear Brothers,

I was dead tired, but somehow I awoke before the alarm. I added a few personal prayers of thanks and requests during the morning prayers. After services, around 7:00 A.M., a few of us gathered around, as usual, for a few moments of what's new. Noos and I acted quite normal. The bombs were set to go off at 8:00 A.M., and I was a bit anxious but was careful not to mention a word that could be misinterpreted.

At home, after getting Moriyah and David off to kindergarten, Orit and I took a short walk, and I filled her in. "Beep, beep, beep," began the radio. "Kol Yisrael M'Yerushalayim [the Voice of Israel from Jerusalem]. It is 9:00 A.M. and here is the news. Bassam Shaka, the Mayor of Shechem, was seriously wounded this morning when a bomb blew up his car. Karim Chalef, Mayor of Ramallah, was injured when his car also blew up." I was talking with the tractor driver in Shilo when he turned on the radio to hear the news. "Ezeh yofi," ["How beautiful"] he quickly reacted. Then on the radio,

"An army sapper, a Druze, from the Galilee was also seriously wounded when he tried to dismantle another bomb that had been placed by the garage of Ibrahim Tawil of El-Bireh." My head sank straight down, but I couldn't show anything. What happened, I wondered, dismayed. What happened at Tawil's place, and what about the others? Nothing was said.

The commentator continued, "The army and police are starting an intensive search to find the perpetrators. It is significant that today is exactly thirty days since the massacre at Beit Hadassah." "You see," the tractor driver said, "you only talk, but the guys who did this are men of action." "Me? What about yourself, you're the one who always says that we have to shoot the leaders and instigators. How come you didn't do it?" I reacted. "You listen to me and you'll see, now it will be quiet in the area. This should have been done a long time ago," continued the driver. "I agree with that," I retorted. After spending some time discussing the tractor work for the day, I went to the office.

Our secretary and about another ten residents and visitors were discussing the news. "Thank God, thank God, somebody had the strength to do what should have been done a long time ago. Those murderers should have been dealt with by the government. . . . Maybe it was the SHABAK [secret security forces]," said our secretary. "No, you don't understand the situation. It's inner rivalry among Arabs. I'm sure that it was the Arabs themselves," said Yair. "You know what? No doubt, it's some of our guys who did it. They deserve one big yasher koach. Now there will be quiet, you'll see," said Yosi. "Who do you think did it, Era?" asked Yair. "I don't know, I wish it would have been me."

About half an hour later I was on my way to Yerushalayim for some meetings. On the way, passing in the other direction, were four or five police vans, portable battalions. I tried to appear natural as we passed the vans, but my heart beat a lot quicker. The news broadcasts were full of reports and the reactions of different cabinet ministers and other personalities. They were asked if it was good or bad for Am Yisrael that such an attack occurred. The majority expressed the belief that the PLO leaders should have been dealt with by the government.

Walking the streets of Yerushalayim was an experience. It seemed that everybody was an expert and extremely knowledgeable as to what had happened. Of course, each expert knew exactly who planted the bombs. I stopped here and there to listen to their opinions, smiling to myself. One thing for sure, they were all pleased with the attack. One group expressed it this way: "Our pride has been returned to us."

The reactions at the government office where my meeting was scheduled were, for the most part, the same as those in the street. It was a really good feeling. It seemed as if most, if not all, of the nation was reunited once again in their happiness that the PLO mayors had been attacked. Yet, on the other hand, I was troubled and bothered, very much so, by the Druze army sapper who had been seriously injured. How could that have happened? All precautions had been taken, and yet one of our soldiers had been hurt. I had to squelch a desire to call my brother-in-law Yehuda to find out what had gone wrong. I had to keep my reactions totally normal. I knew it wouldn't be easy.

I called Yehuda a day later to say hello. Don't forget, I told him, you are meeting me this afternoon at 4:00 in Yerushalayim to help me find a used wardrobe. We had arranged before the attack to meet, if we could, on Tuesday afternoon to discuss what went on. The meeting was to take place in a public park in one of the neighborhoods of Yerushalayim. What a meeting. We gave each other a big handshake, and as we walked, Yehuda filled me in. Five leaders of the NGC were to have been attacked. In actuality only two were: Bassam Shaka and Karim Chalef of Ramallah.

The biggest fashlah [failure] was at Ibrahim Tawil's place. According to the plan, his garage door was wired, and that went okay. We feared that because of the delay of one hour between the car bombs going off and Tawil's scheduled departure from his home, the army might send a sapper to check other members of the NGC. Therefore, a warning was also passed to one of the army officers in charge. He would have gone with the sapper and in some way would have warned him. Indeed the army command did send sappers to check the cars of the other NGC leaders. It seems that there was a misunderstanding and our army officer thought that the car was wired and not the garage door. Even so, he tried to steer the sapper away from the area, but the trip wire was jostled by the sapper, and both he and the army officer were injured.

In Yerushalayim, two problems developed. One of the three guys who was to participate in the attack backed out at the last moment. And Dakak's car wasn't in its usual place. After waiting some two hours, our guys left. It turned out that Dakak had left the country. That was really bad, because he is the brain behind the NGC.

In Beit Lechem, the group involved also didn't plant the bomb. They told Yehuda that the constant barking of the dog in Dr. Natashe's yard made them decide not to pull off the action.

So far, the inside information that we had told us that the police had not gotten on to us at all.

Era

July 1980
Shilo

Dear Avi,

It's unreal. It seems that the only news in the media these days is the attack on the mayors. Even though it's been five days, still it headlines all the papers. All the experts are guessing who were the perpetrators. The day of the attacks, the Knesset decided to discuss the affair. Rav Drukman called out from the Knesset floor, "So shall all of your enemies be banished." The military head of YOSH said, "It's sad that they weren't hit a little higher up." On the other hand, our Prime Minister, Menachem Begin, was furious. He said, "The acts this morning were among the most dastardly kind." It's so typical of him. Because of him and his appointees, like Ezer Weizman, we were forced to act, so, of course, he had to defend himself. If he was a strong and straight person, he would have said that we should have expelled them a long time ago.

Newspapers from overseas are full of pictures, articles, and commentaries. Media representatives are swarming all over to see what's going on, and the English-language broadcasts that I pick up at night, on radio, from all over the world, have made it a top story.

The results so far are amazing. It is as if a switch was turned off. Rock throwing, Molotov cocktails, and tire burning have come to a total stop.

165

There hasn't been a single incident. What a difference. It is hard to believe. Even one of my Arab neighbors said yesterday, "It should have been done a long time ago, and then there would have been quiet." I was genuinely surprised at his reaction and responded, "You mean you're for the hit on the NGC?" "You've given us much better conditions than they have, and we want to continue that. The kind of activities that the NGC are encouraging is not helpful to us. They don't represent us. If someone didn't stop them, they would have continued making things worse for all," my neighbor told me. I didn't believe him too much and said so to him. "I can see that you don't yet understand me or a lot of my people, but many want peace. The militant leaders make problems for us."

Last night, before Shabbat in Shilo, a visitor gave a Dvar Torah, a talk, which, of course, had to do with the attack. He said, in specific instances, one has the right to do what was done. He said that it was not only in the hands of the government or the army to act. The government has the obligation to defend us, and if they don't, then we have the obligation to do so.

The visitor's Dvar Torah reminded me of the words of a military judge in the court case against me when we shot down the telephone lines of the Arab village which had been cutting our lines. "The government that has permitted these settlers to live where they are is responsible for their protection, and it's obvious that the government has not done so." In his decision, he stated that our security situation was indeed bad, and because we acted under duress, he was going to give us a very light sentence. In the courtroom, he stated publicly that our crime was not our action but rather the fact that we used military equipment not in accordance with the regulations. Had we used a knife, he would not have found us guilty!

Our inside information has it that our security forces have not yet picked up the trail of the perpetrators. But they will find out who did it sooner or later.

As the days go by and we feel the total quiet in the area, I realize more and more how important the action was. Once again, we can travel the roads of YOSH and not worry that any moment we will be stoned or firebombed. Orit can once again drive the children to school without needing a soldier or one of us to join her on the trip. Now that there is quiet, I'm sure that a lot more families will come to the area.

166

I've been in the Knesset two or three times in the last week, and it's great to hear the MKs talking about our attack. At least four or five of them have told me, maybe jokingly, "Why didn't your people invite us? We too would have participated." In our meetings with the army echelon since the attack, they constantly talked of how important the action was and how it has quieted down the area and made their work much easier.

Due to the total quiet that has replaced all the violence, the ambivalence that arose in me at times before has not returned. I'm referring to whether we have a right "to take the law into our own hands." We urged, so often, so many government officials to stop the NGC, yet nothing was done. So, when the government did nothing and our lives were in danger, somebody had to do something. How I wish that our government would have acted to protect us, but they didn't, and we had to protect ourselves. We can only pray that the government will learn by example. Otherwise the problem is sure to return!

Shalom,
Era

July 1980
Shilo

Dear Brothers, Shalom,

You told me over the phone that the attack on the PLO mayors is still making headlines in the U.S. and that mainly the reports are negative to Israel. The press in the States is always looking to find wrong with us. I was given a copy of the *New York Times* yesterday by a visitor from the States. Some reporter writes that it's difficult to understand how the Shin Bet, one of the world's best secret service forces, which has solved so many serious situations for Israel, many outside the country, is not able to get to the bottom of this case in its own backyard. The writer suggests that the government of Israel was either behind the act or was interested in the attack occurring. Therefore, the Shin Bet is not seriously looking into the affair.

What baloney! If the reporter were to make just a simple check, he would find out how much the Shin Bet is trying to solve the case. Actually

I shouldn't only blame your newspapers. They follow the lead of our papers. The press here in Aretz is antiright, anti-YOSH, antireligious. It's been that way since the beginning of the State. Anyhow, the Shin Bet is trying really hard to solve this case. Yet it is true that our government would do a great service to the cause of peace if they would let the case drop. The results have been something. All the rock throwing and everything else has come to a solid stop.

The Shin Bet has even questioned me! Yep, believe it or not. This past Tuesday there was a message for me in the office. "Come to the police station in Shechem." I called up the police in Shechem and asked them, "Are you sure that you want me for questioning?" The clerk said yes but could not give me any further information. About an hour later I called back again and this time I spoke with one of the investigators—who happens to be an Arab. If that sounds strange to you, it really shouldn't be. Though the UN, the Arab Countries, and the world constantly call us "occupiers," etc., Arabs living with us in YOSH have more rights than in almost any other Arab country in the world. Consequently, there are many Arab policemen.

Anyhow, I called and spoke to an investigator, who told me to come down for questioning. "Questioning?" I asked. "For what!" "I don't remember but come down. When you get here, we'll open your file and see." "Do me a favor," I continued. "Check for a second, see what it's all about. We are busy with many things here, and if it's not an emergency, I'll come down next week." "Hold on," he said, then came back with the file. "It's quite important. Come down now—something with your car trying to run down a policeman." "What's with you guys? You've got the wrong person." "Is your license plate 649673 Peugeot 404 Blue?" "Yes, it is." "Well that's the report." "Okay. I'll come over later on."

I left my office a bit concerned. I never attempted to run over a policeman. Yet, brothers, the information about the car was correct. I decided that I'd drive first to speak to my father-in-law, Avraham, and get advice from him. I was a bit worried that they were trying to spring a trap on me.

My father-in-law wasn't in his factory in K'dumim, so I decided that I'd go see the investigator anyhow. I parked outside the police station in Shechem, walked inside, and introduced myself. The investigator was amiable enough, offered me a glass of tea or coffee, and then proceeded with his questioning, which went something like the following. After the preliminaries (name, address, age, etc.) he proceeded. He warned me that I had the right to remain silent, but that if I talked it could be used against me. "Do you own a 1972 blue Peugeot 404 license plate No. 649673?" "Yes." "On the night of [I don't remember the date he mentioned] you and another person were driving in Shechem at around 12:00 A.M. Is that so?" "There is a possibility," I answered. "What do you mean by a possibility?" he asked. "Don't you know?" "Let me ask you, do you remember what you did on Monday night, May 3?" "He thought for a moment and said, 'No, I don't'." "The same with me. I don't remember what I did that night, but there is a possibility that I was in Shechem and a possibility that I wasn't." "What would you be doing in Shechem so late at night?" "I'll tell you. I live in Shilo, some twenty-five kilometers [eighteen miles] south of here. I am Mayor of the village. Many times I meet with my fellow mayors, and the meetings last until late at night. Also, my parents-in-law live in K'dumim so maybe I was meeting them. Or maybe I had met with some land sellers at night."

"Land sellers at night! Why at night?" The investigator's voice became a little hurried, as if we had caught me at something. "You should know. The Jordanians have threatened to kill any Arab who sells land to us. There are many sellers, but they are afraid to do so publicly, so we meet at night." "Can you give me the name or names of the people you met that night?" "I never said I was in Shechem that night. I never said that I met people that night. And no, I wouldn't give you the names of the sellers for two reasons. One, the deal could then be in jeopardy and the Arab's life in danger. Second, it has nothing to do with your questions—and tell me please, you told me over the phone that you want to question me in reference to an attack on a policeman. What are you referring to?"

At this point he had to use the facilities. He left the room, leaving the open file on the table. As soon as he closed the door I quickly turned the file around so I could read the evidence that the police had against me. My eyes opened wide as I read. The file was in reference to the attack against the PLO mayors. For a moment I thought that the police assumed I was involved in the attempt on the policeman and somehow that was connected to the Mayor attack. I read the charge sheet, and the evidence led in a somewhat different direction. The policeman in Shechem testified that there were two men in the car, both wearing skullcaps and both with beards. I knew immediately, therefore, that I was not involved. As you know, never in my life have I been able to grow a beard! As I read on, I began to understand the connection. The Shin Bet feels that there was a connection between my car and its two occupants that night and the subsequent attack on the mayors. Therefore they were looking to get information from me about the two and what connection, if any, I had to them.

I quickly turned the file around just a second or two before the investigator returned, just like in the movies. What is interesting was that he asked me only a few more cursory questions and told me that he was finished and if they needed me they'll call. I drove back to K'dumim, hoping that my father-in-law had returned to the factory. I needed advice. I pulled my father-in-law outside of his factory and as we walked I told him what had happened. Understanding the seriousness of the situation, he immediately called one of the lawyers living in YOSH. Two hours later I was sitting in a café in Tel Aviv. We gave the lawyer some background information, and he requested that we talk hypothetically.

The upshot of our conversation can be summed up in the following manner. The lawyer said, "Stop talking Zionism to me about the Shin Bet. They want to solve a case, and they don't care whether the attack on the mayors was good or bad for Am Yisrael. Whoever breaks the case gets a feather in his cap. If you are questioned again, they will promise you that if you talk you'll go right home afterwards, but if not, you'll be behind bars. I'm telling you that they can keep you for up to fifteen days, and only with a special permit from the Chief Justice can they keep you longer than that. Shut up for fifteen days, and you'll be home. If you talk, you sit." If need be, he was willing to handle the case.

What can I tell you, Baruch and Yosef? On the way home I saw myself sitting in jail. I've never been interrogated by the police and now for attempted murder, no less!

Avraham's talking interrupted my thoughts: "Be very careful where and

170

what you say. Your phone will be tapped, and you'll probably be followed. I also think that we should meet with Yehuda, tonight." I realized that my lifestyle would be changed drastically. If I wanted to stay out of jail, I'd have to be supercareful. Who knows, maybe all those garbage TV detective shows I used to watch in the States will help me. I'll look to see if I'm being tailed, both on foot and by car. I'll use diversionary tactics on the phone, etc. Sounds like fun? No way. This is serious stuff. For the time being I don't think I'll be writing any more letters.

Era

July 1980
Shilo

Editor's note: Era's lawyer suggested he keep a record of the continuing investigation, which he might one day need to rely on in court. The following is taken from that diary.

The next day I tried to act normal. In the village, people asked me what happened, and I responded in a joking and serious manner at the same time. I told everything except the parts that had to do with the attack. I acted very angry at the chutzpah of the SB [Shin Bet] and police to accuse me of trying to run down a policeman. Every time I came to the office, I expected the secretary to inform me that the police had called, but all of Wednesday went by with no phone call.

The next day I received a phone call from my brother-in-law, Yehuda. One of the residents of Ofra was Dan Tor, the brother of Ilan Tor, who had been under arrest for eight months for shooting at a mob of stone-throwing Arabs. Dan suggested that I meet with Ilan to get information about Shin Bet procedures. Orit and I thought it was a good idea, so I drove to Kiryat Arba to meet him. He was very helpful, that's for sure. Basically, his point was that the SB will try all types of methods to get you to talk. They start talking about day-to-day matters and slowly move the conversation where they want it. Then if you don't answer questions, they've got you. Second, they'll promise all kinds of things. Better jail conditions, their help in getting a pardon, a chance to go home for a few days after the interrogation. Third, they say, as if to back your actions, "You did the right thing," "We feel just like you," "This is just a job to us," etc.

Ilan's suggestion was simply not to agree to talk about anything. Give my name, address, etc., but nothing else. If need be tell them that on principle I refuse to give information that could lead to a Jew's being arrested for saving other Jewish lives. For example, he said, they can ask for a list of people who used your car. Once you mention a name or two they'll say, "But didn't you allow so and so to use it," or "We have proof that so and so used it," and then they're on the way to cornering you.

Thursday morning, the expected phone call came. This time they wanted me to come that morning to the military command in Shechem to meet with an interrogator named Elbaz. I forgot to mention that meanwhile Yehuda found out from his connections that the Shin Bet feel that I'm very involved in the mayors' attack and are going to do their utmost to break me.

Once again I drove to my father-in-law's and together we went to Elbaz, whom Avraham knew a bit. Avraham told me that Elbaz isn't the easiest guy in the world. Elbaz told Avraham not to worry, that we'll only be a few minutes and that he was sure it was just a mistake and that was what he was going to ascertain.

My father-in-law left the investigation room, and I was left with Elbaz and the Arab detective that questioned me the first time. Anticipating a long morning with delays, I had brought along some Talmudic writings to read. I was also pretty sure that I would be in jail by nightfall, so in my car I had a sheet, blanket, tefilin [phylacteries], prayer book, and toothbrush.

Elbaz started off pleasantly enough. He introduced himself and the detective and told me that they'd ask only a few questions. I smiled to myself. Once again, after taking my particulars, he began questioning me. Although I didn't see anything, I was sure that my testimony was being taped.

The questioning went pretty much like this:

Elbaz: "Do you know Shechem well?"

Era: "What do you mean by well?"

Elbaz: "You tell me."

Era: "I don't really know what you mean by well."

Elbaz: "Do you know where Kikar HaShaon (Clock Square) is?"

Era: "I think so, why?"

Elbaz: "How often do you travel in Shechem?"

Era: " 'Often' is hard to define."

Elbaz: "What were you doing on the night of . . . at 12:30 or so in the morning in the main street of Shechem?"

Era: "I don't remember that I was there."

Elbaz: "We know you were there; what were you doing there?"

Era: "Mr. Elbaz, let me ask you a question. Where do you live?" (I believe he said Tel Aviv). "Do you know what you did on such and such a night?"

Elbaz: "No, but let me remind you, Mr. Rapaport, that I'm asking the questions." His voice now rose with subdued anger.

Era: "Yes, you ask the questions, but just like you don't know where you were that evening in Tel Aviv, I don't know where I was in Shechem or even if I was in Shechem."

Elbaz: "Mr. Rapaport, I told you before, we know you were there. We want to know what you were doing there."

This went on back and forth for another ten minutes or so. In the back of my mind was Ilan Tor's warning, but so far I was enjoying myself. It reminded me of a fencing match.

Era: "You haven't told me why you are asking me all these questions. What am I accused of?"

Elbaz: "I'm asking the questions, not you."

Suddenly, he changed the subject a bit.

Elbaz: "Whom do you allow to drive your car?"

Ilan had called it perfectly. I thought quickly and came to a decision.

Era: "Mr. Elbaz, you told my father-in-law that we would only be a few minutes. Its been almost an hour. You're asking me all kinds of questions as if I'm accused of something serious. Yet you refuse to tell me what. Now you are asking about other people using my car. If you're accusing me of something, fine, then arrest me." I put out my hands so he could put on handcuffs. "If not, then I'm a busy person, the mayor of a village. I don't have time for games, so if I'm not accused, shalom, and I'll be seeing you."

Then, believe it or not, I stood up and started walking toward the door.

There was a kind of roar in the room, or at least it sounded that way as Elbaz yelled something to the effect of, "Where do you think you're going? I'm in charge here, not you. Come back and sit down. Now."

I turned back to the table and calmly told him, "Mr. Elbaz, I know you are not playing games; therefore, I won't either. You're not just asking questions. You're accusing me of a very serious offense, attempting to run over a policeman." Before I could continue, he interrupted: "How do you know that? Who told you so?" Once again I spoke calmly. "He did," I said, pointing to the detective. Elbaz yelled at the detective something fierce.

Then, in his anger, he turned to me: "Let me tell you. You're accused of being involved in something much more serious, the attack on the mayors, and we want all the information from you." Calmly, I don't know how I did so, I turned to him and said, "Mr. Elbaz, you are accusing me of a very, very serious act. So let me tell you right out, I don't know anything about it. I didn't participate in it, and more so, on principle, if I knew anything I wouldn't help you. If they were Jews, then they did a big mitzvah and I won't help you accuse Jews. I have nothing more to say. I won't answer any of your questions. I'm going to study Talmud." I guess it was another five to ten minutes that he prodded me trying to get me to answer his questions. When I refused to cooperate, he left the room and went to speak with my father-in-law.

He came back a few minutes later with Avraham and said to me, "I've talked to your father-in-law. He says that you're probably anxious, and he wants to talk to you. You can also get some advice from a lawyer. Also, you'll be home for Shabbat. Calm down. On Sunday, you'll come back again."

I was surprised, for I was sure that I'd be in jail for Shabbat, but I tried to hide my reaction. During Shabbat I discussed the situation with Noos, and we went to the mountains to talk in private. Saturday night Yehuda and his father, Avraham, came over. Yehuda reinformed me that the SB feels that I was involved but had no proof of it. It was important, very important, for them to break me. The four of us discussed possible lines of ques-

174

tioning. All of us agreed that the best line of response would be total quiet from me.

Sunday, I was to be at the military command in Shechem at 9:30 A.M. Once again Orit prepared sandwiches and a drink for me, along with an overnight bag with lots of clothes for a long stay. I added my prayer shawl and tefilin, and chumash [Bible]. At 9:00 A.M. I gave Orit a good long kiss and headed north to Shechem.

I entered Investigator Elbaz's room and was welcomed by Elbaz and another person called Yisrael. Yisrael took charge of the investigation, and it immediately took a very interesting turn. He introduced himself as a policeman from the research unit in Tel Aviv. "We have reviewed the facts, the investigation, and your answers, and you are correct; we have nothing on you. You are not accused of anything, and as soon as we are finished, you are free to go. As I said, I am from the research unit, and I'm doing a project on relationships between Arabs and Jews, especially in the territories." "Territories?" I questioned. "What are you referring to?" "This area, where you live," Yisrael responded. "Oh, you mean YOSH," I said. "It's not very important what you call it." "Oh yes it is," I interrupted him. "It is essentially different. If you call this area territories, that means you don't see it as yours. I hope you don't allow your personal feeling to color your report." "Of course not, I am doing research, and what we are interested in is, as I said, the attitude of Jews to Arabs and vice versa."

"That sounds very interesting. You know that I am a social worker by profession, and the research you are doing really interests me. Would you be able to send me a copy of the report when you finish it?" I asked him. As this is going on I'm saying to myself, Is this guy for real or does he think I'm stupid? He's doing research like I'm a physicist. Be careful, Era, he's leading you. At the same time I enjoyed the fencing. Although Ilan Tor's warning to be totally quiet was in the back of my mind, I felt I was in control of myself. While studying for my master's degree at Yeshiva University's Wurzweiler Graduate School of Social Work, I studied interviewing. I never dreamt, and I'm sure that neither did my professors, that their educating me would come in handy some eleven years later in a shabby investigator's room in what was once a British and Jordanian prison.

His question brought me back to the present: "What do you think about the relationship between Jew and Arab? How should we act toward them?" "When you say 'we,' who are you referring to? The people in our settlements?" "Yes, but let's start with you." "Yisrael," I said, "I have an idea. I'm just one, and from me you can't get a good idea. I'll go to Shilo and speak to the people there. We'll invite you to a meeting some night, and then you'll get a good idea of the ideas of the people living in the villages. I'm just one and not important."

"I'll accept your invitation, but first, let me hear your ideas. You're an important person, the mayor of the village, one of the leaders of Gush Emunim; your ideas are important to me." I could see that he wanted to corner me at some point, but I was still enjoying the fencing, and so I didn't cut him off.

"Do you think that we should act nice to the Arabs or consider them different from us?" I said, "Considering a person different should not necessarily influence the way we act toward a person. Don't you consider the Arabs as different? They have a different culture than ours. But a person is a person, and we should have respect for everyone, for every human being was created by God."

The questions and answers continued this way for about ten to fifteen more minutes. As I spoke I became calm, and yet I realized that too was a danger signal. I forced myself to be superaware and made a decision to stop the game. Just then Yisrael asked me, "What do you think about the need to listen to Arab policemen?" Red lights were lighting up all over my mind, yet I still wanted to fence—maybe because I wanted him to realize that talking wasn't going to break me, and as for physical abuse, I was sure they wouldn't try. "That's a strange question, Yisrael. What's the difference between an Arab and a Jewish policeman? They're both here to protect us, and we should have respect for policemen," I told him. "I even remember as a kid in the States, walking the beat with the policeman." "So therefore you wouldn't consider not listening to an Arab policeman, right?" "Of course not."

I felt that it was time to stop the fencing. He was closing in and trying to corner me more and more. I could see where he was leading to. "Yisrael," I said, "it's a Sunday morning, the first day of the week, and I have much to do in my village. I would like to help you in your research, so you're invited, once again, to arrange an evening or a Shabbat to come over. It's been nice talking to you." Then I stood up and started to walk toward the door. Once again, suddenly, Chief Investigator Elbaz gives out a real strong yell: "Where do you think you are going? Sit down, you're still being questioned; we'll tell you when to leave." I decided to put the cards on the table. "Yisrael," I said, "I don't understand. You told me that I'm not accused of anything and that you're doing research; therefore I answered you. Yet when I get up to leave, Elbaz tells me I'm being questioned. Now I know that you are playing a game. You're accusing me of something very, very serious. You are accusing me of being involved with the attack on the PLO mayors." Now it was Yisrael's turn to get upset. Before I could continue he asked sharply, "How do you know that?" "Elbaz told me," I answered quite calmly. Then he glared at Elbaz and yelled at him, "Who told you to tell him. What kind of investigator are you? You spoiled everything!"

"Spoiled or didn't spoil, that's your problem" I said. "You are accusing me of a very, very serious act. Actually of two serious acts, attempting to run over a policeman and the attack on the PLO mayors. Let me tell you explicitly that I have had nothing to do with either act, and I don't know who was involved. Furthermore, on principle, if I knew a Jew was involved I could give you no information at all. I wouldn't help you put Jews in jail for protecting themselves. You can now ask whatever you want. I will answer you that anything I have to say, I will tell only to a judge. If you want to lock me up, I'll sit in jail until my trial. If you have anything on me, lock me up. If not, I'll go home." And once again, I stretched out my two hands offering them to be handcuffed.

There was a few moments silence and then Elbaz asked questions. I answered to each one of them, "I'll tell whatever I want to the judge." This went on for about fifteen minutes. Then they told me that I was free to go, and that if needed they would be in touch. I was totally surprised. I'm sure I didn't succeed in hiding it. I forced myself not to ask Yisrael about his research project but stood up and left the room, bidding them both shalom.

Editor's note: Era was never questioned again until he returned to Israel of his own volition in December 1986 and admitted his involvement in the attack on Bassam Shaka.

February 1987
Tel Mond Prison

Dear Brothers,

Now that the case is over, much more is known about the Shin Bet's attempts to solve it. In fact, it turns out that the SB [Shin Bet] stopped at nothing in order to get results. Suspects' homes and telephones were tapped, and in some cases even the parents' phones were tapped. One of the members of the group was allowed to listen to a tape of himself talking about the plans while walking in his orchard! In another instance an SB agent, dressed as a soldier with his hand in a cast, hitched a ride with two members of the group. In his cast was a tape recorder! I had been aware of some unidentified cars parking on the main road leading to Shilo about a mile before the village. With my binoculars I was able to see them using sophisticated listening equipment. Now, it turned out, my fears were right. They were listening to our conversations. In fact, the former military commander of YOSH, Binyamin Eliezer, told us after our arrest that the "SB looked for us with candles for four years."

I can also tell you that my car was tailed over and over by the SB. As you know, Orit and I have many guests over for Shabbat. Some of them are people that we never met before. One day, I got a call from an acquaintance of mine—an Israeli from Tel Aviv who works for the government. He said he had to meet me soon, and since I sensed the urgency in his voice, I arranged to meet him the next day. What does he tell me? He has information that the SB suspects me and is planting a guest for Shabbat in the near future! I thanked him and told him that there is nothing to worry about because I had nothing to do with the attack and that if I had I wouldn't be talking about it.

In retrospect, I think it's pretty safe to say that if the guys who were with us hadn't participated in any other attacks, the SB may not have gotten on to us. I felt certain from the beginning that we would be found. However, now that the facts are in, my thoughts have changed a bit. The SB tried very hard to find us. It may be that they had very strong feelings about some of us, but there is a long road between feelings and legal proof.

Anyhow, all of this is hindsight. Here I am sitting in Tel Mond prison.

In response to another part of your letter, no, you don't have to worry about me. Yes, you are quite right, I do sound pretty good. Remember how in college I used to have ants in my pants? Here, in prison, there's no place to go. So for the first time in a long while I've reopened the books. I love you all.

Thank you for taking care of Ema.

Love,
Era

November 5, 1987
Tel Mond Prison

Dear Sam,

The accusation that our actions undermined the sovereignty of our government has been thrown at us here in Israel also. Even among the leaders of Gush Emunim, there are those who have condemned us strongly for that exact reason. I do not accept, almost at all, their point, and there are a few reasons why. In order to understand my point of view, it is important to review the situation in YOSH some seven years ago, the time preceding our attack.

The Likud government was officially for the development of Judea and the Shomron. That was their platform at the elections and to an extent their raison d'être. I believe I once wrote you that Menachem Begin stood up at Elon Moreh and declared, "There will be many Elon Morehs." However, in action they were very slow and to an extent quite negative. They needed much pushing. We were eager to settle the area, and one can say that we provided the momentum. There were times that we attempted to settle some areas, and the Likud government sent soldiers to remove us. Yet, behind the scenes in the Knesset, we were told by senior members of the same Likud party, "You guys are doing the right thing. We have pressure on us, especially from the U.S., which is telling us not to act. Therefore, it is important that you do so." Even certain members of the opposition Labor party told us that we are doing the right thing—contin-

179

uing the way of their founding fathers. Outwardly our actions could have been interpreted as challenging our government. In reality, we had their blessing and help in our actions. I'll give you a specific example. Publicly, government funds couldn't be given to us. Yet, in reality both the Labor and Likud parties transferred funds to us via the Ministry of Interior through another area council. Although we weren't pleased by the agreement, we played ball and so did the government. There was no undermining of the government. The opposite was true. We were strengthening our government, acting with their backing in areas where, for various reasons, they were unable to. Senior members of both parties met with us, encouraged us, and in many instances joined us in action. And, Sam, I'm not talking about some unimportant members of the Knesset; rather the top echelon: Yigal Allon, of blessed memory, was a major force in the backing of Kiryat Arba; Peres okayed Ofra; Rabin okayed Kedumim; Dr. Burg told us, "You are the NRP's vanguard/spear; keep up the good work." I heard that Moshe Arens himself collected money for the development of Hevron.

Nachon [naturally] there were differences of opinions, serious ones. Soldiers removing us from settlement sites was an ugly situation. However, there were tremendous political pressures on Israel from abroad, especially the U.S., and a certain amount of pressure in Israel. Our government needed our push from the right to counter the powerful left. These are the exact words of senior members of the government. I was there when they told us these things. You can tell those people who claim that our actions were a challenge of authority or disgrace to our government that it just isn't so. In almost all the attempts to establish settlements, we informed government and army officials of our plans in advance.

The security situation was the same in some ways yet quite the opposite in others. You wrote that people complained that we had taken the law into our own hands. I have two responses to that. One, that our actions in terms of security were comparable to our actions in establishing settlements—meaning that our government, for a variety of reasons, was not enforcing the law the way it should and can be done. Here again, much of that is due to American pressures and our hysterical left. The Likud, you should understand, Reb Sam, is not a strong party in terms of action. They're afraid of every shadow that moves. Menachem Begin and the Likud forfeited one of the greatest opportunities, if not the greatest, since the establishment of the State. When he came to power, the world, and the Arab world in particular, was waiting for strong moves. He was called the terrorist by major newspapers and weeklies the world over. And here in Aretz, the country was waiting for major changes.

However, Menachem Begin and the Likud were and are indecisive. They could have changed, within a year, the entire geopolitical map of Israel. New cities and villages in YOSH, annexation of the area, equal rights for Jews on the Temple Mount, expelling all PLO leaders and inciters, closing the PLO universities that we opened and financed. The Likud basically backed away from all of the above. Everything was done with the infamous statement, "What will the goyim say?" That's true of the security situation also. Do you really think it's difficult for my government to impose peace and order in YOSH? It was not difficult in 1979, and it's not so today. All it takes is a simple decision.

I'm writing this letter on a day when the world is yelling at us for putting down the "riots" in YOSH in too harsh a way. Do you know, to some extent, I agree with the complaint. Are we trying to put an end to the riots? Not really. If we wanted to, it could be done, quickly, effectively, and with a lot less bloodshed. How? I'll give you a five-step method. (1) Shut down all the PLO universities/seminars whose establishment we okayed and financed in YOSH. All the "professors" there are PLO members. It's not too hard to guess what they're teaching their "students." (2) Expel, immediately, all the PLO mayors and leaders. (3) Establish policy that any child caught throwing rocks or such will cause the immediate expulsion of him and his family from the country. (4) Stop all illegal Arab building—mostly financed by the PLO. And (5) close down PLO offices in Jerusalem. Yes, Sam, we have them. Amazing, considering the fact that we have asked your government to close the PLO offices in the States. I can go on, but the idea should be apparent by now. We are at war with the PLO, and yet, here in Israel, we don't act as if we are.

Today's government is split along political lines and therefore, maybe, one can understand the government's halfhearted response to the security problem. At the very minimum they should have stopped the PLO from throwing rocks, Molotov cocktails, and bombs. But, as I wrote, due to outside pressure, inner dissension in the ranks, and weakness, very little was done.

Concrete examples. I personally met with the Police Chief in Ramallah numerous times in 1979 and 1980 after our cars were stoned. His reaction? "I have very few policemen and all those on the beat are Arabs. Do you think they will prevent their own people from stoning Jewish cars?" I met with a local military commander in Ramallah. "Do you think it would be difficult for me to stop the attacks on you? Not in the least. However, there are orders from above not to do so. You guys know what to do, so take care of it."

So I approached the Military Commander of YOSH. I met with him a few times along with some other settlement leaders. His reaction: "There's no difficulty for the army to deal with the situation, but we have orders from above to take it easy." "Above?" we reacted. "Ezer," he responded.

We left the meeting, bewildered. The feeling among those present could be summed up in the following way: not only does the government want us to put up settlements for them, now they want us to be the defense department also.

Off we went to Ezer Weizman's office. I get disgusted at repeating his words, but it's important that you understand our frustration with the situation. What does he say to us? "You will not tell me how to deal with the security problems of YOSH; I am the expert. No one told you to go live where you are," and then pointing to me, "You people of Shilo. You have a problem with defense because you settled there. Deal with it yourselves."

Then we spoke to Zevulun Hammer, Minister of Education, who visited us at Shilo. "There are pressures from above, political ones. We can't do more than we are doing right now . . . you guys know now to deal with the situation. Do so yourselves."

"Raful," the Commander in Chief, told us, "if we were the British, we would have solved the problem long ago. Whenever rocks were thrown, they mowed down a row or two of houses with a bulldozer. They effectively prevented rock throwing. But we are not the British, and under the orders we have received, we are doing the best we can."

No, I'm sorry, Sam, I can't accept your constituents' complaints that our actions in 1979 and 1980 were a blow to the sovereignty of our government. Much the opposite. Our actions caused our government to react to the terror situations. PLO mayors were expelled along with inciters. Some of the "universities" were closed. There was quiet, and both the local Arabs and ourselves were able to live side by side and to develop our respective villages.

Sam, you write of the feeling that we are trampling on Israeli law. Once again, I can't accept your congregants' complaints. What law have we here? You'll probably be floored to know that there are some seven laws in this land, and the one with the fewest teeth is Israeli Law. We are governed by:

(a) international law, especially the Hague convention with reference to occupied territories,

(b) Jordanian law—for instance, officially a Jew can't own land in YOSH because Jordanian law forbids it! Only companies can.

(c) British law—many of the laws still in effect are holdovers from the British occupation of Israel, including YOSH. Especially problematic for us are their giving lands to the sheiks,

(d) Muslim religious law,

(e) Jewish religious law,

(f) Israeli Law, and

(g) Military law. Did you know that up until recently, by military law, we were allowed to remain in YOSH for a maximum of forty-eight hours, which was automatically renewed over and over?

A lawyer would have to be an incredible scholar to be knowledgeable in all of the above laws! One could also have a lot of fun with these laws. For instance, when we were first living in YOSH, if you were given a speeding ticket and wished to have a court appearance, it would take place in an Arab court under Jordanian (British) regulations. A Jew was asked to swear on the Koran that he was saying the truth!

So please ask your complainers which law are they referring to when they say we trample on the law. On a much more serious level, that is exactly what our complaint was in 1979 and 1980 and, to an extent, still is. Our government has not been enforcing the Israeli law here. Even more so, when it came to the PLO riots in those years, there was basically no Law being enforced. We were left in an impossible situation! There was virtually no law to trample!

I'm writing this letter almost one year since I entered prison and close to seven and a half years since our action against the PLO mayors. Do you think that the situation is radically different? Outwardly, it may seem so. True, 70,000 Jews are living in YOSH now, as opposed to 5,000 seven and a half years ago. YOSH is ours, and please God it will stay that way. On the other hand, we are still governed by seven different laws. That, indeed, is one of the major reasons that we still have, these very days, a lot of riots, rock throwing, etc. If my government doesn't act seriously and soon, Jews once again may be forced, God forbid, into protecting themselves.

Era

March 1988
Tel Mond Prison

Dear Big Brother:

You ought to have stock in the telephone company at the rate those transatlantic conversations are going. I told you that I'd write, so I'm keeping my word.

Yes, the situation has become a lot hotter in the last three months since the intifada [revolt] has started, but it is not an essential change. The PLO and others like them have not altered their goal—the destruction of the State of Israel. Passover is only one month away. One of the central themes of the holiday is, "In every generation, they rise up to destroy us." Forty years ago it was the Germans. Today it's the Arabs.

What has changed is the PLO method of attacking us. If we want to stop the terrorists, it's possible. Announce that anyone trying to overthrow the State of Israel will be thrown out of the country. That means a rock thrower, firebomber, blockade builder, he and his family. Why his family? Because the elders are hiding behind the youngsters. Close YOSH to the press, just like the U.S., in Grenada and England in the Falklands. Like every normal country in a state of war—which we are in. Immediately throw out the four hundred instigators whose names our Shin Bet possess. After all of these actions, let's see the situation.

If you think about it, Brother, there is such a ridiculous paradox in what is going on. I'm sitting in prison for acting against the terrorists who are presently turning our country upside down. The Arab terrorists, whose entire desire is to kill us, are walking around free! Only we Jews could do such a crazy thing.

Over the phone, you asked me if our lifestyle has changed since the intifada. Yes, it has. You expect, every time you travel, to be hit. Most of the time, it doesn't happen, but it's a daily event. There also has been a change in feelings. At the beginning, people, including the Arabs, expected everything to just blow over. When they realized that our government was not going to do much about their rioting, they escalated their attacks. Every day rocks, firebombs, stones, nails on the roads, roadblocks, all staged for the Western media, which of course leaped at the chance to portray the Jews as the ruthless oppressors.

They have chutzpah. No other country in the world would react with the restraint that we have shown. In comparison, at Kent State University, what happened? Was there any kind of real fear that the U.S. government would be overthrown? Of course not. Yet the National Guard fired to kill. What happened two years ago in Philadelphia? Some twenty terrorists in a house "threatening to overthrow the U.S. government." Don't mind my sarcasm. What happened there? The police bombed the neighborhood, I remember police arrests and roundups in East Flatbush and East New York. The suspects were belted around brutally. The PLO terrorists involved in the intifada are intent in destroying us. We are required to stop them.

You probably heard about the American Oleh, Meshulam Moskowitz, who was almost stoned to death by PLO terrorists. He was passing through the Arab village on the way to Ofra, and he was stoned. He couldn't bring himself to shoot at his would-be murderers (he was also afraid of being put into prison!). So he fired into the air. When they realized that he had no intention of really protecting himself, they charged and started hitting him with huge stones until he was knocked unconscious. By the way, his father was a student of Abba. Meshulam is a karate expert, but he is new in Israel and doesn't yet understand the mentality of our "neighbors." He should have fired directly. This is war.

Yesterday, Dr. Sam Korman's daughter, Jodi, was traveling from Jerusalem to their home in Ma'aleh Adumim. Their car was stoned and their eighteen-month-old baby was hit on his head and passed out. Thank God, he wasn't seriously hurt.

You know Brother, if we hadn't acted almost eight years ago in the manner that we did, the Arabs would have done the same then. Our actions stopped the killings and gave 70,000 Jews an opportunity to move into YOSH.

By the way, I was home for three days during Purim. For the Purim meal, we traveled to Ofra to eat with the Etzions. With us were three "refusniks"—new arrivals from Russia. A couple who were refusniks for eight years, and now they are eight months in Israel. The other was a single fellow, a refusnik for seven years and in Israel for three months. They are the real heroes of our people. What inner strength! When I look at them and hear their stories, I am filled with tremendous pride. What an ingathering of exiles we were. The three Russians, three Israelis, two Americans, and one Ethiopian—besides our eleven kids! all of us sitting around a table in Ofra, celebrating the miracle that God performed: saving our grandparents, generations ago, from total destruction. Here we were, the ingathering of the Diaspora, living in the cities that our grandparents built generations ago, and still the same old song was being played outside. Our enemies trying to destroy us.

Before leaving for Ofra, I gave one of the Russian Olim a gun and asked him if he was against using it if necessary. You should have seen his reaction. He was insulted by my question. He said, "I don't understand your question." When I repeated it in slower Hebrew, he said, "No, no, I understand the words of your question—but not the question!!" So off we went: three new Russian Olim, Orit, the kids, and myself to Ofra. We traveled via Mazraat, the same village where Orit was almost killed. If you're asking yourself why I went that way, I'll answer you in a moment; but first let me tell you what happened. The road to Mazraat winds steeply up the mountainside with a cliff on one side and a deep valley on the other. If a rock is thrown into your car and you lose control, you'll be in the other world. As we are winding up the road, I see two Arab terrorists standing on the cliff. Immediately, one unleashes a rock right toward our van. The rock missed, and I slammed on the brakes. Before I came to a stop, the Russians were out. I jumped out as the Arabs prepared to throw again. We yelled a warning, one shot was fired, and they ran away.

We had made a decision before leaving Shilo that if we were attacked, we would immediately react to prevent the terrorists from continuing to attack us. The strategy proved successful. If those rocks, and they are big, had gone through the windshield, you would have been saying the Memorial service over us—the drop to the valley floor is some 300 feet, straight down.

It seems to me that the newspapers are purposely not emphasizing that the Arabs are out to kill us. Their weapons are as deadly as ours. Your press presents it as a David and Goliath reversed. We are Goliath with modern arms and army, and the Arabs are David with slingshot and pebbles. What a lot of garbage! The roads that we drive are twisting and winding. Around every bend a terrorist with a Molotov cocktail or large stone can be waiting. They hide behind trees and boulders and wait until they see the "whites of our eyes." There is no way to know where and when they'll appear.

If the situation sounds like the Wild Wild West, then, to an extent, it is. Yes, it's more dangerous than before to ride the roads. It is a difficult period. For me, also, it is a frustrating time—for many reasons. I acted against the same terrorist organization that is presently terrorizing a good part of our country and people. Yet I am sitting in prison, and they are free to continue their terrorist activities. Second, Orit and the children travel the roads often, and I can't even be out there to protect them if something happens. I have taught myself to expect that terrible message one day: "Your wife and/or children have been seriously hurt." Does that thought scare me? It sure does. It, however, strengthens my convictions about living here. What's the solution? I can only answer that we have to be strong. The Arabs simply don't want peace. What about the peace treaty with Egypt? you ask. It's a sham. The moment they rebuild their shattered economy, they'll be the first to attack.

I can only begin to imagine the difficult time that you people are going through: being bombarded by the terrible press, hearing such frightening reports of the situation here and seeing it all on TV. You are where it is really hard to be. I know that I have written this to you before, but I'll repeat it again. Being in Israel during these years has been an amazing experience, both difficult and happy. Above all is the fact and the feeling that we are continuing in the ways of our people. There is a weight on our shoulders— a weight of generations. It is as if the millions of Jews from all the thousands of years of our wandering are all standing around us watching, waiting to see our actions. I'm not imagining it, my Brother. I feel it. I can feel our uncles and aunts, Mordecai Shimon and Yehudit, and our grandparents and parents standing and looking over my shoulder, watching me. I hear Yehudit telling me today, as she told me ten years ago, "If I were younger, I would come with you to your work camp in Ofra."

I can also hear Mordecai Shimon telling me, "Era, remember to put things into perspective. The difficulties now are tiny compared to the wars of 1945–48, '56, '67, and '73. The question is, Are you willing to stand up to the challenge? Millions of Jews have given their lives for the dream you are living today. Which Jew didn't say, time and time again, Next year in Jerusalem? Now your time has come. What are you going to do? Are you going to give away what all those generations of Jews prayed for?

Well, you should have seen the kids on Purim. Orit is an expert on dressing up the kids with all sorts of clothes that we have. Moriyah was a cleaning lady; David a soldier; Atarah a princess; Yitzhak a cowboy; Tsofiyah a dancer. Yitzhak didn't want to remove his outfit for days. David came down to Netanya the day before Purim. We had a great time together. We went to a small amusement park, and David took a ride on a machine that turns you upside down. Then we went to the beach. Yes, in the middle of March, and we began to build a sand castle. I haven't done that in so many years. He kept on telling me how good it was to be with me and how good a father I was. I told him that it was fantastic being with him, and indeed it was. It has been years since I spent a day alone with one of the kids. I promised myself, as I have done over and over since my imprisonment, that when I'm released, I'll spend more and more time with them.

While reading over this letter, I realized that I didn't write you why we took the road to Ofra via Mazraat. Yes, we could have traveled via the main road, where the chances of being attacked are slimmer. But if I stop traveling a certain road, then tomorrow, I'll stop traveling another, and in a few weeks, I'll be limiting myself to half of my country. A country is yours not because you say it is but because you live in and develop it. You feel this country when you walk, ride, build, and plant. When you feel a part of this country of ours, you can't leave it. There is no other road.

Love ya,
Era
P.S. Come soon.

4 Native Son

Dear Heshy,

Thirteen days! Thirteen days out of a lifetime. For most people thirteen days go by and have no real effect. For me, they were thirteen of extreme importance. They were the days between the 13th of Nissan and the 26th of Nissan 5744. One year earlier, in April 1983, we had been approached by the leaders of Gush Emunim and the Settlement Movement. After long discussions, Gush Emunim decided that the time had come to reach out to the Jewish community in the Diaspora, especially the U.S., with the message—the time had come for Jews to return home to Israel. Gush Emunim was searching for the proper staff to try and influence the American Jewish community.

The leaders of Gush Emunim thought that we would be excellent "messengers." I, American born and bred, understood the American Jewish scene. Orit, who had visited the States with me some five times, was fluent in English. We hesitated a lot before making our decision. Orit pushed for us to go—not that she wanted to leave Aretz; rather, she felt a responsibility. "Israel has given us so much, and God has been so good to us, we have to help others. We'll go only for a short time to give the starting push."

I wasn't interested in going. I didn't come to Israel in order to become a shaliach [emissary] overseas. On top of that, I didn't believe that we or anybody could influence great numbers of American Jews to come on Aliyah. Our history shows that I'm right. Who was our greatest leader? Moshe. How many Jews followed him out of Egypt? According to Rashi, four-fifths stayed behind.

Ezra and Nechemiah, weren't they top-notch shlichim [emissaries]? Yet only some 30,000 out of nearly 2,000,000 in Babylon followed them back to Israel. Wasn't Herzl charismatic? How many came and answered his call? And how many leaders of the Jewish communities in the States came here hoping that their flocks would follow? Rabbis Dolgin, Riskin, Hartman, to mention a few—their flocks are still grazing in the green grass of America. So, if none of them had a major effect, why should we, I asked Orit.

My wife thought for a few moments and then said "First, we are going as a group, not as one, and there is more chance of getting something moving. Second, I've seen the strong response that Israelis evoke in synagogues when they speak. This time, if it's done in an organized manner, I think we can have an influence." Orit knew, and knows, how to influence me. She was chipping away at my refusal.

My decision to go, however, stemmed from a totally different reason. One that I've written to you about and one that I discussed with you in person: honoring thy father and mother. Since Abba was run over and killed by an automobile in November 1982, Ema has gone through very difficult times. We suggested that she come here to be with us, but so far Ema wants to be with people and culture that she knows. Coming as part of the delegation, we would be able to be around Ema. So, in the beginning of September 1983, the Rapaports arrived in the "Big Apple."

Before leaving, I informed the leadership of Gush Emunim that we agreed to go for six months and no longer. Halfway through, I realized that we would stay until the summer months, three to four months more than originally planned. It would be impossible to find anyone to take over for me during the school year. So in early April 1984, I flew back to Aretz to look for shlichim to take our place in the U.S. in the fall. I was there for ten days and returned two days before Pesach.

As usual, Orit was super. We had rented a house for six months and would have to leave and move before Passover. On top of it all, I was to be in Israel! I don't know how Orit succeeded in getting everything done, but she did, and so when I returned just before Passover everything was ready.

I could not have known how monumental the decision to go before Pesach was until thirteen days after. It was Friday morning and among the headlines on the New York news: Israeli police and security forces have arrested some ten residents of settlements in YOSH. They are suspected of planting bombs under Arab buses as a warning to Arab terrorists. Right after morning services at the Young Israel, two of the congregants turned to me: "What do you think about their actions?" "I don't believe it was Jews who did it. You'll see, within two or three days the whole incident will look different," I responded. I was being sincere. I had heard nothing about it.

The next days some names of the arrested were leaked to the press. Shaul and Barak Nir, Uzi Sharabaf, and Boaz Heineman. The only name familiar to me was Heineman, and both Orit and I were surprised. "You'll see," I told Orit, "in the end it will turn out that no Jews were involved."

Saturday night, the news was full of the arrests in Israel. Now names of people that I was familiar with were mentioned. "Akelah"—one of the leaders of the resettlement of YOSH, a powerhouse of a person. He worked with underprivileged youth and had adopted some others into his family, was one of Bnei Akiva's best schlichim in Israel, and a founder of Ramat Magshimim [a settlement on the Golan Heights]. Yeshua Ben Shushan was one of the elite in the elite of our army—the parachute scouts. In the 1973 Yom Kippur War he had killed and injured tens of Egyptians as he single-handedly blew up an enemy bunker at the Suez Canal. He himself was seriously injured in the action and to this very day suffers immensely. Menachem Livni was one of the main personalities in the redevelopment of Kiryat Arba/Hevron, and Shaul Nir, one of the foreign news reports informed us, was an underwater commando in the Israeli Navy.

The next morning, Sunday, when I returned home from your shul, Orit told me that we had received a phone call from her father. Her brother, Yehuda, had been arrested. Truthfully, I became nervous. Did the Shin Bet have a lead onto our attack, or were they arresting people stam [just] to see if they could get information from them? Meanwhile no one else from my group had been mentioned or arrested. If Yehuda kept quiet and I was sure that he was able to, I was still in the clear. But I was nervous. I listened for updates on the news all day long and called Orit many times to find out if she had heard from Israel.

Sunday, Monday, and Tuesday went by without much information for me. The arrests in Israel continued to make headlines. I was amazed. It seems that only what happens in Israel stays on the front pages for more than a day. You know—we are the size of the state of New Jersey and yet, after the U.S. and USSR, there are more foreign press in Jerusalem than anywhere in the world!

I had many meetings during the next few days. At almost every one of them, the question was asked over and over, "What's going on? Do you know them? Blowing up buses? Lucky you weren't there now, otherwise you'd be involved also." I tried to be calm, but I knew that I wasn't successful. What I didn't understand was, how were the people around me so blind and not able to see my anxiety?

Wednesday morning I awoke to the news that more arrests had been made in Israel. Among those arrested—Moshe Zar. A double red light lit up before my eyes. Moshe Zar was our driver. There was no doubt any longer. The Shin Bet had broken everybody. Yet, I said to myself, something is incomplete. Natan Natanson hasn't been arrested. So it's possible that they arrested Zar but didn't break him, and in actuality, only he and Natan knew for sure that I was part of the team. I said to myself, "Moshe is strong—he won't break."

The morning after the beginning of the arrest—Sunday morning—my brother Yosef had called me. "There are some reports on the radio about arrests in Israel that should bother Rivka's son," he said. Yosef had been giving me a signal. Rivka was our mother's third name—almost no one knew it. Two months after our attack on the mayors, my family and I were visiting the States. While walking down a noisy street with my two brothers, I had told them of my involvement. I wasn't one hundred percent sure they would be supportive of the act or not. One thing I did know—they would back me. Abba and Ema had taught us that family always should remain close, and you always have to help each other. Abba and Ema had drilled that into each of us.

When I came to pick up my mother that evening, Yosef had me promise him that I would make no move to return to Israel without discussing it with him. Then he told me that he was very proud of the act that I had done. We also decided not to tell anything to Ema about my involvement. There was no need or reason—yet—to get her worried.

Wednesday afternoon I told Orit that I wasn't sure I could go ahead with the coming Shabbat plans. Our family was to be guests at a large synagogue in Brooklyn to talk about Aliyah. If my name was mentioned just before Shabbat on the radio, my appearance there would be a disaster for the cause. Orit agreed with me. Only time would tell us how wrong we were in our decision. During the three years we stayed in the States, the overwhelming majority of rabbis, synagogues, and communal leaders received us with open arms and thanked us for acting against Bassam Shaka.

Late Saturday night, somewhere after midnight, the phone rang. I immediately told Orit—it's from Aretz. Orit's father was on the phone. He informed us that soon after Shabbat ended, Natanson and Shlomo Levyatan were arrested. I was taken aback. I had expected Natan's arrest, but Shlomo Levyatan? He had such a very small part. He was to have passed on information to someone; that's it. But even more shocking was that only Natan, Yehuda, and myself knew of his participation. The Shin Bet must have been able to break either one of them. You see, if, for instance, I had to "show" to the Shin Bet that I was giving full information about my attack on Bassam Shaka, I could have done so by mentioning Yehuda Etzion, Natan, Moshe Zar, and myself. If Shlomo's name was mentioned, then everything had totally broken down.

"Do you know if anybody else's name was mentioned," I asked my father-in-law. "No, but it's obviously not important; they know everything. When are you returning?" I was taken back by the question. "Well, you know Gush Emunim wants us to stay until the end of the school year. Has anything happened that we should shorten our stay here?" It was my father-in-law who was surprised this time. "Well, maybe because of all the arrests here. It's still too early to see if they will have any effect on our activities here. We'll wait and see."

We may as well start packing, I told Orit when her father got off the phone. She nodded. We spent part of Sunday packing. That evening, on the way to pick up Ema, I spent some time with my friend Avi and told him of my involvement. "I'm coming to you as a man to his rabbi. Therefore, you are bound by the laws of confidentiality," I opened. Avi was hurt! "Everything you say is confidential to me." "I know, my friend, but as soon as I tell you, you'll understand why I'm emphasizing it." I then told him that I had crippled Bassam Shaka. When I finished, Avi looked at me and said, "You've taken part in a big mitzvah." Avi was of the opinion that I should return to Israel and be part of the trial.

When I reached my brother's house in New Jersey, he insisted that we talk in the streets. "I don't know if the Shin Bet has asked the FBI to look for you, but I'm not taking any chances. In the street, it's much harder to tape our conversation." I didn't argue with Yosef. After updating him I told him that we were planning to go back. "The decision is obviously yours, but hear me out first. You've told me that the Shin Bet in Israel are Zionistic, close to you, etc. That may all be very true, but let me tell you—above all they are professionals. They are taught to be professionals. They would do anything to get their man. Why do you intend to make it easier for them? You're here. They have to find you here and extradite you. That's not easy. You can make a deal for better conditions. They are not friends of yours; they are out to do a job. You can go back in another week or two. First check out the situation with a lawyer. Why hand yourself over on a silver platter? Right now, they want you in their hands—to close the case. Era, the FBI, CIA, Shin Bet—all of the security forces in the world are basically animals of their professions. They have to be; otherwise they would not succeed. I'm not telling you not to go back—but check out the possibility and see if you can make a half-decent deal. You know what? If you're important enough to them, maybe they'll lower the charges on the other guys in return for your coming back."

Tuesday night the phone call came. "Orit, my code name is David, and I'm calling from the jail in M'grash Harusim. Sitting with me are your brother Yehuda and Natan. We know everything that Era did. We think the best move you can make is to come back right now. Staying away is not going to make the situation any better. When will Era be home so we can talk to him? So you know that I'm telling the truth, speak to your brother and Natan." Yehuda and Natan both got on the phone. "They know everything. The relationship here is quite good; they're friends of ours. It's probably best if you come home." David got back on the line and Orit said, "Call back in another two days, and we'll give you an answer."

The conversation from the jail strengthened our resolve to go back. The next day, I believe, the news broke in the States that I was also involved. It was also that day that one my friends in Staten Island became involved in the case: "What do you mean go back? First of all, I want you to promise me that you'll see a lawyer, and I'm sending you to one right now." I was not able to know that the conversation with him would be the first rung in a ladder of steps that were to keep me in the U.S. for three years.

"You have no right to go back immediately," the lawyer said. There are many legal matters involved here. I'm not sure that you can be so easily extradited. And if you can't be easily extradited, then in return for yourself, you can request a shorter sentence, etc. Maybe you can get better terms for the entire group. Besides, you are not allowed, I believe, to be extradited for a political action. It would be interesting to have the Israeli government ask for your extradition. Then you could answer in court that it was a political act. If our courts accept it, it may have a very powerful influence on your court. Maybe the U.S. would have to recognize Israel's control of Judea and Samaria before they could return you to Israel."

I explained to Orit what he said. My friend, who sent me to the lawyer, agreed with his evaluation: "We could use your court case here to get across the importance of YOSH to the American public." Saturday night I traveled with my brother and Avi to meet with one of America's "super lawyers," a prominent New York attorney. One of the members of his firm, Mark, was also a member of Avi's synagogue. He was adamant in his resolve that we stay in the States to see what develops. "Meanwhile I recommend that you and the family go on vacation for a while. That way the press or extremist Arabs here won't get to you. If you return to Israel, whatever we could have done from here will have no strength. Wait awhile and see. Who knows, maybe this can develop into a major case, in a positive way, for Israel's claim to YOSH." The influence of the lawyers was having its effect.

I was coming to the decision that our return to Israel to be part of the court case could be delayed so we could see if indeed we could have a positive influence from being in the States. Orit wasn't at all satisfied with my changing thoughts. She, however, told me, "*You* have to sit in jail; *you'll* decide when to go back." It was a thought and a statement that Orit repeated many a time in the three years that we stayed in the States. She wanted very much for us to return but wanted the decision to be mine.

Meanwhile, one of our "friends" from the Shin Bet decided to call back to find out when we were returning. When Orit's answer wasn't to his liking, he sent us a veiled threat: "You know we can easily request his extradition, and that won't be very pleasant for you." Orit answered him, "I suggest that you speak to our lawyer in Israel," and with that she ended the conversation.

It was time to tell Ema. I knew it wouldn't be easy telling her, yet there was, at this point, no choice. "Ema," I said, "those white hairs on your head, many of them are from worry. Well, you're about to have some more." Then I told her. She was against what I did. That I expected. Ema was brought up in a certain generation. To rebel, to act against or not with the authorities, was strange to her.

The phone calls to my mother's apartment, to our kids' school, and to the offices where I worked started coming in the next day. Barry Slotnick was right. If we wanted some quiet, and for the kids' safety, it was imperative that we go on vacation.

Once again, two of the many friends of ours in the States offered us the use of their summer homes outside New York. "Here's our car. I'm paying for your gas—go travel," one told us.

Toward the end of the week, we took the kids out of school and began our travels. One or two weeks, at the most, we told my mom. Indeed, we expected to return to Aretz right after.

Things wouldn't be so simple.

In the shock of the wave of arrests, Orit and I hadn't had the opportunity to evaluate the situation in Israel. I didn't understand the relationship between our attack on the PLO mayors and the attempted attack on the buses, their arrests and ours. A special-delivery letter sent to us by my father-in-law made things a lot more understandable.

There really was no connection, save for the fact that Menachem Livni, who was involved in the attack on the mayors, was also involved in the bus attack. Yet the SB [Shin Bet] was "using" the situation. They arrested some twenty-seven people, called us the "Jewish Underground," as if we had acted together, and presented the public with a very grave situation. It turned out that the SB knew for a long time the identity of many of us who were involved in the attack on the PLO mayors. Yet they also realized that the public, who for the most part were for our action, would not allow us to be "hung." The "attack" on the buses gave them the angle they needed. Menachem Livni, Shaul and Barak Nir, and Uzi Sharabaf were charged with planting bombs under some Arab buses. Women and children could have been hurt. The public would be angry and would not object to a "hanging." The SB planned things perfectly. They followed Barak, Shaul, and Uzi the night they planted the bombs and arrested them on the spot. If, indeed, they were only interested in stopping the attack, there was no need to allow them to plant the bombs. It was obvious from the newspaper clippings that my father-in-law sent that they were after a different result. "National disaster prevented," "Lives of hundreds of children saved," read another. "SB prevents one of the worst mass murders in our history." They had shifted public opinion behind them.

My father-in-law included one other important fact. Just a short while before, the SB got into trouble when two PLO terrorists were taken alive off the bus they had hijacked and were later found dead. By their "discovery" of the "Jewish Underground," they were getting the press off their backs. They decided to arrest all those who were involved with the attack on the PLO mayors, along with those who they arrested for the bus "attack," and others for supposedly plotting to blow up the Temple Mount mosque; and created the "Jewish Underground," when in truth many of us never had met in our lives.

My father-in-law's letter continued with his dissection of the situation and his strong recommendation that we return to be part of the trial. He didn't see any positive reason for us staying in the States. Her father's letter didn't improve my wife's unhappiness about our decision to remain awhile. "You don't have to be upset," I told her. "We're going back in two weeks."

The SB would not have to come looking for me. Neither, in actuality, could I make a good deal for my return, for I had one major factor going against me: I was going back no matter what. The security services knew this—not by tapping my telephone, by simply asking anyone who knew me.

Era

July 1987
Tel Mond Prison

Dear Cousin,

We had decided not to tell the kids of my involvement in the actions against the PLO mayors until a week or so before our scheduled departure. If we were forced to go on "vacation," then let us enjoy it. My friend's ranch was a superb place. In a small town outside New York City on the banks of a lake, he had inflatable boats, games, quiet—in short, everything to help make an enjoyable vacation. Except it was hard for us, if not impossible, to enjoy. Our thoughts were 6,000 miles away. Orit's brother was behind bars; so was her cousin. Their families and twenty-five others were suffering. How could we enjoy?

I especially was quite nervous, although I tried to hide it. I was sure that at some time and place, the police would try to find us. I taught myself to be supercareful. Phone calls to my brothers were made from a pay phone to a pay phone. I would call them at work, and they would give me a code number. After deciphering the code I would call the number, and then we could talk somewhat freely. I would teach myself to keep an eye on the cars behind us to see if we were being trailed. That truly was a super-precaution and not necessary. I was more concerned with the press than with the police. If the police wanted to arrest me, it would be easy for them to do so.

I wasn't hiding out, and I wasn't intending to stay away from Israel. The press is another story. They were trying to reach me. When they didn't succeed in doing so directly, they began to phone my mother, brothers, and friends. TV shows, radio, feature articles—all promised to me to give me the opportunity to express our side of the actions. Many offered very fine sums of money for my trouble. It was not easy to say no to the offers— mostly because we wanted the world to know the reasons for our actions. The guys in jail were prevented by the laws of sub-judaica [interference with a court case] from talking to the press. We, however, could talk. Our lawyer warned us over and over to stay clear of the press.

We were having the opportunity to be together as a family. Never before did that happen. Orit and I were always too busy with our work in Eretz

Yisrael in one way or another. To go away, even for two days, with the kids, that didn't happen. Suddenly, we were all together.

Toward the end of the two weeks, we received another phone call from my father-in-law. The lawyer representing us in Aretz suggested that we wait a little while longer. When things "quieted down," he wanted to suggest a deal to the prosecution for my return. The deal might include better conditions for me and for the entire group. But nothing could be done until official charges were pressed. In how long? Approximately one or two months. My father-in-law was pessimistic. He didn't believe that the prosecution would be dealing for anything.

A friend told us to continue using his car as long as we needed to. When I tried to thank him, he would yell at me: "Thank me? What have I done? Nothing! You did what I should have done."

The newspaper articles on a member of the Jewish Underground being in the States had a very interesting effect—one, I admit, that I didn't expect. My mother and brother began receiving phone calls from Jews all across the States offering help, money, and a place for us to stay. Some of them were people we knew. Some we didn't. One was a long-time acquaintance of mine, with whom I had studied at Yeshiva University, now a successful doctor in Cleveland. "We have a basement for you. Come for as long as you want."

"You know, Orit, I have an idea. If we have to be here for a month and a half, let's travel West."

Thus we were off on what was to be one of the most memorable trips of our lives. Describing it would take pages and pages, so I'll just emphasize a few of the highlights. We traveled from New York to Niagara Falls, Cleveland, and St. Louis. From St. Louis on, we camped out except for Shabbatot, which were spent with people all across America. Denver, Rocky Mountain National Park, Zion and Bryce and the Grand Canyon, Las Vegas and Los Angeles. In Los Angeles, we met with some of the important rabbis of the "West Bank" (the West Bank of the Mississippi). We tried and were somewhat successful in enlisting their help to counterpressure our government to consider the intolerable security situation which led to our actions.

While staying with the Mauers in Los Angeles, we received a copy from my brother of the "confessions" given by the guys. The driver of the car testified that he had driven me and another person whose name he didn't know to Shechem, waited for us near Bassam Shaka's house, and drove us back to Shilo.

It's interesting. I guess you would expect yourself to be upset, even angry, at a person who because of his talking you were liable to spend years of your life behind bars. Over the phone, my father-in-law had hinted to me that the confession would hurt me, and I told Orit that among the many requests that I have of God is that He give me the inner strength to continue respecting, in the way I have until now, the person or persons whose testimony is liable to put me behind bars for many years. There were many reasons for that request. Among them a statement of the rabbis: "Don't judge your friend until you stand in his place." I don't know what kind of difficult times my partners went through before they confessed. And, on a deeper level, we did something for the security of our people. If we have to sit behind bars for that action, we knew from the beginning that we could end up in prison.

The trip, for us, was one of the best times that we have ever had. Since we were camping out every night, save for Shabbat, everyone had his/her job to do, and it required everyone to help one another. The long hours in the car were a lesson in confined-space interaction. Above all were the conversations that we had with each other about so many different topics. And Orit and I had time to strengthen and deepen our own relationship. If one had to go to prison, Orit and I often laughed, this is the way to get prepared.

Almost immediately we told the kids about Yehuda's involvement, what he did and what's happening to him and the others in Israel. Moriyah and David especially were very involved and constantly asked for more information. One of the mornings, the conversation was really special, and Orit and I taped it for the future.

Moriyah: "I don't understand Ema, if what Yehuda and his friends did was correct why are they sitting in jail?"

Orit: "I know it's hard for you to understand. It's also hard for us to understand."

204

Moriyah: "Yehuda and his friends hurt some very bad Arabs, right? Those Arabs, you told us, killed Jews in Hevron, so why should they sit in jail?"

Orit: "Sometimes the government doesn't agree that it is the right thing, and sometimes even if it is the right thing, the government has pressures on it not to do the right thing."

Moriyah: "You mean that maybe the government doesn't agree that what Yehuda and his friends did was right. Isn't saving Jewish lives a mitzvah, and isn't Israel a Jewish country? It's not like here in America where there are just a few Jews and a lot of non-Jews. In Israel there are mostly Jews."

Orit: "You see, the government is made up of different people with somewhat different ideas. Some of them think what those PLO Arab mayors did was very bad; some of them think that it wasn't so bad."

Moriyah: "Wasn't so bad? Killing yeshiva students is not bad! Ema, that's wrong!"

It was a beautiful conversation and maybe a good opportunity to let the kids know that I was involved. But, on the other hand we had another one and a half months to go before returning—or seemingly so. Why spoil their "vacation"?

Era: "Well, because the government of Israel didn't do what they should have done, some Jews stood up and did it by themselves."

Orit: "But listen to us. What Abba has said is not easy. Going against our own government—a Jewish government—is a very serious action. There are many rabbis who think that it's forbidden to go against our government even if they do things wrong."

Moriyah: "But once before I remember that we went against the government."

Era: "When?"

Moriyah: "In Yamit."

Orit and I exchanged quick glances. I was floored at the statement and wanted to see how much they remembered of our efforts to stop the withdrawal from Sinai.

David: "I know why we went to Yamit!"

Era: "Why?"

David: "Because our government wanted to give it away to the Arabs—the Egyptians. And that's part of Eretz Yisrael, and it was forbidden for them to give it away. So we went there to try and stop our government."

Moriyah: "We were with some families from Ofra, also among them the brother of our Rav from Shilo, Rav Yoel Bin-Nun. And he told us before the soldiers came to take us away that we are not allowed to touch a soldier, because they are holy and because our government has sent them. We were in Talmei Yosef to protest against the government's actions but not to touch a soldier."

David: "And I remember that Abba and Ema went up to the roof of our house in Yamit and the soldiers came to take us down. When they brought the ladder, you lowered us down to them."

I was extremely surprised at their memory of those very difficult days at Yamit and the villages in the area. The kids remembered almost everything.

Moriyah: "And when finally we all left the village and the bulldozers started destroying the city, Rav Bin-Nun and everybody tore their shirts as a sign of mourning because a village in Eretz Yisrael had been destroyed. Then all of us who had cars traveled with our lights on, on the way out of the area."

David: "In Yamit, Abba, no one was arrested when we went against the leaders of the people, so why now were people arrested?"

Era: "David, Moriyah, you've asked a very, very good question. Let me try and explain. Most of the time, it's forbidden to go against what our government says. But there are situations when our government is doing something so wrong that maybe it's a mitzvah to protest and to try and prevent their actions. The "when" is a very difficult question and should only be done when rabbis are asked, because the rabbanim are understanding of the holiness of the government and also of Eretz Yisrael. Therefore, they can recommend, or better, they can tell us when we are allowed to go against the government. Yamit was, indeed, a very special situation. The government wanted to give away land that is part of Eretz Yisrael. That's a very big sin, which is forbidden. Many rabbis told us that we can go and that we should go to Yamit to protest. But they also warned us not to touch a soldier because that is forbidden. So when important rabbis advised us to go to Yamit and even they themselves were there, we had to go. There are times that the government makes big mistakes. We have to be on guard so that they don't make mistakes."

Moriyah: "If so many Jews didn't want Yamit to be given away, how come the government did so anyhow?"

Orit: "You see, many times the government will do what they think the people of the country want. Had 20,000 or so Jews gone down to Yamit and if another 200,000 to 400,000 protested in Yerushalayim, then the government would have understood that the people of Israel didn't want to give away parts of Eretz Yisrael. But only some 5,000 Jews were in Yamit, and there were no major demonstrations, so the government understood that the people didn't mind."

David: "But, Ema, Abba, why don't more Jews care about Eretz Yisrael?"

Orit: "Oy, David shelanu [our David] have you asked a question! Where have we lived this past year—in the U.S. Do you know that there are more Jews living in America than there are in Israel, and they're here, staying here, and not coming to Israel? Maybe they do care about Israel but not enough to really do something about it, like coming to live in Aretz. It's probably that a good part of the people are nonbelievers who don't believe enough in God, who commanded us to live in Aretz. Also, for many of the Jews in the U.S., the life is easier than in Aretz, and it's hard for them to leave an easy life."

The U.S. is a country that is breathtakingly beautiful—yes, from sea to shining sea. You don't know which way to turn to grasp the exquisite beauty of this country. It stuns you, some of the places. Many of them have no words to describe them. Bryce Canyon. When we arrived there, I warned Orit that she will see one of the amazing sights in the world. What was Orit's reaction? Tears came down her eyes upon seeing the place. Being next to nature makes one learn to relax, to appreciate, to be close to one another.

Sometimes I just wish that all our problems in Aretz would pick up and go away. I just want to live a quiet normal life. I don't want to go on fighting all my life. I don't want my kids to fight. I want to be able to travel the width and breadth of Israel as we travel the U.S. and not to have to worry about PLO terrorists attacking us. I don't want to go every year to the army. Leave me alone, let me be a normal person. I and Israel are not supermen, yet we are doing a superhuman job. I don't want to go on fighting my neighbors for a piece of land. Just a few short years ago, I never would have imagined myself being in the forefront of the battle for Eretz Yisrael. That's not for us to do, that's for others—greater, much greater than us. We are just simple run-of-the-mill Jews. I'm not a hero and I don't want to be a fighter."

I see the kids, and I think, What about them? Will they have to fight throughout their lives? I want to be able to go back to Aretz and ride a bicycle with them through the mountains of Shilo without a pistol at my side. I don't want to worry that their school bus will be attacked by PLO terrorists.

You know, the American Jew has it so easy. He stays here, raises his family in the most modern society in the world, sends me a few dollars which makes him feel good and does his thing here. He has none of the day-to-day real-life problems that we face. Yet I know that all that I hope for is a dream. It's not reality. For back home our neighbors will keep on fighting us for they have one dream: to drive us into the sea. And we also have no choice, or maybe we've made our choice. We will build and live in Eretz Yisrael. God will hear our prayers. "He who makes peace in the heavens, He will make peace on us and all of Israel."

And so we traveled to Seattle where we stayed close to a week, and we headed east to Glacier National Park. We planned to spend Shabbat at a motel near the park. We were scheduled to return to New York within a week and a half, for we decided that we would return in any situation. We saw nothing to be gained by being away from Aretz, even if returning there meant my going to prison.

It was while we were all together in the motel at Glacier National Park that we decided to tell the kids of my involvement. After sitting them down, I began, "You know the attack on the PLO Arabs that Yehuda is involved with. I want you to know that I am also involved with it. When we go back to Eretz Yisrael, most probably I'll have to sit in jail for many years, and you will have to do without me for many years."

"Abba, what did you do to the bad Arabs?" Moriyah was the first to react. "Well, I don't want to tell you exactly what I did, but I hurt one of the very bad Arabs." "But if he was very bad, why should you have to sit in jail, Abba?" Moriyah immediately questioned. David was sitting on his bed extremely quiet, and then I could see the tears coming down his cheeks. I moved over to him and put his head in my arms and I kissed him time and time again. Then Moriyah started crying. Orit held her tight. "Abba, I don't want to go back, and you'll be separated from us, let's stay here," David finally said with much pain. Moriyah picked up her head and wiped the tears, "But David, we live in Eretz Yisrael. We are just visiting here as shlichim; we don't want to stay here." David broke in, "But Abba will have to go sit in prison, I don't want him to leave us." "But what do you want—for us to stay here in America?" questioned Moriyah. "No, but I don't want Abba to leave us." David held me tight.

It was a difficult time for all of us, that hour we spent together telling the kids. We all fell asleep in the big motel double bed.

There was a transformation in the kids. We could sense it right at the top of the morning. They tried spending a lot of time with us, realizing that the time that we had together from now on would be limited. Toward the end of Shabbat, Moriyah and David both told us that they were angry with us for telling them of my involvement. "You should not have told us on Shabbat! It made Shabbat a very sad day, and that is not proper." That was a reaction that we never expected.

From that moment on, the kids became even more full of questions and thoughts about the attack on the PLO mayors. They wanted to hear particulars. Suddenly I became more important in their eyes. I wasn't sure whether this was a result of my action and their admiration of it, or because of their realization that I would be around a lot less, if at all. Orit and I once overheard a conversation between Moriyah and David. Moriyah said to David that Abba is a real hero for doing what he did and only very few would do so. David answered her, "That's right, but now he will be away

209

from us so much, and it'll be so hard without him." Then Moriyah told him, "David, yes, it will be very hard without Abba, but we'll help Ema with the house and that will be our part in what Abba, Yehuda, and the others did."

Orit and I talked at length of the options available to us upon our return to New York. We both felt that staying in the States was no longer doing us any good. We had agreed to hold off our return to Israel, so that we could see if the prosecution would be willing to lessen the sentences of the others in exchange for my return. No such deal seemed imminent. Meanwhile, the time the guys in Israel were sitting in jail awaiting the trial would be taken off their final sentence. I was traveling around and wasn't gaining time. So our plan called for us to return to New York, close up shop, and return home to Aretz.

As the days passed and we came closer to New York and returning, I became more anxious, knowing that soon I would be behind bars. I didn't know what to expect, and the fear of the unknown had its negative influence on me.

Our last week on the "wagon-train" had us returning via St. Louis and Chicago. We planned to arrive before Shabbat at our friend's summer house, and we arranged to have Ema and Baruch be there with us. We hadn't seen them for the entire seven weeks of our trip. It would also give us the opportunity of breaking the news, especially to my mother, that we were planning to return to Aretz within two weeks.

But a short conversation with my brother Baruch changed all our plans. He told us that during the weeks that we were traveling, Ema had undergone a battery of tests. Baruch had paid attention to a dropping of Ema's lip and weakness on one side of her body. The tests were still going on, and the doctors were not one hundred percent sure of what Ema had—most probably Alzheimer's disease. We would delay returning until the final results of the tests would be in. It was an obvious decision. Abba and Ema had taught us through their actions that you don't leave your parents in their time of need.

We were now two weeks away from the beginning of the school year. We had no plans at all. Everything was up in the air, for we were awaiting the results and a change for the better in Ema's condition. Orit and I were really in a squeeze. We could not leave for Israel. To stay in limbo indefinitely was also something that couldn't be done. It would be unfair to the kids to spend more months out of the school system. I hadn't worked for close to four months, and our savings were about to empty out. For us, as a family, the best move would have been to return to Aretz. After a few days of decision making, which included discussions with Orit's parents and a lawyer in Israel, via the phone, we decided to delay our return for two months. However, before finalizing that decision, we asked the rabbi of Shilo for advice.

Not that there are no rabbis in the U.S., but in this situation we could not accept advice from them. We needed an opinion from rabbis who understood the necessity for Jews to live in their own land. Rabbi Elchanan Bin-Nun of Shilo listened over the phone to our dilemma. "Give me a few days to discuss it with other rabbis here, and I'll let you know," he requested.

We waited and enjoyed every moment that God was giving us together. It really was an unusual time for us. On the one hand the thoughts of the future and the uncertainty and fear of prison and Ema's disease. On the other hand, we were spending unhurried time together now, swimming, rowing and canoeing, and taking walking trips with the kids. We had never spent so much time together. It's going to make the parting, afterward, even more difficult, I said to myself, and immediately was reminded of King Solomon's amazing words: "There is a time for everything under heaven." Enjoy, I said to myself. Spend as much time as you can with the kids. Prison is right around the corner.

One week later, Rav Elchanan called us from Shilo. He had spoken to two of the most important rabbis in Israel. They both recommended that we stay near Ema until we see what developed with her. Even though it would be difficult for us and even though it would mean us having to stay away from Eretz Yisrael, the mitzvah of honoring thy mother took precedence in this situation.

The rabbinical advice was very important to us. Having to make a decision to stay away from Israel, is the best of situations, is difficult. In this case we could not have decided to stay without rabbinical backing. Maybe it's difficult for you to understand that, so let me try and explain. Living in Eretz Yisrael is a halachic [Torah] requirement—part and parcel of being Jew. Halachah governs a Jew's life from the moment he gets up until he goes to sleep. If a Jew is uncertain how to act halachically in a certain situation, then he is required to receive advice from the proper halachic authorities. To an extent, it can be compared to a person needing medical advice. The same can be said in halachic situations. We are not all experts in the field and need advice from experts. The rabbis to whom Rav Bin-Nun had turned to for advice were among the most learned in the world. It made our decision easier.

After Rav Bin-Nun's phone call we discussed our options and came to a decision. We would remain in the States for a month or so, until we could ascertain what's going on with my mom. During that period, we would return to my mother's apartment and the kids to HAFTR [Hebrew Academy of the Five Towns and the Rockaways] elementary school. The kids were quite unhappy with our decision. They wanted to return to Israel even though it would mean our being separated. "Abba, we have to live in Eretz Yisrael. That's the place for Yehudim to live. We've talked about it too much. When we first came to the U.S., you said it was only for a half a year as shlichim. Okay, we agreed to come, but now the half-year is already one year, and now you want us to stay longer. It's not fair. We want to live in Eretz Yisrael, even if you have to be in prison."

"Moriyah, to an extent you are right, and we all want to be in Aretz. There are times that certain situations are beyond our control. Savta [Grandmother] is ill. We don't know what it is. If I go back to Aretz, and then Ema needs my help, I won't be able to come to help her," I told her. Moriyah broke in, "But if Savta is ill, then they'll let you leave the prison to be with her." "Moriyah, when I go to prison, I won't be able to leave even to visit the house for a long time, and of course they won't allow me to go to visit Savta. Prison means that I'm behind bars, locked up. You know, Moriyah, that before we decided, we asked Rav Bin-Nun, who spoke to very important rabbanim in Aretz, and they told us that we have to stay

212

right now. They said that helping Savta is more important for me than returning to Aretz to sit in prison. Just as it won't be easy for you, it won't be easy for me or Ema, but it's a mitzvah and, please God, my Ema will feel good soon and then we'll be able to go back."

Moriyah didn't give in so quickly. "So at least let me go back to Shilo. I'll stay with my friends and learn in the school in Shilo. Here I have no friends at all, and I don't enjoy a moment in school here," she tried to convince us. "Moriyah," said Orit, "we understand your wanting to be in Aretz. So do we, but right now Savta is ill, and we have the opportunity and the responsibility to help her. When Abba's Ema is ill, we just can't pick ourselves up and leave her. That's not what the Torah teaches us. Also, please God, Savta will get well soon, and then we'll be able to return. Meanwhile, we'll try to make Savta happy."

So once again, our plans for returning to Aretz changed and we joined Savta in her apartment and the kids returned to HAFTR. About one month later, Orit's father, in a phone conversation, told us to freeze any plans of returning. I was really shocked because he had been upset at our staying in the States after the summer. At that time he was very strongly set on our returning. He told us on the phone that it seems the investigators didn't have all the information and they are quite sure that I have knowledge which no one had given them. The "knowledge" that I have can possibly put some other people behind bars for a long time or can be used for a good deal; therefore it was important that I stay in the States. While talking to him I made it sound as if I really had special information even though from the written confessions, copies of which I had received, I realized that I knew nothing more than what had been told to the investigators by the others.

We had gone from sea to shining sea hoping to be away just two weeks or so. Those two weeks had already been stretched to three months, and it was difficult for us to see when we would be on our way. Then the results of my mother's tests crushed our hopes for a quick return to Aretz.

Era

August 1987
Tel Mond Prison

Dear Cousin,

The second round of tests on Ema were also inconclusive, yet the symptoms were still there, and so the doctors ran another battery of tests, and we eagerly awaited the results. One month later, I took Ema to the doctor to hear his conclusions. "I find nothing seriously wrong. It's most probably, Mrs. Rapaport, that you're simply getting older and the body is protesting a bit."

"You see, Ema, I told you that you have nothing special to worry about," I told her, while giving her a big kiss on the way home.

"I hope you're right, but I feel that there is something wrong with me. I feel a loss of control on the left side of my body every so often and headaches which I've never had in the past."

Planning our return, we were all excited, although I had mixed emotions. I wanted to return to Israel, but I didn't want to go to jail. Two weeks later, Orit's father gave us the okay to return. The lawyer who represented Yehuda, Yossi Yeshurun, approached the prosecutor to see if some kind of a deal could be made. However, the prosecution did its homework. They didn't have to make a deal for my return. Everyone they questioned about me assured them I couldn't stay away from Israel for long. They told Attorney Yeshurun no deal. It didn't faze us, and we continued with our plans to return, ordering tickets, beginning to say goodbye, packing.

It happened just two weeks before our scheduled flight. We had told Ema of our plans to return, and she took it very well. "Yes, you should go back. Your life is there. I know it'll be hard for you there, especially now that you'll be in prison, but Israel is your home. Go and God should take care of you." I said to myself, "How super my mother is. She's getting older, not feeling too well, and yet tells us not to worry about her—she'll get along!" "Ema, why don't you come along with us? We'll be able to live together. You'll have privacy, and yet you'll be able to help us out and be with us. It'll be a good deal for the both of us." My Ema thought for a while. "I have my sisters and brothers here, my friends, I know the language, the people, the area. Most important, I have Baruch and Yosef here. If I go to live with you, it won't be fair to them." "But, Ema, what about us? If you don't come with us, then we'll be without you, and who knows when I'll see you again? Also, you have some friends in Israel, especially Mrs. Hoffman, and you'll spend a lot of time with the kids. And, if you want, you'll come back. You know what—spend two to three months with us, and then return here for two to three months, and then come back to us."

My mother thought for a while: "Let me think about it." I thought that maybe things would work out well. The next day brought me back to earth. Orit told me over the phone Ema was holding our baby, Tsofiyah, in her hands and suddenly Tsofiyah just slipped out of Ema's hands and fell on the floor. Ema told Orit that she didn't even feel Tsofiyah slipping out of her hands. Ema also complained to Orit that her eyesight was beginning to fail. "Orit," I said, "something is wrong with Ema and we have to get to the bottom of what's going on." As a first step, Ema called and arranged with a specialist for an eye examination the next day. The examination lasted about half an hour and then the results: "Mrs. Rapaport, your eyesight has gotten significantly worse in just the half-year since your last examination. From what I can determine you have macular degeneration. There is nothing in medicine that can help you. There is a possibility that it will get worse, but it seems to us that the present degenerative actions are slowing down. It is a disease that comes from age, and basically we can't prevent it."

That evening I had a long discussion with Orit. Once again our plans to return were delayed. How can I leave Ema in her present situation?

"Something troubles me with Ema's situation. I have this feeling that there is really something seriously wrong with Ema and the tests have not been able to diagnose what," I said to my brother that evening. We decided to wait another week or two to see what developed. During the week we received a phone call from Israel. My father-in-law wanted to know when we were returning. I told him of the developments in my mother's medical condition and that we temporarily had put a freeze on our plans. He was not at all pleased with our decision. Neither am I, I responded, but I see no other option right now.

During the next month, Ema was checked by two other eye specialists—world famous in their field. Their reaction was the same: Ema had macular degeneration of the eye and basically nothing could be done about it. After Ema stayed by Yosef for Shabbat, Yosef pointed out that he noticed a marked weakness of her left side. That Saturday night the three of us decided that Ema would have to go through a battery of tests to see what was going on. Ema agreed, and the tests were scheduled for early the next week.

During the week I said to Orit, "It seems to me that we are going to be here for a few more months. Ema obviously has something seriously wrong with her, and I don't see us leaving until it is clear to us what is going on. I haven't been working for five months, and we don't have any more savings. I'll find some temporary work that'll keep us going, but I don't see any other options." And so I found a job working in a welfare agency.

It took another two weeks until the doctor called my brothers and me into his office: "We have the results of your mother's tests. I'm sorry to inform you that we have found a tumor in her brain. It is a very large tumor situated above the pituitary gland, and I am 95% sure that it is cancerous. I'd like your Ema's permission to take a spinal tap to be sure."

The three of us were totally quiet. Then Baruch broke the silence: "Doctor, tell us bluntly, what is our mother's situation?"

"It looks bad, very bad, but first we need the results of the spinal tap," he responded. "Your mother's situation is extremely serious, and I am not optimistic about the chances for her recovery. If the tumor is cancerous, then maybe we can use radiation therapy and/or chemotherapy to reduce it."

We had the very difficult job that evening of breaking the news to our mother. I don't know how, but she took it so beautifully. She was very strong and agreed to the spinal tap. One week later we were once again gathered in the doctor's office when he broke the bad news about the results: "The tumor is cancerous, and I have discussed the possibility of an operation with one of the best neurosurgeons in the country. He is not optimistic and does not recommend an operation. The tumor is very large and very deep. To reach it through an operation, he would have to cut away so much of the brain that nothing would be gained by the operation. We can try chemotherapy, and that is what we are recommending—an immediate intensive dose of chemicals with the hope that it can reduce the tumor. The experts that I have spoken with are pessimistic and believe that your mother has only a few months to live. But this is one of those cases that one never knows, only God, and we have to do our utmost."

"Doctor, maybe there is no justification for giving our mother any treatment at all. If the chances are so small, then why should Ema suffer through chemotherapy? You and others have told us that it is extremely painful, and if the chances of survival or betterment are so small, then why put my mother through the ordeal?"

"If your mother does not get treatment, the odds are extremely high that she won't live more than a month or two. Yet if she gets treatment, it will not be easy for her, and there is a chance that it will not help her. However, on the other hand, there is a chance that the chemotherapy will reduce the tumor and allow your mother to live."

"What kind of life? Will she be a vegetable? What will she be able to do and what not? If she gets treatment and remains a vegetable, then what has been gained?" It was my brother Yosef who asked the hard questions.

The doctor thought for a while: "No one can answer the questions that you asked. There is a chance that your mother's health will improve for a short period of time and then, once again, will get worse. She can only receive a specific amount of chemicals and no more, for too much of the drugs destroys the healthy brain cells. Everything is a risk, but one thing is almost for sure. If we don't give her any treatment, she'll die very soon." After listening a bit more to the doctor, we told him that we'd think about the options, talk to our mother, and get back to him soon.

The next few days were the first of many difficult days that we were going to have in the next three years. We realized immediately that Ema would have to make the final decision—it was her life, death, struggle, and pain. We decided we would turn to an acquaintance of the family, who was head of oncology in a Brooklyn hospital, Dr. Sam Korman, to get his advice. After looking over the charts and results of the CAT scan, he was very emphatic: "You must go ahead with the radiation therapy and the chemotherapy for your mom. She has a bad case of cancer, but the treatment can possibly reduce the size of the tumor, stop its spread, and give your mother more years. Yes, it is a difficult treatment and the results may not be good; yes, your mother may become a vegetable, but if she doesn't receive treatment, there is almost no chance for her."

Before presenting Ema with her options, we turned to Rabbi Dr. Moshe Tendler, the son-in-law of Rav Feinstein, a halachic scholar and also a researcher in cancer. We asked him what the halachah would demand of Ema to do. After listening to our description of Ema's condition and the doctor's recommendation, he asked for a few days in order to discuss Ema's condition with the doctors. Three days later, he gave us a very definite yes. Halachah requires Ema to undergo treatment in her situation. There is, in halachah, a situation of "sit and don't do anything," but in this situation the doctors dealing with Ema are of the feeling that something can be gained by treatment. Albeit, one of the doctors felt there was no reason for treatment, for it would not help, but that doctor was in a minority, and from experience, there is a possibility, however small, that the treatment would help. Therefore, Ema was required, halachically, to choose the treatment.

On Saturday night, in Yosef's house, we all sat with Ema and explained the situation. Ema understood what was facing her and chose to receive treatment. It was obviously a very difficult decision for her. I feel that our being close to her strengthened her resolve. Maybe, to an extent, it was as if we were going through the treatment with her.

On the fifth day of Ema's treatment, everything started going wrong. Ema lost control of her brain and started acting in a way as if she were totally drunk. It was a very degrading experience, one which I would prefer not to write about or, in fact, remember. It lasted for two months, when the hospital told us: we have basically finished our treatment. There's nothing more we can do. You can take your Ema home!

The only reason that we agreed to take Ema home—well, don't misunderstand me, we wanted Ema home more than anything else, but when the hospital released Ema, Ema was in no condition to come home—was that we felt that her continued stay there would only worsen her condition. Ema was home for two days, and her condition was so bad that one of the world's leading cancer treatment centers, Memorial Sloan-Kettering in Manhattan, agreed to Ema's undergoing treatment there.

Before Ema's hospitalization, we had received many letters from neighbors in Shilo and acquaintances throughout Israel. The overwhelming majority of these letters backed our staying in the States. "There is no justice or moral reason for you to come back and sit in jail," was the basic gist of the letters. Orit's family differed. Her father, brothers (one in and one out of prison), and uncle were adamant that we return: "Every day that you stay behind in the States has no purpose. You belong in Israel, even if it means going to prison." All the rabbis in Israel, save one, whose advice we sought, advised us to stay in the States. Neighbors of ours from Shilo, who knew how hard it was for us to stay away from Israel, continued to urge us to stay in the States.

It was indeed very hard for us to stay out of Israel, and the encouragement that we received helped, just a bit, to reduce the difficulties. People in the States could not understand how we were contemplating returning, and they were not able to understand how Orit's family in Aretz was insisting that we return.

When Ema's disease was diagnosed as cancer and we understood the meaning of that, Orit and I made a decision—a difficult one—to stay with Ema. Truthfully, at that point we thought we were talking about a few months, for that was the time allotted to Ema, at the most, by the doctors. During this time my father-in-law wrote a letter which, when we read it, we knew it to be true, yet we could do nothing to change the situation. "You will sit twice—once in the States and again in prison in Israel." To a real extent, our "forced" exile was as difficult to us and even more so than my prison sentence afterward. I know that it's extremely difficult, if not impossible, for you to understand that, but it is so. My real prison term was served even before I entered Tel Mond, for we were being kept away from the land which we loved.

The decision was a hard one for the kids also, but they understood. Ema's illness became part of their life, and they wanted to be involved in her treatment. And so, when it became possible, we rented a house and Ema lived with us. After four months of intensive treatment at Sloan-

Kettering, the doctors said, "We've done what we are able to. Take your mother home." Ema came home on a stretcher, unable to walk, move, or eat. From the hospital, we bought a feeder pump, which pumped food into Ema's stomach. And when Ema came home, she was sleeping twenty out of twenty-four hours a day. The doctors were very pessimistic.

Then the kids took over. They gave back to their grandmother the love she'd given them when she was well. During the first year that we were in the States, Ema read to them, went with them to the playground, and bought them the chocolates and ice creams they enjoyed so much. Now it was their turn. They were not going to allow their grandmother to just lie in bed.

The ambulance personnel hadn't even left the house, and Yitzhak and Tsofiyah were jumping on her bed from one end to the other and even on Savta. In came Moriyah, David, and Atarah and started singing to Savta. Even though she asked them to let her sleep, they refused to do so. For over an hour they made simcha [joy] on her bed. Then they allowed Savta to relax, only to return within two hours to jump all over her again. Savta came back from the hospital on Sunday, and by Tuesday she was no longer using the food pump. The kids were feeding her by spoon. Miracle of miracles, Friday night, the kids forced Savta to come off her bed and sit by the Shabbat table. Orit and I both had tears, hearing Savta sing once again.

Savta couldn't read well any longer, and so the kids started reading to her. One or two days later, we were pushing Savta down the street in the wheelchair and she was holding Tsofiyah in her hands! One month later, we returned to the hospital for a checkup, and Savta was walking with the aid of a walker and gave the doctor a big "good morning." He did a double take—he didn't believe what he was seeing. Ema got stronger and stronger and began to visit a senior club four days a week. One of those nights, Orit turned to me and said, "Your Ema is getting better. Shouldn't we consider returning to Aretz? She goes to the club during the week, and on weekends she'll be with Yosef and his family. Besides that, her sisters are very close to her and will be with her a lot. We'll go back; you'll do your term in prison. God will be good to your Ema, and when you are released she will be able to come and live with us in Aretz." It took me a few days to digest Orit's suggestion. The more we talked about it, the more sense it made and the more I was able to consider it.

Once again I asked Rav Bin-Nun, from Shilo, to give us a Torah opinion as to whether we should return. Two days later he called us back. "The rabbis are of the opinion that you are to stay with your Ema. Your mother's medical condition is still of primary importance, and since her recovery so far is due, in part, to your family being with her, it is important that you stay."

Orit and I had difficulty in accepting the advice. Simply put, we were sick of being away from Eretz Yisrael. Since we had asked the rabbis for advice and not for a halachic decision, we were not bound by the advice they had given us.

Two more days of agonizing discussions and then we decided: We would return to Aretz in about three weeks. Once again we informed Orit's father and the people in Shilo and began preparations. We started packing, ordered tickets. Telling Ema of our decision was not going to be easy, yet once again she took it very well: "You have your family, a future to take care of. I'll be okay." And she gave a big hug and kiss.

Two of the newspapers in Israel wrote that they had information that we were returning. One night we received a phone call from one of the Shilo families. They were extremely surprised to hear our voices. "What's going on? According to one of the papers, you flew out of New York last night and should be landing this afternoon," they said to us. "Then why are you calling us?" Orit asked. "Who believes the newspapers?" "Well this time, to an extent, they were correct. We plan to return next week."

Orit's father passed our decision to our lawyer in Israel, and he was going to inform the prosecution. We did not expect any deal, and indeed none was offered. Facing me were many years behind bars. Facing my wife and children were many years without me.

Four days before our flight it happened. I was preparing to shower when I suddenly heard a loud bang from my mother's room. I rushed inside to find Ema lying on the floor, having great difficulty breathing and then she began to turn blue. I quickly began mouth-to-mouth resuscitation while

Orit called the emergency ambulance. In the hospital it was determined that Ema had suffered a cerebral hemorrhage. The next day, Ema was transferred to Sloan-Kettering. The doctors had no idea how long she would be there.

"Orit, we are being told something from on high. Whenever we get close to leaving, something happens to Ema. We can't leave now," I told my wife. So once again we changed our plans.

Ema was in the hospital for close to two months. When she returned, her spirits were low, and again the kids took over. They jumped on her bed, sang and read to her and made her laugh, and within a few days had Ema walking around. But the cancer was taking its toll. A woman had to be with Ema twenty-four hours a day, and we had to rent a house for the woman and special equipment for Ema. It was harder for Ema to walk around, and her concentration span was growing shorter. But the kids wouldn't give up. They kept on nudging Ema to go for a walk to the park with them. The kids even convinced Ema to take them out for hamburgers. When the spring came, Ema joined us on some Sunday riding trips to the mountains. As Ema told us a few times, "I never believed I would see these places again."

In Israel, after a court case of over a year, verdicts were handed down in the trial that I had missed. The case itself had been in the headlines for its entire duration. The courtroom was packed time and time again. Bakeries and delicatessens in Jerusalem sent the prisoners the best they could offer. Every day, like clockwork, a boy of around thirteen, who sold candy bars and ice cream for his father on the street, came running over to the police van bringing the accused to the court and gave them ice cream. There was no doubt that the typical Israeli on the street supported our actions and didn't want to see us in prison. The judges, by a two-to-one verdict, felt differently. My partners in our attack on the PLO mayors were sentenced to three years behind bars. Yet, after a year of a totally negative press and huge pressure on the government, we expected an even more severe punishment.

Sitting in New York, I now knew what I could expect—basically. Three years away from the wife and kids. Three years behind bars. It would not be easy. To me, the very fact that we would be sitting behind bars for defending ourselves was a disgrace.

The days were flying by, and the summer was in front of us. Ema was holding her own, and Orit and I discussed the possibility of returning. Moriyah, all ten years of her, put her foot down. She would not remain anymore in the United States, even if it meant living with our neighbors in Aretz. At the end of the school year, she was returning for good. It was another one of those difficult decisions for us—to let our ten-year-old go to Israel by herself. Yet we knew it was for her good.

Moriyah was missing her friends, her language, her culture, and the holiness of Israel, an intangible ingredient, understood only by those living in the holy country. Moriyah understood it, and so did we.

Yet I wasn't anxious to let her go. I had a feeling that the next time I would see her would be months away and from behind bars. But Moriyah was insistent. To an extent, it was a classic conflict between the needs of the parents and those of the child.

The next afternoon I drove over to the beach with the kids, and after running around with them for an hour, I walked to the side so I could do some thinking alone. I watched Moriyah with the others, and a flash came into my eyes. I saw her coming to visit me while I was behind bars. As Moriyah came running by I reached out and pulled her down and gave her a big hug and kiss and my eyes were a little wet. "Why are you crying, Abba?" she asked. " 'Cause if you go to Eretz Yisrael, I won't see you for a long time."

"Abba," she said, "We have to go back to Aretz. We came for six months, and soon it will be three years. That's not for us. Our home is in Aretz and not in the U.S. I don't like anything in this country. Everything is better in Israel."

I released her. "Can I really leave my Ema?" My God, who has created everything, please give me the strength to make the proper decision. What is more important: another year in Israel or to be with my very sick mother? A flashback came into my mind: lying on a small folding bed in Ema and Abba's room, with a high temperature, bad stomachache, and next to me in the middle of the night was Ema washing me down, giving me toast and tea. In the midst of that flashback another came. Riding in a car on the way to the Catskills. All of my sandwiches were finished, and I was hungry. Ema gave me hers. Still another flashback: one o'clock in the morning and I was returning from a date. I unlocked the door, and there was Ema sitting in the kitchen, waiting for me to return safely.

Ema took care of me always. How could I consider leaving her in this, her real time of need. "Honor Thy Father and Mother so that your life may be lengthened on the land that the Lord has given thee," says the Torah. Isn't this the exact moment that the Torah is talking about? If not now, when? Yet, on the other hand, it is written, "Therefore, shall man leave his father and mother and cling to his wife." I have a wife and a family. Can we continue living in limbo this way? Ema can go live with my brother Yosef. Boom, my thoughts were interrupted by David and Atarah jumping on me. "Look what we found, seashells," they said. "Say three times fast, she sells seashells down by the seashore." Then we were off running into the tide . . . laughing.

Era

October 1987
Tel Mond Prison

Dear Ema, Shalom,

Baruch spoke to Orit this past Monday and told her the bad news in reference to your medical condition. I don't know if you will ever be well enough again to have this letter read to you, but with hope and prayer I am writing.

There are parents, many of them, who preach the Biblical command, "Honor Thy Father and Mother." There are few, so few, who abide by that command themselves. You, Ema and my Abba, may he rest in peace, personified the performance of that commandment. I grew up not only with you, Mother, as my mother, but also with Bubbie, your mother, as my mother. Bubbie had five children in the U.S.A. (two or three passed away in Russia/Poland). But there was only one with whom she could stay—you, my dear mother. To you and Abba, there never was a question of, "How can we do it? There is no room." When my grandfather, whom I never knew, passed away, it was natural that Bubbie would stay with you.

No, it was not easy. In fact, it was hard. You and Abba had a bedroom, Bubbie shared a room with Baruch and Yosef, and I shared the living room. Actually, until the age of ten or so, I slept in your room, with you. There was not a single private corner for any of us. Bubbie was a very strong and controlling individual. Sometimes she would go against your wishes and tell us to do something which you did not want us to do. She didn't necessarily appreciate your method of raising us. And as Bubbie got older and more ill, the little time that you had was shared more and more with her.

Ema, I thank you and Abba for the lesson you taught me. The lesson that no words, only actions, can teach. In the U.S.A. of today, sadly, even the American Jewish world, you would have been an oddity. For we are the generation of the NOW: Love Now, Peace Now, Money Now, Gratification Now. We are the generation that is not willing to delay or suffer. If a marriage doesn't work—get a divorce and remarry. If the game one bought wasn't satisfactory, then throw it out and get a new one. If children are hard to take care of, send them off to dormitories or have fewer children. And yes, if parents are hard to take care of, get rid of them: send them off to the old-age home.

In this world, where words speak louder than actions, you taught us by actions. The amenities of life, the time off for yourselves, that was not part of your plans. You had children to raise and a mother to take care of. For you, they were first and only.

A year and a half after Abba was killed in a car accident, five years ago, we came as representatives from Israel to New York. A major factor in our decision was the opportunity to be with you. I felt that in a small way, I was following your path and actions. Suddenly, Ema, you were struck with a terrible disease. Whatever enjoyment you could still have in life, we wanted to give you. You loved the kids and they you. In the past you had pushed them in their baby carriages and now they pushed you in the wheelchair. When you couldn't eat, they helped you do so. They made you laugh and made you sing.

We were faced with one of the most difficult decisions I have made in my life. On one hand, staying with you, Ema, and the other, returning to Israel. Returning to Israel was not easy. We wanted you to come with us. But I was returning to jail. It would be basically impossible for Orit, pregnant with our sixth child, to be able to care for you also, Ema. Staying in the States? Until when? Please God, you will live to be 120 years old! But our home is in Israel, and we had to return.

Every day away from Israel was difficult to us. On the other hand, if we returned and then the cancer started spreading again, what would I do? I would be in jail!

In the most difficult time of your life, while you are ill with cancer, I left you. I can't even tell you truthfully that I had to, that I had no choice. The rabbis I asked advised us, some even commanded us, to stay with you, Ema.

As I wrote about our "now" generation earlier, I am one of them. I could not suffer any longer being outside of my beloved country.

Day after day, night after night, I twisted and turned. What to do? You, Mother, realizing our dilemma, told me over and over—you have your life; go do what you must do. Yet how can I leave my mother in her time of need? How long could I stay away from Israel? We had been gone for three years. I really had no one to speak to and seek advice from—no one, of course, save for Orit. Orit, with a deep understanding, told me, "Era, it has to be your decision. She is your mother. Whatever you decide, I'll stand beside you." I know how hard it was for Orit being in a foreign country and away from her homeland. The big burden was on her, taking care of the kids and you, Mother. If I was homesick for Israel, then all the more so Orit, whose family was waiting for her every moment.

We compromised. Orit and the kids would go back for the beginning of the school year. Yosef invited you, Ema, to be with him. I would stay some two months to ease the transition period—to see, Ema, if your being away from the kids would have a negative effect on you.

Once again you surprised us. You continued to go to the senior citizens club and kept your spirits pretty high. When a month had gone by and you were doing well, Orit and I decided, over the phone, that I would finalize plans to return in about another month. During the week, we stayed together in your apartment. As you got stronger and stronger, the days got closer to my leaving you. Then, on Shabbat in Yosef's home, you fell and broke your back and were confined to bed in Yosef's home for at least two months. At the same time, the date for my return was around the corner. You urged me to go. "Your family is in Aretz—they need you—go where you belong," is what you told me, Mom.

The night before leaving you, I lay in my bed in your apartment wondering if tomorrow would be the last time that I was to see you, God forbid. I arose during the night, sat and looked at a picture of Abba on the wall. "Abba," I asked, "am I doing the right thing?" Of course, he could not answer me. Conversations with acquaintances during the year came to mind. We had talked about Aliyah, and that often the problem of leaving parents was a major reason for not coming to Aretz. I understood them but responded, "In another twenty years, that's what your children will say in reference to you!" I was facing the biggest test. I couldn't go, yet I knew that I had to go. That night I cried for hours.

I think that leaving you, Ema, was even more difficult than leaving Abba, or maybe it was equal. I never told you of my leaving Abba. I didn't want to open up a deep wound.

I had flown to Abba's bedside two days after you informed me, and six days after he was run over by a car. For four weeks I was by his bedside and with you. I don't know if Abba knew I was with him. I wanted him to know. I wanted him to know that just as he never would leave us, we would not leave him. Yes, I was returning to my family in Aretz, but I wasn't leaving Abba.

I was to leave on an afternoon flight, and so I went to the hospital late that morning to part from Abba. In my heart I knew that I would never see him alive again. He had been in a coma for a full month and was getting worse. As I stood by Abba's bed, holding his hand, the tears came as water. I kissed Abba over and over, more times than I had ever kissed him during our life together. I promised Abba that I would go to his parents' grave the day after I arrived back in Aretz and pray to God that their merit would give him a complete recovery.

I rested my head on Abba's chest, gently touching his face and asked him for forgiveness for leaving. I confided to him that although I didn't fulfill his aspirations for me as a son, in my own way I followed his path. I squeezed and squeezed his hand, hoping for some sign of recognition from him. I told Abba that once, in a rare moment of confidentiality, he had told me, "I was born a small person and have remained so." I told him, "Abba, you may be physically short, but you are a giant to me."

Ema, I couldn't leave Abba, but I had to. King Solomon said, "There is a time for everything under the sun—a time for crying . . . and a time for building." As I kissed Abba once more and rose from his bed, I remembered what Abba told me at his parents' grave, to teach my children to love the Torah, so they would teach their children afterward. I hugged my Abba for the last time in my life and whispered to him, "Abba, I will tell my children, over and over, who you were, and I will teach them, to the best of my ability, to continue in God's ways, as you have taught me."

I turned and backed out of Abba's room. He dedicated his life to Torah and Israel. I backed out as a sign of honor to a father who gave his all for his children.

As I rode down the elevator, I recognized the face of Dr. Tendler, son of Rabbi Moshe Tendler. I had spoken to him over the phone a few times, and he had looked in on Abba during his rounds. I introduced myself and thanked him. In response to his question, I told him that I was returning to Israel. He noticed my red eyes and took me aside and told me a part of that week's Torah portion. It is written in the Torah that Jacob's sons returned and told their father that Yosef was killed by an animal. The Midrash Rabbah states, "The brothers were busy with selling Yosef; Yosef was busy with fasting and mourning, Jacob was busy with mourning and fasting, and Yehuda was busy taking a wife, and God was busy creating the light of the Messiah." Dr. Tendler told me, "When God saw that Yehuda was continuing the process of building, then He, the Almighty, continued and began the creation of the Messiah. One must continue building and

creating. You have to return to your family and Israel and continue building and creating."

I remembered his words as I drove to the airport after saying Shalom to
you, Ema. We both knew what we were facing. I had to return to my home
and enter jail so that afterward I could continue building. Did I do right?
As I sit here in my jail cell six months later, unable to be at your side while
you battle cancer, I don't know the answer to my question. I will never
know . . . I'm upset for leaving, and I would have been upset had I stayed.
In the final analysis, my dear mother, I had to leave and come back. For
that is our command: "Honor thy Father and Mother so that your days may
be lengthened on the Land that the Lord Your God has given you."

By doing so I have continued yours and Abba's way, in my way. From my
jail cell, I promise you, my dear mother, that on my first "vacation" from
here, I will go to the Mount of Olives, to Abba's grave, and ask God to grant
you a complete recovery in merit of the good ways and deeds of my Abba,
your husband.

Your eternally loving son,
Era

5 Prisoner

Dear Cousin,

I guess you are surprised to hear from me. We have a funny relationship. First we were, to an extent, close in our youth (especially since we lived three blocks away and were about the same age). Then each one of us went our own way. Since I've been in Israel, I'm not even sure that we've written each other. On my visits to the States, I would call you. We would talk for a few minutes and that's it. Three times, while in Washington, D.C., I visited you, and three times when you were in New York City we saw each other. With all of that, I feel a closeness to you.

The last time I spoke to you was about six months ago, on a visit of yours to see my mother. You were taping my mother, Aunt Glenda, and your mother. I remember your words—"searching for your past," especially about your father. We also talked a bit about our attitudes toward Judaism and my involvement in the "Underground" in Israel.

Since we only had a few moments then, we really didn't talk in depth, but both of us expressed a desire to do so.

Sitting here in prison in Israel, I have had the opportunity to think. To think about two cousins. From the same grandfather/grandmother. Two second-generation Americans going two different ways.

There is an episode I remember. It happened in your house. We were visiting during the late summer. Our eldest—Moriyah—mentioned that we have a beautiful menorah, and then your oldest son responded. "We have a Chanukah bush." That cut right through and hurt. I said to myself that night, "Here I am living in Israel, physically living a much more difficult life than you; spending at least six hours a week on guard duty, a month and a half in the army every year and living in a two-room caravan. The result? My four-and-a-half-year-old daughter talks about Chanukah in Israel. On the other hand, you are in a comfortable house, working at a good job and Susan is involved in the Jewish community. The results— your son talks about a Christmas tree.

But, my cousin, it wasn't a personal hurt—rather a hurt of our people on one level and a hurt of our parents and grandparents on an individual level. Our grandparents on our mothers' side, of whom we only knew Bubbie, clung fervently to Judaism—for us to be Jews. Yet you were throwing it out the window. For thousands of years, Jews all over the world gave up their lives to live as Jews, and in the U.S.A., where the choice is yours, you were not giving it a try.

I'm not saying, cousin, that my brand of Judaism is the only way, but you yourself told me that you were worried about Jay and that you didn't think he'll remain Jewish. How can you expect him to? America is the great "melting" pot, and your family is in real danger of assimilation. I'm blaming your situation because you are part of me and I love you.

About eleven years ago, Uncle Bob brought his son Alex to Israel. The day after their visit to the Western Wall, Alex spoke up. "My father wanted me to feel something, and yet I could not." Both he and Uncle Bob were upset. Yet I wasn't surprised. What did Uncle Bob expect of Alex? What did he teach him?

And then, memories once again. I don't know if I ever told you that two of our uncles did their utmost, when I was a child, to make me feel ashamed about being religious. They used to make fun of my beliefs and practices—*ancient*, *outdated*, were the words they used. They didn't want to understand how my parents were willing to spend a very high percentage of Abba's income to send us to yeshiva.

Both of them laughed at our very crowded little apartment. As you remember, we lived in a two-bedroom flat—Abba, Ema, our Bubbie, and the three of us, along with Hadassah bazaars, JNF [Jewish National Fund] charity boxes, and bookcases of holy books. Privacy? We didn't know what it meant. As a kid, I didn't have the answers to their sarcasm. I didn't tell my parents, for I knew that they were trying so hard.

Uncle Bob prided himself as being the modern Jew and Uncle Sidney the successful American lawyer. Deep down I had a feeling that my parents were doing the right thing, the future would tell. What has the future told? Sidney's two boys married Christian women, and his daughter married a Christian man. Out of Bob's four children, only one is married, and he has little contact with the others.

My Abba and Ema didn't talk to us much—they just did. When our grandfather passed away and Bubbie needed a place to stay, Abba and Ema opened our very little apartment. Bob and Sidney laughed at that. Today? My mother, who is ill with cancer, stayed with us, and now she is with my brother Yosef. My father taught us Judaism by his actions, and Judaism says to "Honor Thy Father and Mother."

You remember in East Flatbush, I was one of the very few who wore a yarmulke, and I was embarrassed. Whenever I could, I took if off so other kids wouldn't make fun of me. Mark and Susan, whether or not my children wear a yarmulke, one thing is for sure—here in Israel, they would never be embarrassed by it.

I have lived as a Jew in two places. In the U.S. I existed as a Jew, fighting just to keep whatever Judaism I had. In Israel, I live as a Jew.

My kids' backyard is not the stick-ball yard that we played in. Down the road is the village of Gofen—the capital of the Maccabees. Traveling along the road northwest is Ma'aleh Livonah, the site of the first major battle between the Maccabees and the Greeks. In the middle is our village, Shilo—the first capital of Israel!—I look out my window and see the ancient city of Shilo, where the great High Priest Eli lived and where the prophet Samuel practiced. When I look out my window, I have the feeling that Samuel is smiling and saying, "My people have returned." Every step that I take is one where my and your grandparents of two hundred generations ago also stepped! They knew that they were building for themselves and for a future. The proof is here—the future is me. That's a weird statement. Generally the future is someone after you, but in this case I am the future.

To me, my cousin, Judaism is not, as our uncle stated over and over, a book of outdated laws. Toynbee, the historian, wrote that Jews are fossils. In a certain regard, he's right. A large number of Jews all over the world are intermarrying (in the States, some 50%) and are fast becoming fossils. Yet for those who live as Jews, Judaism is living. Anyone who has learned it knows how special it is.

Judaism tells me that I must keep the land of Israel. You know, cousin, Maimonides says that over 200 of the 613 commandments cannot be kept outside of Israel. Even here in prison, Judaism tells me how to act, and I'm not referring to prayers and studies. There is only one pay phone here in prison, and each one of us has the privilege to use it for about ten minutes a day (when it works!). Almost always, a prisoner not from my ward passes by and asks me to allow him to go first for a two-minute call. For me, it's a dilemma. I only have ten short minutes to speak with Orit and the five kids—that's less than a minute and three-quarters per person. If I give him two minutes, what am I left with?

On the other hand, a fellow Jew is asking for help. What do I do? When the village rabbi came to visit, I asked him what to do. His answer was, "If only you were involved, you could give up your two minutes, but who gives you the right to give up your wife's and your children's two minutes!"

The rabbi is not drumming up his answer. It is based on rabbinical response to questions over the generations—since the beginning of Judaism. Thousands of learned rabbis have passed down that answer. It was learned from Moses, who heard it from God. I know I sound mystical to you; our uncles told me so also. If my mysticism means continuing Judaism, then I plead guilty! To me, my action is, in actuality, continuing my grandfather's paths—if you like it, my roots.

You remember, Mark, I was here in Israel during the Six Day War when we freed the Temple Mount and Western Wall. As I am writing you, I remember the exquisite feeling I had when, some two weeks later on Shavuot, we walked, at dawn, through the streets of Yerushalayim to THE WALL. We were, in actuality, tens of thousands of Jews at the Wall. But cousin—that's not all. As I walked, I looked around me, all around me; there they were, walking with us. They? The millions of Jews, who throughout almost 2,000 years in the galut [exile] could not go to Jerusalem because the peoples of the world would not allow them. As we got closer to the Old City and the Temple Mount, the steps I heard running were not only mine. No, cousin, I'm not a mystic; I'm a realist. They were with me: the Maccabees, Bar Kochba, Rabbi Akiva, Rashi, Maimonides, my grandfather and grandmother. I was in a dream—but a living dream, experiencing a "high"—one that can only be experienced in Israel. That is part of the special relationship that we have here.

Suddenly, I understood what I had not understood all of my "synagogue life": the specialness and importance and unity of a congregation at prayer.

I used to ask myself, why are we required to pray in a quorum of at least ten men in order to recite certain prayers? As I reached the Wall, I understood. My words fused together with tens of thousands of my fellow Jews, who were presently with me and with the millions who were persecuted throughout the generations and couldn't be there. As the tears of joy ran down my face, I looked at the Temple Mount, with the strange mosque on it. In my eyes, I saw the Temple in its place, and as I gripped the wall and held on, kissing it as I kiss my kids today, I felt my words of prayer being lifted up to God.

Yes, I felt a hand coming down and picking up my prayers. What twenty years of Diaspora education couldn't teach me, I learned in a few minutes at the Wall. That is the specialness of Yerushalayim and of prayer at the Wall. Why is it so? Throughout the Torah and Bible, that specialness is mentioned over and over. Yet although I "studied" in yeshiva, it was beyond my understanding, the special holiness of our Land. Try and explain to a single person what a successful marriage is; you may explain, but he can't feel it. The comparison is one thousand times stronger in reference to our land.

At that moment, another mystery of our religion and practice unraveled before me. I had always wondered, as maybe you have, why the same liturgy and prayers? Why not change them a bit, modernize them? As the words of my prayer, memorized over the years by repetition, came out of my mouth to God, I realized that those very same words were being said by the tens of thousands around me at that moment! And that they were the very same words said by our people throughout all the generations! The words of the Torah in Devarim, Chapter 29:13–14, came alive: "For those who are here, with us, today, before the Lord our God and for those who are not here with us today."

I was truly thankful to my Abba for the forced lessons of so many years. I was part of my people. A link in a never-ending chain. Who has the right to break that chain? Me? You? The commandment of "Honor thy father and mother" is our key. Honoring them by continuing their ways in Judaism, so that, to quote the Torah, "You may live long on the Land God gave you."

The prayers that I was saying and that the tens of thousands were saying became one. I turned and joined hands with a Jew I had never seen. We danced—for how long? I don't remember. How long does one dance for millions of people? It seemed forever. My feet didn't tire, and my voice never wavered. How else could a Jew have experienced what we were experiencing?

It was ecstasy that could be reached only in Israel. Mark and Susan, how does one thank God for so much good that He has done? Here I was, a twenty-one-year-old boy who didn't deserve this privilege, and yet I was given it. I had to turn to the words of yesteryear—but they were also the words of this year. Who was I to thank God for everything, without including those who brought me to that moment—our parents, grandparents, and onwards? Try and understand, it was their words, generation after generation, praying EVERY DAY OF THE YEAR, at least three times a day, "and return with mercy to Jerusalem your city and reside there as you have said and rebuild her soon in our days." They brought me to Israel. For if they didn't cling to Judaism as they had, as they had been taught from their parents, then the link would have been broken and we would not have our own land today.

Cousin, from my jail cell, I see you over there—breaking the link. Depriving yourselves and your children of your past. And so my cousin, while searching for your father, remember: there is a link about to be broken—forever. Mark, at least you felt the need to search. Your children won't even feel that. For the link will have been broken, and they won't know where and what to search for. There are hundreds of thousands and maybe millions of Jews in the States who have broken the link. They may be happy, but they won't stay Jews.

This letter started out being a short hello and has ended up as a reaching out for us to reconnect again. Maybe it is also a "sermon from the mount."

If I have hurt you in any way, I'm sorry. There was no intent to do so. If I succeeded, somewhat, in explaining the "I" of Era and therefore getting us somewhat closer—okay. If you have the time and inclination write me. Not directly to the prison. Send the letter to Orit and she'll bring it to me.

With "family" love,
Era

March 1987
Tel Mond Prison

David and Florence, Shalom,

To you it is still the holiday, so Chag Samayach [Happy Holiday] to you. It's been a long time since I wrote you. I've had the dubious honor of spending my first Passover, the holiday of our freedom from bondage, in jail. I've told you that being in prison in Israel is better for a Jew than being free in the States. I remember my last Passover in the Diaspora. I'll take this year's Passover anytime. Here in Israel, no matter what you are doing, you feel part of the process of "restoring our days as of old." Even here in jail, the jailers are Jews. We speak Hebrew all day, we argue about things that affect the future of our people. When you listen to the news on the radio, you know that everything that happens influences the fate of our people. That is a tremendous feeling of responsibility, but also something which makes you feel a sense of wholeness, not like in America where you always feel schizophrenic if you care about your Judaism—a Jew in synagogue and an American at business and on the train.

Here there is a deep meaning to life, to pleasure and pain, which lies far beyond the immediate. As you know, some two and a half months ago, Orit gave birth to our sixth child, Dvir Meshael. For the first time I was not present at the birth. I received the message here in prison, while I was sitting in our beit midrash [study hall] learning Torah. All of us started dancing and singing. The prison authorities were nice! They allowed me three hours at the circumcision ceremony. They are required to do that by law. They also wanted to be sure there would be a minyan, so they sent five jailers to guard me. At Shilo, three hundred people gathered. Some 3,500 years ago, Hannah came to Shilo to pray for a child, and God gave her Samuel the prophet. The Philistines came and went. So did the Babylonians, Persians, Greeks, Romans, Crusaders, Turks, and English (the Arabs never ever had a state or government here). And now we've returned, and a son has been born to us in this ancient capital of Israel.

So, my good friends, what's it all about, I ask you? You work hard, very

239

hard, and for what? Another car. A bigger shul in the community, a fancier private school for the kids? A better kosher deli in town?

But it has to be more than that. The State of Israel has changed all that. The Lord has reopened the way back home. HOME. We are building our home here. Your home. You act as if nothing has changed in the last thirty-nine years. Where are you? By choosing to make America your home, you're choosing it as the home of your children. Maybe their children will make it to Israel. If they remain Jews.

You are giving up too much by being away from here. Come and build yourself and your family. God wants more from us than Cadillacs and kosher delis. Come home and build, my good friends. Come home and build.

Thanks for all of your help when we were in America.

Era

April 1987
Tel Mond Prison

Dear Brothers,

Yesterday was a difficult visit. In fact, the visits in general are difficult. I thought of writing this letter to my seven-year-old son, David. It's hard to write him a letter he can understand now. But after yesterday's visit I felt a need to.

Why are the visits difficult? The most difficult part of being in prison—besides the crazy situation that I am incarcerated for protecting my family and other families from PLO terrorists—is being separated from my family. I just want to wake up one morning and know that this bad dream is over.

Have you ever thought what the job of a father is? Or of a husband? I'm not referring to the breadwinner part. The fatherhood part. One of the most important acts is to protect your children and to be with them at their difficult times. Here I am, a forty-two-year-old father of six, not able to comfort my children in their time of need.

It's written in the Torah, "As an eagle stirs up her nest, broods over her

young, spreads abroad her wings, takes them; bears them on her pinions."
This is Moses, our teacher, telling how God takes care of the nation of Israel. In the same way, I would like to take care of and protect my own children. It's the special moments between father/son or daughter, when the
two need each other, which gives meaning to the exquisite relationship. If,
at these moments, a father is unable to be with his child, it hurts. It prevents you from being alive.

Yesterday was one of those times when you want to throw down the
physical gates of the prison which are keeping you from your children. Yesterday when they left, I stood watching them leave, and inside I was
yelling, it's not fair! Let me go home with my children!

Visiting time with them is approximately two hours a week, two of the
most precious hours that one can have. My children and I decided that I
would give them each, individually, ten minutes. During those ten minutes, each one can do whatever he likes with me: read, talk, learn, play, or
walk around the "yard." Yesterday an acquaintance of the family came to
the visit. So we all played together, and we didn't have time for our usual
ten minutes alone.

Fifteen minutes before the end of visiting time, I suggested to Moriyah,
David, Atarah, and Yitzhak, that I spend four minutes with each of them,
or we all spend the fifteen minutes together. Moriyah and Atarah said together, Yitzhak didn't care, but David wanted separately. So I went along
with the majority and said we'd spend the time together. David suddenly
ran away and sat down by a tree near the fence. He started crying. I went
over to him, sat him on my lap, and held him as close as possible, as if to
protect him like that eagle.

When he didn't calm down, I asked him why he was crying so much, but
he wouldn't answer. Finally, I asked if it was hard for him without me. He nodded yes. Like a knife cutting through my heart. I knew that I had to remain
strong, even though inside I was crying. I called over Moriyah and Atarah and
we all sat down together. Orit joined us. It was a beautiful five minutes, until
the guard announced the end of the visit. During the final few minutes, what
was I going to tell the kids? In the past, I had told them why I was here, that
I had done a mitzvah to stop a murderer from killing more Jews. This time, I

knew that wouldn't suffice. So I held all three and told them that in another three weeks, I would finish half the time I would be in prison, until my first home visit. Then Moriyah started crying and said, "Yes, you'll be home for Shabbat, but everyone in Shilo will come to visit, and you'll have no time to be with us." I assured her that the people in Shilo all knew that I wanted to spend the time with them. Then she said, "But you'll go right back to jail and we won't have any time for the trip that you promised."

The guard once again called out that visiting hours were over. We all stood up and walked to the gate, the one which in a few scant seconds would separate us once again, for a full week, and again I'd be a father in absence. I picked up each of my delicious presents from God and hugged and kissed them. Yitzhak shrugged and stood by the fence. He didn't want to leave. In the "words" of a three-year-old, his sitting down inside the fence and not speaking was his way of expressing himself. The guards yelled, "Everyone out." One of the guards came over to take Yitzhak out. Instead of being able to hold him, hug him, and kiss him like a father should, I had to pick him up and put him down outside the gate—and he was gone . . .

Suddenly I saw David once again outside the gate. He was crying and I signaled him to come over to the fence. Between the holes of the fence, I put out my lips, and he puckered his, and we kissed. I told him a quick funny story, he smiled, and then he ran off.

Era

April 1987
Tel Mond Prison

Dear Bob and Frances,

The average traveler to Israel is generally overwhelmed by the historical connection between the land and the Jewish people. Indeed, it is impossible to visit our country without literally falling over our ancestry. As a teenager growing up in New York State, I remember my days at Camp Hatikvah in the Bear Mountain Park area. Some of my walking trips were along the Appalachian Trail. As a counselor in camp, I told my campers, "Just think, 200 years ago, battles in the Revolutionary War were fought in this area." I could feel that they, as I, were impressed by that fact.

For three summers, from 1981 to 1984, the Bar-Ilan University Department of Archeology explored Tel Shilo, the ancient site of Shilo. When I took visitors to show them the dig, I would point out, "The path you and I are walking on now was used by our grandparents of three thousand years ago, during the period of Joshua."

However, to ascribe our special relationship as "merely" a historic one is to center on one dimension. To understand us as a people you must understand that the basis of our love relationship with our land is a religious one.

I admit that trying to explain this love relationship is a formidable task. It is comparable to the age-old questions of: Can a blind person feel what it is to see? Can the deaf imagine what hearing is?

I suggest to you that you open yourself and come with me for a small "trip"—a religious one. Perhaps you'll see and feel more.

Our Bible commands us to live in Israel. It was God who commanded my father of almost 200 generations ago, Yitzhak: "Live in this country and I will be with you and bless you, for to you and your children I will give all these lands" (Genesis 26a).

Everyone knows of the Biblical command to "Honor thy father and mother." What is the reward that one receives for doing so? "So that you may live long on the land that the Lord your God has given you."

There are twelve major holidays in the Jewish calendar. Eleven of them are intrinsically bound up with the Land of Israel. During the holidays, we are constantly thanking God for giving us Israel. There are three major holidays during the year when every Jew is required to come to Jerusalem.

The devout Jew prays three times a day—morning, afternoon, and evening. In his prayers, the Jew requests of God that He return to Jerusalem the Holy City and rebuild it. He requests God to gather the exiled Jews to Israel. He reminds God of His promise to give Israel to the Jews.

At every meal that a Jew eats, during the Grace After Meals, once again he requests God to rebuild Jerusalem. A wedding is considered to be one's happiest moment, a time of ecstasy. At the end, which should be the high point of happiness, suddenly a glass is placed under the shoe of the groom, and he breaks it to fulfill the age-old vow: "If I forget you, oh Jerusalem, let my right hand be forgotten, my tongue should stick to the roof of my mouth, if I do not remember you, if I don't place Jerusalem at the head of my happiness," and that same vow is repeated at the circumcision of one's son. The rabbis stipulate that if one partner in a marriage wants to go to Israel and the other refuses, it is grounds for divorce by either side!

In Judaism, when a family relation dies (father, mother, brother, sister, son, daughter) the mourners tear a piece of their clothing near the heart as a sign of mourning. When a Jew sees a city of Israel destroyed, he rends his garment as a sign of mourning. Conversely, when one erects a new town or village in Israel, he recites the blessing, "Blessed Art Thou, King of the Universe, Who Has Returned Glory to the Widow." Israel without Jews and villages is considered to be a widow. A Jew is allowed to leave Israel for only three reasons and even then only for short periods of time.

Of significant importance to our times is the fact that the Jewish people are commanded by God not to relinquish control of Israel to another people. It is interesting to note that even though Israel has been conquered time and time again, never has it been inherited by a foreign people. Never have they succeeded in developing the country. That also is God's promise to us. For the nations that conquered our country saw Israel as a faraway land, part of their dynasty. It was not of intrinsic importance to them.

In the entire history of the Land of Israel, only when the People of Israel were in control of Israel was it a totally sovereign country. Indeed, only during Israel's sovereignty did the land flourish, did the country bloom and become enriched. That fact can be seen over the last forty years. Jordan illegally occupied Judea and Samaria for nineteen years. What were the economic results during this occupation? There were no universities; the Arab villages had little or no electricity; major Arab cities used generators; very little water was available, and there was no sewage; the paved roads were from the period of British occupation; and there was a minimum of agriculture. Even on the east side of the Holy City of Jerusalem there was little progress. No major Arab leader visited Jerusalem during the nineteen years of occupation save for King Hussein. The Dead Sea remained the "dead sea." The world gave a name to the line marking the separation between the State of Israel and Jordan—the Green Line. On the east side of that line, the land occupied by Jordan, the mountains were bare because Jordan didn't plant any trees. On the west side of the line—Israel—all of the mountains were green. Israel planted tens of millions of trees. That fact is still obvious today.

In Judea and Samaria today, there are, established by Israel: Arab universities, electricity in Arab villages, newly paved roads, millions of newly planted trees, the highest overall standard of living in the Arab world. All of the Land of Israel has undergone a rejuvenation and rebuilding that could be compared only with the periods of the great Kingdoms of Israel, as is prophesied again and again in the Bible.

Enter a synagogue anywhere in the world. The ark with the Torah will be facing toward Jerusalem, a reminder of our desire to be in Israel. And in many Jewish homes the world over, part of a wall remains unpainted and on it the words, "If I forget thee O Jerusalem."

It is interesting to note that Theodore Herzl (considered the founding father of the modern State of Israel), an "assimilated Jew," was shocked into Jewish action by the antisemitic Dreyfus trial in 1886. It was then that he decided that the Jews needed their own country—for survival needs—so that the peoples of the world would not continue to destroy the Jews. Therefore, in 1903, at the Zionist Congress in Basel, he was at the forefront of a proposal to establish the Jewish State—in Uganda. After much debate, the proposal was accepted by the Jewish leadership, but it was never implemented—the Jewish People didn't accept it. For them, for us, there is only one place: the Land promised by God to the People of Israel—Israel.

Over the generations—some ninety—since the destruction of the Second Temple, 1,920 years ago, and even during the periods of the Temples themselves, there were always "progressive" Jews. They tried to reinterpret Judaism to fit their needs, which were inevitably secular. Their attempts have been recorded to some extent in the history books throughout the years. Today, more than ever before, "progressive" Jews are being lost to the Jewish nation, assimilating all over the world in numbers defying imagination. What has kept the remainder Jewish? Traditional Jewish values and practices.

So, when it came to building a country for Jews, the attempts of secular/progressive Jews to "change" Jewish destiny by finding another geographic place for Jews to run to for protection was doomed to failure.

For the Jewish People, the Land of Israel is not only a place to run to for protection. First and foremost, it is our Homeland. It is like, in the words of Rabbi Kook, "a lion cub returning to its Land." The lion can survive outside his kingdom, but he can't live and flourish. He can't be a true lion in a zoo. So it is with the Jew. He can exist, he can survive, outside of Israel, but he can't reach his national glory.

It is only in the Land of Israel that the Jews as a nation can attain and fulfill their calling. If you like, only in Israel can I be a full Jew. Anyplace else is a guest house, where I am a minority with a foreign citizenship. So when trying to understand us, realize that Israel is not just a place for us; it is a part of us. Israel is us. Just as we are orphans without the Land of Israel, so the Land of Israel is a widow without her children—us. To us, giving away part of Israel is giving away a part of our body. Our relationship with our Land has no comparison in the history of mankind. When I work the earth of Shilo, I feel that the earth responds, is happy, smiling, as if saying, "My children have come home to me." And it is precisely for that reason that when I come to Israel from abroad, I kiss the earth of my beloved Land.

Even the secular Jew is connected in a religious way to Jerusalem. On the holiest day of the Jewish year, Yom Kippur, Day of Atonement, you will find almost every Jew either fasting or coming to the synagogue.

At the very end of that day, as darkness begins to descend and we are all gathered together praying and crying for God to seal us in the Book of Life for another year, as the Heavenly Gates begin to close, Jews the world over rise in prayer.

The cantor, a messenger of the people, sings out, "Hear O Israel, the Lord our God, the Lord is One." It is repeated by the entire congregation. The cantor continues, "Blessed is the Name and His glorious kingdom forever and ever"—three times and that also is repeated by the entire congregation.

The cantor sings out with a gradually rising voice "THE LORD IS GOD" seven times and that also is repeated by the congregation.

And as their fervor reaches a crescendo, the shofar—the ram's horn—is sounded: one long blast, and then, just as the Gates of Heaven are closing, the entire congregation of Israel—millions of Jews the world over, shake the Heavenly Gates with a resounding:

NEXT YEAR IN JERUSALEM!

Era

> *May 1987*
> *6 Iyar, 5747*
> *Tel Mond Prison*

Dear Nephew,

Independence Day in jail! The Gemorah would say, "Two contradictions at the same time—an impossibility!" Outside, the country is celebrating. One hundred thousand at the Kinneret [Sea of Galilee]; tens of thousands traveling across the country; tens of thousands marching at Jericho to express our adamancy that the area belongs to us; special holiday prayers in the synagogues; so many of my fellow citizens celebrating, each in his own way, this amazing miracle.

At the same time, here I sit in my jail cell at Tel Mond Prison. With four other members of the "Jewish Underground." I would have to admit that we are a contradiction to the Gemorah's statement. For even though we are in prison, we feel the happiness of our Independence Day. Last night we had a festive meal with all of our ward, totaling sixteen people. We received food supplies from the main kitchen and prepared special delicacies for the occasion. Then we sang for about forty-five minutes. Songs of praise to God and love for our country. Shaul Barak, sentenced to twenty-four years, gave a Dvar Torah. If you expected to hear a complaint about our Eretz then you would be most disappointed. Shaul pointed out that our country is still in the beginning stages—like a baby—and until we grow up, we go through growing pains. He said that we have to look at the many positive things that our country has done so far. Yes, there have been mistakes, but that's part of the development process. If you didn't know where you were, you would never believe that these are the words of a prisoner sentenced to twenty-four years by his government. This is the special love of Eretz Yisrael.

This morning we said the Hallel prayer with a bracha [blessing]. The shaliach tzibbur [prayer leader] was Menachem Livni, also sentenced to twenty-four years. What a contrast, I thought to myself. Where would you find a prisoner celebrating, from deep in his heart, the independence of a country that has decided to put him behind bars for twenty-four years! For protecting his wife and children against PLO terrorists. Absurd, I said to myself, yet here he is celebrating. Suddenly I caught myself—I also am behind bars, sentenced to thirty months for my part in assaulting the PLO mayor, Bassam Shaka, who was responsible for the massacre of tens of Israelis and the maiming of many more.

My thoughts wandered from the jail to Cedarhurst, Long Island, where I spent the last three Israeli Independence Days during my time in America. Those were days of pain for us as a family and for me individually. I could not feel any simcha or independence. How could I? First, I was away from Eretz Yisrael, and try as I could, I did not feel any real simcha on a personal level. I actually felt sadness, for around me were millions of Jews, living in the galut, not taking any real part in the building and ecstasy of our country. The family as a whole decided not to join the Israeli Independence Day parade in New York City. We couldn't bring ourselves to do so. To reduce our country to a Fifth Avenue parade.

At 2 P.M. I went into the prison's TV room to watch the special Bible Contest that is shown every year from Jerusalem on our Independence Day. What a great feeling it gave me. I went to my cell to call my brother-in-law to watch, and what was he doing? Listening to the radio to the pilots of two of our "Lavi" jets talking to Am Yisrael as they flew over Yerushalayim! At the same exact moment, the two strengths that God gave us: Torah and Gevurah [valor]! Correct, I was sitting in jail, but at the moment how could one not be filled with the pride and fire of independence? As I write this letter, I am listening to a program about the beginning of our country and the War for Independence. We declared Independence on Friday. That evening the Haganah [defense force] needed the Jews in Jerusalem to come out and prepare bunkers, supplies, ammunition for the fight. They went to the chief rabbi, Rabbi Uziel, to get halachic permission to do the work on the Sabbath. What did he do? He went out himself to the streets to help! He said this is not a profanation of God's name but a sanctification of His name!

Yes, we have problems in our country, but this is only the beginning of the way. The labor pains which are needed to bring new life to the world. Yes, there are 350 Jewish men in the prison here, and they shouldn't be here. To an extent we have failed them! All of this is part of the realities of building a country. We will overcome our problems. In the meantime, do I not celebrate? Exactly the opposite. I will celebrate because God has allowed me to be part of our rebirth.

I hope that you are still planning to start college in Israel.

Era

June 1987
Tel Mond Prison

Binyamin, Shalom,

I am writing on your second day of Shavuot. Your letter arrived about two and a half weeks ago. So the American/Israeli postal service is not at fault; rather, I am, for not writing earlier. Actually, this letter may not even reach you in the near future. I just realized that your school year is ending. I don't know if letters are forwarded via the university.

I am, thank God, holding my own. I have been in jail for over five months, which is a long time. Orit and our six kids are doing okay. The real pressure is on them. The two oldest ones, aged ten and eight, know why I'm here, and I believe it makes it a bit easier for them. The more that I am here, the more I am convinced that it is better for a Jew to be in Israel in a jail than "free" in America. Here, wherever you are, one feels Jewish. You can say that the air is full of Judaism. Even our arguments have to do with the way to best run the Jewish State.

I was in prison for the seder. We had a communal seder for the ward— half the ward went home, and the rest of us ate together. Last year I spent the seder with my family and mother in New York. This year in jail, "alone," in Aretz. If I had to choose again, I'd take here anytime.

Our ward is officially designated a religious one, and therefore the majority here are somewhat observant. You don't have to be observant to get into the ward. You do have to be Shomer Shabbat [a Sabbath observer], wear a kippah, and pray. Within the ward we are allowed to communicate freely. There are four cells in our ward with twenty prisoners. Officially, we have little contact with other wards. In terms of our treatment, we in our ward are treated okay. Thank you for your offer to help in that area.

In reference to your learning Torah in Israel, there was a time that the possibilities of learning in Israel were nil or very little. At that point, one could have put forth a logical argument for learning in the Diaspora. Today that is obviously not the situation. There is more Torah learning going on in Israel than in any other country in the world. Moreover, the level of learning here is higher than in the galut. Also, the danger of assimilation and intermarriage in the States is so high that in numbers we're losing more than we are gaining. Galut is a stranger to true Judaism, and the Judaism that is practiced in galut leaves out one-third of the mitzvot, which can be done only in Israel. Today, Judaism in the galut is illegitimate. There was a time when one could see it as forced—no choice, rape if you'd like. Today, the choice is ours. Aretz is waiting. This is the only land where Judaism can and will reach its pinnacle, its goal, its raison d'être, if you like. There is no substitution for our national land. Or are you proposing to establish the Kingdom of David in New York?

I'm not sure that I can accept the Lubavitcher hasidim's position that for a person who knows nothing about Judaism and Israel, before you can bring him to Israel, teach him Judaism. Why not bring him to Israel and teach him Judaism here? The chances of succeeding are so much better.

By the way, the Bir Zeit University—at which all the professors and teachers are members of the PLO!—was a small seminary of some twenty-five girls when we came to the area. We financed and paid to build it into a full-fledged university! We are a crazy people, indeed.

The leftists in our country have had much, if not all, of the press power since the establishment of the State until this very day. They use every opportunity to wield their power to try and convince the populace against Yehuda V'Shomron [Judea and Samaria]. Sadly, our leaders on the right have been quite afraid of them and many a time have not acted properly due to that fear.

I am not surprised that your fellow residents have little sympathy for our cause. Where does their knowledge come from? Mostly from ignorance and articles in very anti-Israel papers and press/media in general. If some of them are open enough, when they are finally confronted with the facts, then maybe they'll open themselves up for change. For instance, the "West Bank" being part of Jordan. Do they know that only three countries in the world recognized Jordan's occupation of Judea and Samaria (Pakistan, Great Britain, and Jordan!)? Do they know that the PLO was established in 1964—some three years before we freed Judea and Samaria in the 1967 war? Do they know that the PLO wanted to do then what they have been trying to do since then: massacre us and force us into the sea? One can go on and on, but that is the idea.

But, Binyamin, be strong and stay with your convictions—that will make your students think about God. Let them come and see how the words of the Prophets in the Bible have come true in Israel today.

I'm going to learn now with my fellow prisoners. Write me soon and I'll get back to you, quickly this time.

Era

July 1987
Tel Mond Prison

Dear Tova and David, Shalom Rav:

This isn't or wasn't a planned letter, meaning that I wasn't intending to write to you now, but rather in another few weeks. The events of this past week changed things. I am referring to, obviously, the savage murder of one of our children, an eight-year-old boy from Elon Moreh. My thoughts went immediately to a conversation that we had, Tova, last year. It was soon after the murder of a Long Beach yeshiva student. If I'm correct, it was on Shavuot. Your reaction then was something like, "I said to myself, what would Era be thinking, for one of my reasons for not coming to Israel is my fear of my children being hurt or, God forbid, killed in the army, and here down the road, a yeshiva student gets murdered."

In a moment of frankness I once told you that it's really "nice" of Amer-

251

ican Jews to stay in the States and allow us to fight to keep the land safe—
as if the blood of our children is okay to give for our homeland while the
blood of American Jews is given to the Red Cross. Do you think I don't fear
the day that our David will be a soldier (it's only ten years away) and have
to fight, God forbid, the Arabs in a war for our survival? That I don't think
of the day that there will be a knock on the door and outside will be two or
three army personnel with the dreaded message? I do think of those days;
it is somewhat "natural" in our country. It has been part of our legacy since
we were a people some 3,500 years ago. We were never able to run away
from our killers.

In comparing the two murders, I am reminded of the Gemorah discussing the mitzvah of loving God. It's a famous story of Papus Ben Yehuda
who found Rabbi Akiva teaching Torah even though the Romans declared
that any Jew found teaching Torah would be killed. Papus asked him,
"How can you teach? they'll kill you?" Rabbi Akiva answered with the example of the fox and fish. It's a dry season, and the fish is struggling in the
near empty river. From the bank, the fox calls to him, and says, "Come up
on land, and I'll help you get by." The fish answers him, "You are supposed
to be the smartest of the animals, but you are the stupidest. If I can't survive in my home, how can I survive out of it?" I would paraphrase, and
Rabbi Akiva added, that the Torah tells us that it is possible that danger
will accompany your living in Israel. However, Israel is like the water to the
fish. Only here can we live normally and come to achieve the special holiness that Hashem [God] has given us. So if it is dangerous here, then so
much more so outside the land.

I'm not sure that you really allow yourself to digest the enormousness of
our having a Jewish State the last forty years. I've said this before, and I'll
say it again; for close to 1,880 years, God kept us out of Israel, and at last
He has given us another opportunity. You and I—of the same generation—
have a privilege that Jews, millions of Jews, throughout close to ninety generations didn't have, and . . . the great majority of us are acting as if
nothing has changed. True, there are dangers living here in Eretz Yisrael.
Are there no dangers living in the States? Both spiritual and physical? True,
more Jews have been killed here in wars than Jews have been killed in the

States. It is also true that so many more Jews in the States have been "killed" due to assimilation, while here assimilation is almost nil. Of course, no one is likely to be "killed" by assimilation in your family, but aren't you living apart from your brethren, Am Yisrael? In other words, by your staying in the States you are giving credence to other families who say that since you, a religious Jew, aren't going, it strengthens their decision not to go. And the strengthening of the U.S. Orthodox community is a strengthening of assimilation. True, you are involved in the building of a nice Jewish community in Woodmere. Hundreds of the same kinds of small Jewish communities came and went in America. Their synagogues today are churches.

Right, you'll have quite a few years of a pleasant Jewish life in the U.S. That too will end. I remember my Abba and Ema, may they rest in peace, telling me, "Don't worry. East Flatbush will remain Jewish—'they' are on the other side of the tracks." I remember my grandmother telling me about the great Cantor Mordechai Hershman who prayed in the Amboy South Synagogue in Brownsville. I have pictures of the Amboy South shul which I took three years ago with a cross smack in the middle of what was once an Aron-Kodesh. I have with me here a picture of the gate of the synagogue that my grandparents built in East Flatbush. My grandmother's name is directly under the new sign, "Holy Tabernacle Church."

I have with me here drawings of the ancient Shilo—the first capital of Eretz Yisrael—and next to it I have no pictures—only the new houses and new synagogue of the rebuilt Shilo. And so to paraphrase, "You work hard and we work hard". . . you work hard and reap the pleasantries for a few years and leave the rest to others while you run. We work hard for a great and lasting future.

On the positive side, how can you compare the quality of Jewish "life" in the U.S. with here? Even my "jailers" are Jewish, and we talk together about rebuilding Aretz. When I first visited my parents in Cedarhurst (1971 and on) I walked with my Talit [prayer shawl] to the Beit Knesset, Beth Shalom. The president of the shul told my father, may he rest in peace, "Tell your child, please, that this is not Israel. The Jews don't like it when he wears a Talit in the street!" A very dear friend, to this very day, feels uncomfortable wearing a yarmulke in his neighborhood, and of course he doesn't wear it to work. Why does a Jew who owns his own business not wear a yarmulke at work? You won't find that here. It is the difference between living in your home and being a nervous guest.

To a very big extent you are teaching your children a double standard. You pray for something—to come back to Israel—but don't act it out. You lived here for two years; you know the great feeling it is to live here as a Jew without the falseness of the Diaspora. True, it is easier in some ways in the States. But is that what is important to you? You and I have an opportunity to rebuild Eretz Yisrael—it's like a dream. Do you have any kind of idea what an Aliyah of 1,000,000 of you would do to both this country and yourselves? We could finally make real headway in solving some of our serious problems and you could feel, finally, what it is to be a Jew without a mask! Even more so, the Arabs would begin to fathom that we are here for good and that Jews from all over are coming. The world's attitudes toward Israel would change! You have a part in obstructing that.

Sorry for the harsh words. Take care.

Era

February 1988
Tel Mond Prison

My Dear Son David, Shalom,

Once again, yesterday, you asked that question. The same question that you've asked time and time again. The same question that I've answered every time you've asked. And, I wonder to myself, maybe I don't know how to explain or maybe the explanation makes no difference—because you want me home with you.

Oh, how I love every moment I spend with you. Now that I'm on "rehabilitation," I get to see you so much more. I'm home once every other week for eighteen hours, and once a month for forty-four hours. But that time flies so fast that it feels that before arriving, I'm leaving to go back to jail. This Friday night, when I was the shaliach tzibbur at the Shabbat

254

evening prayers and you stood next to me and helped me a bit, I looked at you and remembered another little boy of your height and age standing next to his Abba in the Beit Knesset and helping his Abba during the prayers. The little boy was me, and the cantor was my Abba. How I loved every moment I spent with Abba, and I knew he enjoyed it—he told me so.

I know that the separation from you is very hard on you. It is for me also. How I want to sit and learn with you. How I want to hike with you, ride bicycles with you, play ball with you, and just be with you. It has been nine and a half months already since I've been separated from you. Nine and a half very difficult months. Whenever I come home and you see me, you hold me as tight as I hold you. Moments of ecstasy. Having you and being with you is an amazing blessing from God.

Sometimes I wonder at myself—that I had the strength to attack Bassam Shaka. I knew so well that I would go to jail and leave you for a very long time. You ask me, David, over and over, why did I have to do it. I feel that you know the answer, my eldest boy. Maybe your asking the question is your way of expressing your anger at what I did. This time when you asked, Moriyah also asked that I tell her exactly what I did. Maybe you're a bit too young to understand what had to be done.

You have a right to be angry, David, for by acting against the PLO man Shaka, I left you "alone" for nine and a half months, actually a whole year if you count the time that I stayed with Savta.

What I want you to try and know, my son, is that I took into consideration, before acting, the possibility that I would sit in jail separated from you. But even though I knew that, I acted. Not because I don't love you. I acted because I do love you—so very much. If I didn't act and didn't protect you, I wouldn't be doing my job as an Abba. Your life was in danger, so I did what I had to do, to protect you.

But, David, I wouldn't be telling you the truth if I didn't tell you that I acted also to protect Eretz Yisrael from the Arab terrorists who don't want any Jews to live here. We have a mitzvah to settle Eretz Yisrael—a mitzvah that every Jew has to be involved in. If we were to allow the Arabs to continue to hurt us, it could be that a lot of Jews wouldn't come here and then we wouldn't be fulfilling the mitzvah. Fulfilling mitzvot sometimes means personal sacrifice. In my case, it meant the possibility of sitting in jail, but even so I had to do it.

You could say that I should have asked your permission because you are also suffering by my sitting in jail. There are many things that a parent does without asking his children. That, if you'd like, is the prerogative of the parent; it is also his responsibility.

I know, I believe, how much it hurts you when I am around. I can feel it when we kiss hello, and I can feel it when we kiss goodbye. Even more than that, I feel it every moment that we are together. I want to hold on and not let go. When the time gets closer and closer for me to leave, I keep thinking about that terrible moment.

Yet, my David, there is happiness even in our situation. Last night when I left, after being with you for a Shabbat, when I walked toward the bus, I sang out to you, "You are very nice children." You sang out, "Abba, Abba, nice, nice, nice."

When I sang out, "I love you all, all, all," you sang out, "We love you, you, you." When I got on the bus I was really smiling and thanking God for being so good to me for the gift of my children.

I love you my dear son.

Abba

December 1987
Mount of Olives, Jerusalem

Ema, Words at Your Grave:

You prepare yourself, for Ema was very ill. Ill with cancer of the brain for over three years. The doctors warned us, your mother has only a few months to live—at the most.

But . . . there is no preparing—for we had only one mother and all the preparations are worthless. And when my brother Yosef informed me, over the prison phone, that you had passed away, Ema, we both cried like babies.

When we were babies we had Ema to take care of us. Now the three of us are orphans from both father and mother.

Ema was a mother in the best meaning of the word. Maybe we can describe you, Ema, in today's "modern" world, as an Ema from the old generation. Ema, you took care of our every need. When we went to school, the sandwiches were ready—all wrapped for us; and when we came home, supper was always waiting. When we were sick, Ema, you always had a special medicine for us. You would always be ready to play or read to us.

When we were reprimanded at school, it was you, Ema, who came to school to straighten out the situation. When the three of us fought between ourselves, it was you who came running in as the peacemaker.

And when we grew up and started dating, you would stay up to make sure that we came home safely.

Throughout all of my life, I don't remember you, Ema, ever raising your voice—everything was done gently. You told me, Ema, that before Abba's death, he told you that he was not sure of what the heavenly court will say about the way he fulfilled the commandments between man and God, but he had no worries about what they will say in reference to his behavior between man and man. He acted kindly to every man and woman, rich and poor, learned or not, "important" or not. Our Ema, we say the same about you.

I don't know of anyone who had something against you—even the smallest complaint. Ema ran away from arguments. "We have to instill peace," she said so often.

Ema, you tried to influence us to take certain paths, but you knew very well to let us decide and to live with our decisions. My moving to Israel was difficult for you; you "lost" your baby. But the moment I decided to come here, you helped with everything, preparations, packing, shipping. After I was living here, you constantly looked for people to bring packages to us. There was hardly a week that we didn't receive a letter from you—like clockwork.

You and Abba were from the lower-class income bracket. Yet during the last ten years of your life you managed to save some money. Yet you didn't use the money for yourselves—you wanted us to enjoy. Our house in Shilo was built, to a large extent, with your money. We decided to add an apartment downstairs so that you could live with us. The good Lord didn't will it that way . . . you, Ema, won't enjoy the home. You never even got to see it. It's so typical—you did everything for us.

Ema, you weren't "only" an Ema. You were an exquisite wife for our father, may he rest in peace. King Solomon wrote in "Woman of Valor," "Her husband's heart trusted in her." The "Ein Yosef" commentary explains this as meaning: "When the man was not in his home, he trusted in his wife that she would guard over everything in the house." That was exactly the relationship between you and Abba.

"She did him good and not bad." Abba knew all the time you would try and do things that were beneficial for him. There were no questions in his mind.

"Her hand was stretched forth to the poor." Ema, you were like your mother, my grandmother. You walked the streets of New York in the snow and rain, the heat and the cold, to collect yet another penny for the poor, for the Jewish National Fund, and other worthy causes. Hours, days, nights, weeks, months, and years, you dedicated to Hadassah, and you became president of one of its large chapters in New York. You taught us, Ema, and we grew up with charity in our hearts.

"Her husband was known by the gates of the town." Ema, modest as you were, you preferred to put yourself in the background and allow Abba to use all of his strength and time to teach almost 16,000 students in over sixty-three years of teaching! And Abba returned the honor to you. In every public gathering, Abba made sure to honor and praise you.

When Abba passed away, you told us, Ema, that "the best friend of your life had gone." You and Abba were not only husband and wife; you were close friends. Being with both of you and seeing how you treated each other was like being in a school of honor, love, and behavior.

For our Ema, being a supermother and wife wasn't sufficient. To these you added being a superdaughter. "Many daughters have done well, but you were above them all." In this, our generation, along with our other sins, we throw away fathers and mothers to poverty, loneliness, and old age homes, because, seemingly, there is no room in our (large) houses. You, mother, were way above them all. When my grandfather—your father—

passed away at a young age and you and Abba had recently been married, you both invited and requested Grandmother to come live with you. And so it was—not for one year or two or three, but for thirty years! For thirty years of your married life you continued to be a daughter, in a small two-bedroom apartment, where we were six: both of you, Bubbie, and the three of us. Abba and Ema had very little income, and Savta was not very healthy. We learned from our Ema and Abba what the mitzvah of honoring thy mother and father is. One part of the mitzvah is not to leave a mother. In our home it was much more than that. We learned to honor Bubbie in the proper manner. If she requested something, you, Ema, and Abba taught us to listen to her and fulfill her request.

There was another field in which Ema was outstanding. As a grand-mother. Ema had the strength, sensitivity, knowledge, love, and ways with her grandchildren till the very end. Never were they a bother to her; never were they too noisy for her. Ema always had time for her grandchildren. She would sing to them, read to them, play with them, walk and teach them, change them, feed them, help them in every way possible. At the age of seventy-four Ema had more energy and patience for children than most young mothers at the beginning of their motherhood. And her grandchildren returned that love in kind. When Orit decided to go to New York four months ago to see Ema for what turned out to be one last time, she took with her three of our kids. They all asked, very strongly, to go and be with Savta. They wanted to return, just a bit, of your love and kindness, Ema.

"And she will be happy on her last day." The great interpreter, "Ein Yosef," says, "All her life she will be happy on the honor that she will have on her death day." I'm not exactly sure what the Ein Yosef had in mind. Possibly, Ema, that finally, on this day, we can tell, to all those assembled, just a bit about who you were. Maybe, also, my dear mother, that you have been honored and have been buried in Eretz Yisrael.

Or maybe the honor that the heavens are receiving now, our dear mother. There will be no need for a heavenly tribunal to judge you. From on high it has already been decided: Ema of ours, you are going directly to the Garden of Eden to sit next to your father and mother and the best friend that you had, our father, may he rest in peace.

Ema, two days before my marriage to Orit, I came up to this mountain with my father to visit the graves of my grandparents and great-grandparents which are located directly opposite the Temple Mount. Abba pointed to the graves and said, "Era, here is your past. You are the present, and your children, please God, from you and Orit, will be the future. The essence? Teach the Torah of God, that my parents taught me and I to you, to your children, so that they can teach it to their children." Neither Baruch, Yosef, nor I is a teacher like Abba was—no one was like him—but Ema, tell Abba that we will do our best.

Thank you Ema, for everything, for raising and caring for us and for giving us, totally of yourself. And now, go rest in peace. Go to God with your pleasant voice and your sensitive ways. Tell Him that it is difficult for us— so difficult without you both. Shalom to you our mother and teacher.

January 1988
Tel Mond Prison

Dear Uncle,

Two weeks ago today, we went up to the mountain for the unveiling, and once again the wound opened even more. Sadie wrote in her letter that she is "consoled" that her sister is no longer suffering. I am not consoled, for how can one be consoled over his Ema? On the other hand, man is born and dies. My Abba and Ema have left their stamps on this world, both in their own special ways. Abba, as a teacher par excellence, of over 16,000 students and some sixty-three years of teaching. Ema, as we wrote on her tombstone, was an example of a wife to her husband, a mother to her children, and a child to her mother. We have been left with memories, but maybe more important, the message and the challenge. The message—to continue to teach the Torah to our children that our parents taught us. The challenge—to follow in their steps by being caring and good people to others. Abba and Ema did that from their hearts.

No, my uncle, I am not consoled. But my parents helped give me the inner strength to accept the ways of God and to forge on—with gratitude and happiness. Abba said to us so often, "There is too much sorrow; don't get wrapped up in sorrow. God doesn't want us to be sorrowful, rather to be involved with happiness, even, to find happiness in a sorrowful situation."

And, you know what? Even as I sit here in Tel Mond Prison I try to implement their advice.

No, I don't know that my parents would have agreed with my action. I tend to feel they would have disagreed, maybe not against the action but my involvement. That, however, is not the point. I am continuing what they have taught me—in my own way. In this instance, they taught me that one has to fight for Eretz Yisrael.

Now the Rapaport family surrounds all of the Mount of Olives. On the west facing the Temple Mount are my great-grandparents. Southward, Abba's sister and her husband. Eastward, protecting the road from Jericho to Jerusalem and overlooking the Dead Sea, are Abba's brothers, Abba, and, now, Ema.

The kids ask for you whenever I'm home, so you'd better come before they start forgetting.

Take care of yourself, my dear uncle.

Love,

Era, Orit, Moriyah, David, Atarah, Yitzhak, Tsofiyah, and Dvir

6 Israeli

January 23, 1996
Shilo

Dear Ze'ev:

I hope you don't mind my calling you by your Hebrew name. You've asked me a number of questions about difficult problems, and I'm going to respond through a series of letters.

People ask me how I feel now that there's a peace agreement. Well, to tell the truth, I don't believe we have peace. We've created conditions where it looks like peace, but beneath it all, it's a sham. There have been so many closures of Judea and Samaria, as well as Gaza, that the reason there's no terrorism is because no one's being allowed in. If they were allowed in, you'd have lots of terrorist attacks. But if they had a true peace, you could let anyone in, and nothing would happen.

In every other part of the world when you sign a peace agreement, it means you can go anywhere. When Germany and France made peace after World War II, Germans could walk around in Paris without getting killed and the French could walk through Berlin without endangering their lives. But is that true here? No way! A Palestinian can walk around in Tel Aviv or Haifa, but if a Jew is seen by an Arab in Ramallah or Jenin, he's taking his life into his hands. This is peace? If it's peace, why do we have to have rock-proof million-shekel buses? Why are all the water pipes in the Shomron being encased in cement to prevent the Arabs from poisoning the water supply? Why does a tunnel have to be built from Jerusalem to Rachel's Tomb in Bethlehem so that Jews can be protected from rock throwers? And why are we building an electronic fence between Kfar Sava and Kalkilya?

People argue that the army will patrol the area. But if it's peace, what do you need all these patrols for? If you don't have real peace, where people can go wherever they want to in safety, then the whole thing can't work. Let me give you an example: *National Geographic* wrote that there isn't enough water to supply the needs of the Middle East. Until God will do differently, that's the situation. This is the opinion of world-renowned water experts. Who said it's not a problem? The head of the water company from the Labor party. Now let's look at reality, Ze'ev:

265

There's a law in Israel that you're not allowed to dig your own well because of the severe water shortage. And if you dig a well in Samaria, it takes away from the water in Caesarea because 70% of the water comes from our area. So in the Oslo giveaway, one of the conditions was that they can't dig wells without our permission. Five days after the agreement, the Arabs in the Jenin area alone had dug twenty wells. Twenty wells! So there was a big thing on TV. The government found one well. That leaves nineteen. In Gaza, they dug twenty-five wells in five days. And Gaza has almost no water.

What does Israel say? It's okay! We can't stop them anyway. We can get water from Jordan or Turkey, or from icebergs that we'll tow from Alaska. What country in its right mind gives away its water? What country gives away the only oil it has, like we did to Egypt? Only Israel. You surely don't read about it in the American newspapers, but all the new border areas have been suffering from automobile and tractor thefts, and whatnot. Nobody in these towns can even hang out their laundry on clotheslines. They steal it all—shirts, underpants, whatever—and then they run back into their own towns while the Palestinian police do nothing. One kibbutz lost half its milk supply just two weeks ago.

You see, we have open borders now, just like you do with Canada. But that can only work if both sides genuinely want peace but not if one side thinks this is just temporary until they get back everything. According to the agreement, there will be soldiers on the main road. But that will only be beneficial psychologically. If a guy from the neighboring village of Turmos-Aya fires at me, how will the soldiers on the main road protect me?

You've asked me if the peace agreement can work, and I have to admit that I'm very skeptical. Right now, arms are coming into the Arab-controlled territories all the time. The Palestinians have enough arms to make life miserable for us for a very long time. They don't have an army, but they can commit many acts of terror simply by traveling into Israeli cities. A middle-range cannon fired from the Shilo area can travel more than thirty miles and knock down a house in Tel Aviv. And for a missile it would be child's play. They're three miles from the airport. If they fire a rocket at a plane coming in from New York, Peres will call Arafat in and say, "Zeh lo yaffeh [It's not nice]. You can't act this way to a blood brother of yours, a nice guy like me." And he'll say: "I roundly deplore all this."

What I am really afraid of is that the Palestinians will mount a campaign of terror that will sap Israel's ability to resist. But, you see, they won't be able to throw us out of here like they did to the Jews of East Flatbush or Canarsie. That's the difference between the galut and here. In America, one day we're here, and the next day we're not. But in Israel we stay. They'll try to move us out; why shouldn't they? We're a detriment to peace. Don't you know that?

The problem is the West doesn't understand that the Middle East operates by different rules. A word in Arab culture isn't necessarily a word. Actions mean much more. Our government wants to change the collective psychology of the Middle East. But I doubt they can.

Look at how the Arabs treat each other. It's true that we had an assassination, but Jews killing Jews is the exception, not the rule. That's why everyone was so shocked when Rabin was killed. In the last three years, at least 1,000 Palestinians have been killed by their brothers and sisters. And how many wars have there been over the years between Arabs in Yemen, Jordan, Syria, and Lebanon? There's a psychology there that I just don't understand. My culture doesn't teach me to kill thousands of brothers.

I have no problem if Ahmad, who has a piece of land down the road, wants to stay on it, as long as he lets me live on my land. I can even be friendly with him, but I recognize that it's a different culture with different values. There will always be a fear and lack of trust between us. The reason is they want something which is mine, and they claim that we want something which is theirs. What I really want is ten million Jews here tomorrow developing the land. The problem is that some of my people don't believe that we have a God-given right to this land.

Part of Arafat's genius as a tactician is that he finally realized that what the Israelis were telling him was correct: Stop the killing now, and we'll be able to give you land. But in essence I see no change. If anything, he's gotten a present for being violent. Basically, the government's policy makes the Palestinians think: "Look what we got for killing Jews, so let's kill some more. But first let's not do anything as long as they're giving us land for free. We could wait a year or two."

We have a government that's willing to go to tremendous lengths to deceive itself. It confuses what it wants to believe with what's true. And Arafat says: "Look, it's working." We always said, and it was a joke but not a joke, that the day the Arabs put down their arms, they'd get everything. And believe me, they won't be satisfied until they have everything.

This is what we hear from the average Palestinian as well as from their leaders: that peace isn't on the agenda. As an example, there's a guy here in Shilo building a house. He and his fellow Arabs were having a conversation with us, and he said to me straight out: "You know, this house we're building for you now will be ours in the future. It's just a matter of time. And not only that, my grandfather's house in Yaffo that your people stole, I'm going to be living there in the future too." And this is not the exceptional case. It's the rule. Under such circumstances, we're not going to have peace for very long, if at all.

Shalom,
Era

January 28, 1996
Shilo

Dear Ze'ev:

The changing situation has created all sorts of dilemmas for us, such as, do we take the bypass roads or not? If we don't go through the Arab towns, then it's like we don't have the land anymore. But if you go through with them controlling it, then you've accepted their control. Before, they threw rocks at us, but at least our government was in charge. A bypass gives you a way of going through in which you don't have to be subject to their authority.

"So what are we going to do?" you ask. Why we haven't done anything is the million-dollar question. We marched with thousands of people. The police came and bashed our heads in. The beatings in America were nothing compared to what happened here. We have pictures of one of our guys, a forty-six-year-old man, handcuffed behind his head, being dragged down the mountainside by his feet with his head banging against the rocks on the ground. Not every policeman is brutal, but you just need ten bad guys to mess everything up.

So why do I say we haven't done anything if we marched? Because it wasn't enough. We should have had 50,000 people out there, and every day. If we'd sat down outside the Prime Minister's office and said we're not moving, it might have helped a lot. It's very frustrating to me. The situation is so confounding today that it has to be the hand of God. It can't be the hand of man. I say God is hiding His face, just like in the Holocaust, though I in no way equate the two.

How is it possible that people can be so blind to what's happening, to the danger we're all in? It must be that God, for His own reasons, doesn't want them to see it just yet. The optimists like myself say we've got to go down before we go up. It happens over and over again in Jewish history. God comes along and says: "You think you can give away the land of Israel. It ain't that easy. You're intertwined with the land." And then, when it doesn't work, the Jews who thought otherwise will be convinced in a way that I haven't been able to convince them.

We will also have to continue appealing to our fellow Jews in America. We hope they'll give to us directly, not to Israel bonds because through bonds very little of the money gets to us. When I was in New York, I found that a lot of Jews were sympathetic to me. Satmarer hasidim offered to hide me out if the police came looking for me. Ditto for Lubavitch. I had friends who said: "Come hide in our basement till it's safe. No one will find you there," et cetera, et cetera, et cetera. For many people it was sort of a thrill to hide out a bandit type who they thought was a good guy. There are Jews who grew up with antisemitism who see what we're up against in Judea and Samaria as a continuation of that. Now that they live in the suburbs, they don't have the fights they had in Brooklyn, and their kids don't either. But the memory of the fear is still there, and to them we're heroes.

When you get right down to it, I'm not sure what will happen, but as a person who's been here, I'm sure you realize that there's no way we're leaving, no matter who controls the area. People who wait almost 2,000 years to come back don't leave because a Jew who wanted a Nobel Prize made a deal. We're back, we're here, and we're staying.

Shalom,
Era

February 7, 1996
Shilo

Dear Ze'ev:

The decision to come here had a lot to do with my grandparents, who died from starvation in Jerusalem. They simply could not bring themselves to leave their holy beloved city. In those days, when the Arabs attacked the Jews, and they did, there was no Israeli Army to defend them, and the possibility of death was very real. Yet they remained. Our family roots are in Jerusalem. There's even a street in the city, Rechov Baruch Rapaport, named after my grandfather.

When I think about the love I have for Israel in a personal sense, I'd have to say a lot of it comes from my father. He was born and raised in Jerusalem but came to the U.S. for a degree in education. Life in Palestine was very hard in the 1920s and 1930s. But even though he lived in America he remained a Yerushalmi [Jerusalemite] to the core. He was a teacher at the Ramaz Yeshiva for many years, and it was his idea that the students should dance down Fifth Avenue on Israeli Independence Day. Naturally he led the way, dancing with them.

Israel was part of my father's very essence. My uncle would send an etrog or citron [a fruit that one says a blessing over at that time of the year] from Jerusalem every year before the holiday of Succot. And my father would look forward to that time the whole year. He would talk about it, wondering aloud how it would look, whether or not it would be in perfect condition and so on. My tefilin bag was made for me in Jerusalem. It was all those things together.

My mother's influence was less pronounced, but it was there just the

270

ISRAELI

same. She worked for Hadassah, and I still remember her own mother standing on the streets of Brooklyn, collecting money for Israel with a pushka till she was ninety-one. It was very hard for her when I left, though, because she was hoping I'd marry an American girl and stay in the U.S. with her. But then again, she was the same person who told me on her deathbed to go back to Israel.

The truth is that not going back to Israel would have meant that the familial chain was broken, not to mention the Jewish one. When my father taught me the Bible, the love for the land seeped into my very being through a process of osmosis. And when I was here in 1967, the Six Day War became the match that ignited the charcoal that was burning in me all the time.

So why didn't I stay in Jerusalem? After all, it's a holy place too just like Shilo, and it was where my family came from. Everything that a person could want in terms of his past was there. The reason was that there's building work to be done here. This was my tsav, my commandment. My grandfather did his thing, and this is my thing.

The fact is, my personal life had a great deal to with how my general philosophy developed. Without a really deep religious and historical belief in the holiness of the land, there really is no basis for living here. It's subjective, but isn't all true belief subjective? Let me try to convey how I feel about it emotionally.

In the first days, when we rebuilt the ancient village of Shilo, I remember glancing at the hill outside as we recited the evening prayers, and saying to myself: "Samuel, the Prophet, is smiling now—your children have returned home." For me this wasn't an imaginary vision. I really felt it and I even "saw his face." It's as if the prophet told me: "We've passed the scepter to you."

The eyes of all the grandfathers and grandmothers of all the generations are upon us. The eyes of the Jewish people of more than 170 generations are looking at us. How much would a Jew from Aleppo, Syria, or from Yemen or from Russia, any time in the last 1,000 years, have given to be in our situation? To us has fallen the unbelievable merit of being the guardians of Eretz Yisrael. What an honor! It was not given to those greater

271

than us—Maimonides, Rashi, Rabbi Yosef Caro, or other famous rabbis. Don't ask me why. That's what was decreed from the heavens. Accept it!

This is the gift that the large majority of Jews never received: the opportunity to rebuild the land and to guard it. The merit to return to the empty mountains that are filled with glory and majesty; that are filled with our forefathers' footsteps, with our parents' houses, and with their graves. And right under our houses lie the remnants of our first capital, Shilo, the place of the Ark. It's as if God says to me: "I've given you the land, the land that I promised to Abraham and to the settlers of Shilo who follow in his ways. Don't miss the the opportunity to rebuild your land—*My land.*"

I believe that I hear the voices of the "choir of the generations," of all the Jews who walked through these valleys and who climbed to the tops of these mountains, who brought the sacrifices and danced on God's holidays in Shilo. They are in front of us and around us, and God is above us.

I believe, when I step on the holy ground here, that sometimes I can converse with our ancestors and ask if we are fulfilling their expectations, and they respond. And out of my heart there escapes a prayer to the Almighty. There are no words to explain that feeling, so I simply smile . . . and cry. And I know, just as I breathe the air of Israel, that *there is no way* for the Israeli Government, together with their PLO partners, to deliver this land to our enemies.

One star-filled Friday night, at 2:30 A.M., I climbed high up, to the top of the water tower in Shilo. I turned toward the north, south, east, and the west. From the east, the lights of half the tribe of Menashe shone from the other side of the Jordan River. From the west, the lowlands of the shores of the Mediterranean. From the north, the mountains of "blessings and curses," and from the south the mountain of Ba'al Chatzor and the direction of Jerusalem.

And that question again: How did we merit to be among the guardians of our Holy Land? The head doesn't grasp, but the body shivers and the tears flow. There is no answer, and there are no words with which to thank our Father in heaven. "Even had our mouths been full of song we would not have been able to praise Him," [a quotation from the Sabbath morning prayer] and so all that's left is the feeling, the love, and the gratitude toward the Creator of the world.

You see, the commandment to live here is what drives me. I could have lived in a nice house in Vermont, maybe on a river bed, and it would have been beautiful. It's certainly more peaceful there. But that's not what we Jews were commanded to do. I am a link in a chain. And when, and if, I go up to heaven, I'll be asked: "What did you do? We handed you the key. What did you do?" And the Great Judge is sitting there. Look, I wasn't created to do nothing. I've got a chance to do what Jews haven't been able to do for thousands of years, and if I don't seize it, I'll have no excuse. Even sitting in prison in Israel is better than living free outside of Israel.

But to see that, you have to have vision, the vision that I'm afraid Sandy, living in New York, doesn't have. Those Jews who live in the U.S. and along the Israeli coastline are going to have to answer why they didn't come here. And I'll have to answer why I wasn't more successful in getting them to come. But the bottom line is a Jew has no right to give away Eretz Yisrael. I was given it to watch over it. It's incomprehensible that a Jew should just give the land away. If so, then why did we ever come back?

Shalom,
Era

February 11, 1996
Shilo

Dear Ze'ev:

You've asked me if I have any regrets about what I did to Bassam Shaka. I'd be a hypocrite if I told you I did because I really don't. At the time it was a necessity, 100%. Knowing that you're going to maim a person is not an easy action to take, but under the circumstances, nonaction would have been harder.

First of all, you have to understand our process. If a rabbi whom I believe in and respect tells me to do something, he would find in me a responsive audience. We consulted with rabbis about whether this was permitted by the Torah in terms of saving lives and protecting ourselves. The decision to harm another individual is of such magnitude that I don't have the strength to do that on my own. They approved it, but don't ask me which rabbis because I won't tell you. Thank God it was decided that it was only necessary to hurt him rather than kill him to attain our objectives.

I want you to know that while we knew there was a risk that Shaka would die, our experts know how to set a charge in terms of how much damage it will do. You can prepare a bomb so that only one car will explode, and you can prepare one that'll blow up ten cars. We checked Shaka's actions for weeks. When does he get up? Is his wife with him? What about his children? Is there a bodyguard? The bomb was prepared to do minimum damage and to explode only when the car moved.

It should be understood that Shaka was no random target. He was picked for a very specific reason, namely, that he was one of the heads of the National Guidance Committee which was made up of mayors of West Bank towns. This committee was the PLO in the area in all but name, and they were directly responsible for the loss of life and attacks on Jews that occurred in the two years before the murders of the six yeshiva students in Hevron in May 1980—and let's not forget that, as opposed to today when the PLO is legitimate, in those days it was completely terrorist, not political, and the Israeli government had totally outlawed it. Now, Bassam Shaka was the most active member of the Committee. He publicly applauded the massacres of Jews in terrorist attacks, and it had been reported that he was directly involved in planning the murders of Aharon Gross and the others in Hevron. More than that I don't need. At one point our government expelled him, but because of politics the decision was reversed.

People asked how we could take the law into our own hands. And I say we picked up the law that had been thrown to the ground and was no longer in effect. You go into a car and have Molotov cocktails or rocks thrown into it, and you tell me it's not life threatening. And if our government fails to protect us, what are we to do? Die? I remember the case of two people who threw rocks from the bridge of a freeway near Washington and were sent to jail for something like fifty years because the judge considered it like murder. And they didn't even kill anyone.

If you were a Protestant in Kansas and the government didn't protect you, if I remember my American law, you have the right to bear arms to protect yourself. Here, in Israel, it's certainly so. You're talking about a people who were almost totally destroyed in the Holocaust, and this is only thirty-five years later and the government isn't protecting them. So obviously, at the minimum, you have to defend yourself.

People ask me if I'm worried that Bassam Shaka might go after me, especially given the importance of revenge in Arab culture. Perhaps, but let's remember that we know his address too. We're not wimps out here. I also know the Arab who in 1972 exploded a bomb in a refrigerator planted in Kikar Tzion in Jerusalem which killed thirteen Jews. He lives nearby. And the person who set off the bomb in Dizengoff Square in Tel Aviv under the bus came from the village on the other side of the mountains. It's a two-way street. They know who we are, and we know who they are.

You see, I don't like to live this way. But the fact is that Shaka is a man with no regard for human life. My government should hang him tomorrow, but they won't.

I don't have any comment about what the other guys did in terms of random targets because we were not coordinated in all of our activities. But we are in a war. No one has to tell America how many innocent people were killed in their wars. And today the U.S. even admits that some of those wars were wrong. But in a war innocent people die, sad as that is.

Shalom,
Era

February 16, 1996
Shilo

Dear Ze'ev:

You've asked me to comment on the political situation today. This is a really painful subject, and I'll try to be totally honest. In my opinion, people like Rabin and Peres have no appreciation of the uniqueness of the

Jewish people, which is why if it continues this way, it won't continue. It can't. You had a man like Rabin who said, "There's no place in Israel that's holy for me." He made his infamous statement that he would use his passport to travel in the West Bank. He had no understanding of Judaism. Ben-Gurion and Golda Meir had much more feeling in this area than he did.

Interestingly, when you ask those who know better than I do, they say that Peres is more Jewishly inclined, but, from the outside, I'd say no. He should have pride. When you ask a Jew to sign an agreement to give up your land . . . he should have cried. He should have ripped his clothes as a sign of mourning and said he was doing so only because he had no choice. Instead, he smiled and there was a celebration.

And we learn from this whole Oslo debacle that if you take a political position, it's important to do it for the right reason. Rabin was a security hawk, right? So it followed that the minute he started to believe that there was no real security problem, he could give away the whole store. If he'd wanted to hold on to the land because it's ours, which is the only reason that counts, he wouldn't have signed the agreement under any circumstances.

I can't say whether Rabin was someone who, according to Jewish law, turned Jews over to non-Jews, a moser. That's for the rabbis to judge. But if you ask me, did Rabin have a hand in Jews being killed? then the answer is yes. He did it also in 1948 with the Jews who got shot on the Altalena. And therefore for him to be involved directly, or indirectly, was nothing new. The fact that he allowed PLO terrorists to get out of prison, the fact that he didn't use his power as Minister of Defense to stop that, it's obvious he bears responsibility for Jews' being killed later by these terrorists.

Peres is even more of a snake. He lies straight out. The reality is that people have been killed, and more will be. The dangers of what he is doing now have not even begun to seep into anybody in this country, except for those who are intimately involved. He is simply destroying our security. Those who are in the army who know what's going on would be lying to you if they didn't tell you. I, who live in the area, am not going to lie to you because I do know what's going on. We have to pray to God that something awful doesn't happen to our people.

This is all related to Yigal Amir too, since he said that he wanted to hurt Rabin because of what Rabin had done to the people of Israel. If you consider the lost lives that Rabin is responsible for because of his policies, you can understand why Amir did it. When you get hit with rocks or shot at, you can understand the man's action. I'm not agreeing with it. Understanding doesn't mean agreeing. Maybe Amir was just hurting so much that he felt a need to lash out. Did it stop the peace process? In the short term it certainly didn't, but you never know. Ben-Gurion once said that to be a realist you have to believe in miracles. I have no idea how this looks in God's eyes. There's an immediate effect, there's a long-term effect, and then there's an effect min haShamayim [from the heavens]. The most important, in my opinion, is the third.

You could say the same about Baruch Goldstein. He saw what was going on and probably hoped the peace process would grind to a halt. People in the Hevron area say there was a cache of weapons that the Palestinians had hidden in the caves. The truth is that under our system you don't really find out the truth, because the commissions don't really go deep enough. Even in America, do they know everything about the Kennedy assassination? And that happened so long ago.

All that interests me in connection with Amir is, to what extent did Rabin know about what was going on? Within one and a half minutes after the assassination, the radio announced that Avishai Raviv's group had said: "This time we missed; next time we won't." And we all know that Raviv was an agent provocateur who headed a so-called right-wing organization. But, in reality, as the newspapers reported, he was working for the government. And don't forget, a million people heard it on the radio. Obviously the plan was to miss and just fire blanks. That's why one of the security guards yelled that it was only blanks. Amir was supposed to have been given blanks. Only he wasn't, and the rest is history. The only question remaining is: Who gave the order?

I don't want you to get the wrong idea, Ze'ev, that I favor these types of actions. It's too soon to judge the outcome of all these things. But of one thing I'm sure. We have to learn not to solve our differences within the Jewish people through violence.

Shalom,
Era

Acknowledgments

Our rabbis tell us, rather command us, that one is to render thanks to those who have helped. However I am unable to do so. Over the years, the PLO, Hamas, and other terrorist organizations have threatened the lives of the members of the "Jewish Underground." My family and I live with that threat every day of our lives. However, it would be unfair to subject others to the same threat. With the present Israeli Government's policies and the murderous actions of the PLO, those threats can be realized at any moment. The long arm of the terrorists can reach a bus in Jerusalem as well as the World Trade Center in New York. Mentioning those who have befriended me, and without whose help I could never have had the honor of acting to protect Jewish lives, would endanger their lives. However, there are a few who are on the PLO list anyway. They have given me permission to publish their names.

Rabbi Avraham Weiss of Riverdale, N.Y. The Rabbi has risked his life countless times to fight for Jewish causes. He stood by me, a friend in need, after my action, guiding and strengthening my family and me.

Rabbi Hershel Billet of Woodmere, N.Y. Rabbi Billet is one of the few who is not afraid to speak out on topics that the "establishment rabbis" run away from. He and his wife and family opened their hearts and home to us.

My wife's parents, Avraham and Yaffa Mintz. True builders of the Land of Israel. It would be hard to imagine Judea and Samaria without them. On a personal level, they have been unbelievably good. My brother-in-law, Yehuda Etzion. His twenty-four hours a day are spent battling for Israel.

And then there are those who are no longer with us. My father, Rabbi Yitzhak Yehuda, and mother, Yocheved, of blessed memory, who instilled within me the love of Israel and the Jewish People. My uncle, Mordecai Shimon, who taught me the meaning and the how of fighting for Israel. Rabbi Tzvi Yehuda HaCohen Kook. My rabbi in Israel, where I studied during the Six Day War, Rabbi Kook was the leader of "Gush Emunim." His students changed the face of the land of Israel.

And most important, my wife, Orit. All that I have done, simply stated, is through her support, teaching, and love Our seven children—the next link in the chain of the generations. My brothers Baruch and Yosef—no one could ask for better ones. And to Kenny Fishman, who encouraged me to write and didn't relent until I did so.

Above all and without comparison. The Holy One Blessed Be He.

Era Rapaport
Shilo, Israel
1996